LIFE LESSONS

Life Is an Upward Spiral

THE HUMAN-CENTRIC PATH FOR PERSONAL GROWTH

Ansar Yawar

Published by Ansar Yawar
Dubai, The United Arab Emirates

First paperback edition July 2024

Developmental editor: Crystal Nero
Copy editor: Vanessa Ta
Book design: Christian Topac
Book layout design: Mannan Muhammad

ISBN 978-87-975468-0-2 (Hardcover)
ISBN 978-87-975468-1-9 (Paperback)
ISBN 978-87-975468-2-6 (eBook)

www.ansaryawar.com

For my mother

What if every setback you've faced wasn't pulling you back, but lifting you upward—guiding you along the spiral of life?

Let's begin this journey with a riddle:

Riddle

I am the path you tread upon each day,
With me, your purpose finds its way.
With twists and turns both light and dark.
Not a straight line, but round I go,
Higher with each step, even when slow.
Though sometimes steep, you must not tire,
For each challenge takes you higher.
With lessons learned at every stage,
I am your path through every age.
You can approach me seriously or playfully,
That's your decision to make.
If you choose seriousness, tears will flow more than laughter.
If you choose playfulness, laughter will bring tears.

What am I?

The Five Knots

In life's intricate web, there are
Five knots that tightly bind:
The vessel, the soul, the truth of life,
Love and relationships—yet true contentment in God, we find.

Untangling these knots with care,
Unveiling the truth with a human-centric flair,
Lesson by lesson, we shed each layer.
In the vessel of our earthly frame,
Lies wisdom, waiting to claim.

To grasp the roots of human suffering,
We must unlearn, relearn, and keep elevating,
Transcending our life's spiral courageously,
The essence of life we must seek playfully.

Threads of ignorance we unwind,
In detachment's wisdom, treasure we find.
Shackles of fear—we break free,
Ego humbled, true self to see.

Deep connections, hearts entwine,
In this dance, everything is beautifully aligned.
Through each bond, God's presence gleams bright,
In the fabric of our dreams, as a guiding light.

So let us weave with hands and hearts,
A tapestry of love, a sacred art.
For in our essence, we find the key,
To unlock the universe and truly be.

Sometimes, I find myself journeying far beyond where I've ever been, without moving an inch. It was on one of those days that this poem came to life, and from it, *Life Is an Upward Spiral* was born. This poem reflects the entire book, captured in a few lines. But if you listen closely, it may take you even further than I've ever traveled.

Contents

CONTENTS

The Fifth Knot: The Great Orchestra

Dear Seeker

Life is a rich tapestry, woven from moments that challenge, inspire, and transform us. Deep within, I've always been captivated by the profound questions of our existence: questions about identity, origins, the complexities of human suffering, and the mysteries that lie beyond our mortal world.

A vivid childhood memory shaped my worldview in a lasting way. While riding the train with my mother, I often found myself gazing at the faces around me, wondering why people seemed so unhappy. As a child eagerly looking forward to growing older, I couldn't understand why aging seemed to extinguish the spark in their eyes. Why weren't people more joyful now that they had the freedom to explore the world on their own terms? What had happened to their sense of wonder and curiosity?

My mother—whom I affectionately call Nana—often cautioned me against staring at strangers. But one day, unable to contain my curiosity, I asked her, "Nana, why are people so sad all the time?" She responded with a gentle smile, "That's a good question, my son. Let me know if you find out one day."

My Nana is an extraordinary woman. Though she never received formal schooling and cannot read or write, she carries a wealth of wisdom no book could contain. Her simple yet profound explanations always ignited my curiosity. She compared life to a card game: sometimes you are dealt good cards, sometimes bad ones, yet with the right perspective, every card has its value. As a child, I could not fully understand this lesson. Today, it resonates deeply. Life is less about the hand we are given and more about how we choose to play it.

Curiosity has been my constant companion, guiding me from those early questions to the present, as I prepare to share the answers I've uncovered through my journey toward enlightenment in this book. What a journey it has been. Within these pages, I offer a guide to untangling the knots that constrain our souls. As each knot is loosened, the soul rises and reconnects with the rhythm of breath, freeing you to once again embrace the melody of your existence.

In life, we navigate through contrasting threads of joy and sorrow, triumph and defeat, love and loss. Through these highs and lows, we contribute our unique stories to the vast mosaic of humanity.

Yet today, there seems to be a reluctance to acknowledge our struggles. We often rush to overcome challenges, hasten the healing process, or act as if we are fine, all while burying issues that need to be truly resolved. Ironically, we admire those who have faced significant trials. Stories of real struggles not only capture our interest but also earn our respect.

Through deep introspection and personal development, I've learned to embrace the invaluable lessons hidden within life's ups and downs. My sincere hope is that the insights drawn from these experiences will inspire and transform you on your journey.

One key lesson is the recognition that our evolution and the challenges we face are ongoing. As we grow, so do life's complexities. No wisdom can make one feel completely wise, no bliss is ever permanent, and no strategy can fully eradicate life's challenges. The journey of self-discovery and learning is endless—a blessing in itself. I hope this insight fuels your curiosity rather than dampening your enthusiasm. I ask you to trust me and follow me down the rabbit hole, where true transformation awaits. I am excited to share the treasures I've gathered with you. Though each person's journey is as unique as their fingerprint, we all share access to a universal wisdom that lies dormant within us, waiting to be awakened and lived.

Exercise: Before we begin, take a moment to reflect on three challenges or recurring patterns in your life — the ones that seem to circle back no matter how much you try to grow or change. These are not just obstacles; they are your thresholds — the points where growth is waiting, where healing is asking to begin. Write them down with honesty and detail. Name them clearly, not to define yourself by them, but to bring them into the light of awareness. As you journey through the sessions of this book, return to your list.

You will begin to see how each challenge aligns with the Five Knots — how awareness brings clarity, truth brings release, love brings renewal, connection brings understanding, and transcendence brings peace. By the time you reach the final pages, you will no longer see these challenges as burdens. You will recognize them as sacred teachers — catalysts that guided you toward becoming who you were always meant to be.

The Way Forward

As I set out to write this book, my intention is not to establish myself as an author. Rather, I am driven by a profound sense of duty shaped by my own trials and tribulations. I believe that wisdom is meant to be shared generously, not guarded.

This book does not aim to impose beliefs or dictate a specific path. Instead, it is crafted to challenge and expand your thoughts, offering guidance if you are open to receiving it. Throughout history, our innate curiosity has driven us to seek truth, meaning, enlightenment, and a deeper understanding of ourselves and the world. This curiosity has led us to explore various belief systems, engage in introspection, and dive into spiritual realms. I encourage you to approach this book with an open heart and a critical mind. Reflect on my thoughts and assess how they resonate with your own journey and unique starting point for personal growth.

I write as a Muslim, and throughout this book you will encounter verses from the Qur'an. They are not placed here to convince, but to illuminate. The Qur'an speaks in a language that reaches beyond boundaries of faith, offering truths that resonate with human nature itself. Many of its messages align with the discoveries of modern science and the timeless patterns of life, making them universal in their relevance. The aim is not conversion, but clarity.

Life Is an Upward Spiral is not meant to be read with the simple goal of finishing it. Instead, take your time, allowing each lesson to unfold naturally. Let the journey progress at its own pace, trusting that you will reach the end when the moment is right. Ideally, reflecting on a few lessons each day will deepen your understanding and enhance your journey. The lessons in this book are interconnected, and it is crucial to fully grasp each one before moving to the next. Every life lesson concludes with a call-to-action paragraph titled *Spiral Upward*, designed to distill the essence of the lesson and encourage you to integrate its wisdom into your life.

This book offers facets of my life, insights, and valuable perspectives to guide you toward personal empowerment and an exhilarating journey of self-discovery. It is organized into five sections, which I call *The Five Knots*. Each Knot contains lessons that help illuminate the origins of human misery, inviting you to unravel them and move upward with deeper awareness.

May this book serve as a sanctuary in times of hardship, uncertainty, or doubt, a faithful companion from which you can seek solace, draw strength, and find inspiration. As you immerse yourself in its words, I hope you discover resilience, compassion, and clarity, empowering you to face life's challenges with determination and profound insight. Let the lessons within act as a compass, gently guiding you back to the essence of your being whenever you feel lost or overwhelmed. Think of this book as a wise and steadfast friend, always there to remind you that you are not alone in your struggles.

As you embark on this journey, I encourage you to move slowly. Reflect deeply on each lesson, allow its wisdom to take root, and integrate it into your life. This is not a race; it is a dance. Trust the process, for transformation unfolds in its own time.

Before you proceed, take a moment. Reflect on the challenges that brought you to these pages. What knots are you ready to untangle? What truths are you prepared to question? Write these down. They will be your guideposts as you ascend the spiral.

Prayer First

Before We Begin Our Journey

Have you ever wondered why God invites us to pray? Surely, He does not require our prayers, for He is whole and complete. Yet, prayer is God's way of instructing us that the first step toward manifestation is visualization. Prayer enables us to envision the best possible outcomes; manifestation cultivates belief in our capabilities; and action propels our motivation forward.

With this insight, let us initiate our journey with a prayer for transformation. Prayer is more than a mere call. It is a powerful declaration, the first step on a path into the unknown. By imagining what we seek, we lay the groundwork for its achievement. By repeating our prayers, we turn them into a force that fuels our actions, transforming thoughts into reality.

Dear God,

May my deeds enrich those around me as rain nourishes the earth, reflecting your boundless love. Let me be a vessel for compassion, kindness, and understanding. May my presence remind others of Your divine grace that infuses all existence. As rain quenches the earth's thirst, let my actions soothe and nourish the souls I encounter, planting seeds of love wherever I tread.

May my true essence, like the moon reflecting the sun's radiance, align with my heart's pursuit of purity. As I navigate the complexities of life, guide me to harmonize my thoughts, words, and actions with the deepest longings of my soul. Through introspection, I am committed to unveiling my true essence and embracing the transformative power of personal growth. May the spirit that I embody, reflecting Your divine light, illuminate my path of self-discovery.

Guide me to embrace surrender as a caterpillar trusts in its metamorphosis at its most vulnerable. True transformation indeed lies within surrender. Like the caterpillar that discards its cocoon to emerge anew, I too relinquish my doubts and limitations, trusting in the transformative journey of life. Amid challenges, sustain my faith, affirming that true beauty is indeed unfolding.

If nothing in this world truly belongs to me, let me find contentment in simplicity. In a world obsessed with material wealth, I seek detachment from the illusions of materialism and transient desires, finding joy in life's simpler moments. Liberate me from ownership and allow space for gratitude, humility, and a deeper connection to my essence.

Allow me to pursue extraordinary goals with selfless intentions, faithfully employing the talents You have bestowed upon me. My abilities are sacred gifts, meant for service to better the world, not for personal recognition. Guide me to honor this sacred trust with unwavering dedication, or, should I falter, remove it from me, as I place my complete faith in Your boundless wisdom.

I am profoundly grateful for everything You have given me and everything You have taken away, as each moment has taught me vital lessons. May I consistently embrace blessings with humility and perceive hardships as opportunities for growth, recognizing that resilience is forged in the crucible of adversity. With gratitude, I surrender to Your divine plan, trusting that every detour is the right tour, enriching my journey and revealing wisdom beyond my comprehension.

In prayer, surrender, and gratitude, I discover the essence of life's profound lessons. You are the All-Knower, the epitome of wisdom, so by elevating my thoughts and unraveling the mysteries of life, I ascend to a higher plane. Each step upward brings me closer to You and Your eternal wisdom. With an open heart and a willing spirit, I therefore delve into the hidden beauty of life's teachings. My greatest desire is to be guided, for the more I comprehend, the more I can love You selflessly. Your love and guidance are the ultimate rewards in this life and the hereafter.

Let us begin with the core of our journey: understanding human misery. For how can we ascend if we do not first uncover the roots of our pain?

1: Human Misery

Man, skilled beyond all other creatures,
can think in time, travel to the past, and imagine the future,
yet often perishes before his death.

He is born with an inner light capable of illuminating the world,
but he buries his shine in darkness
and extinguishes his joy with momentary pleasure.

His brain can map the universe, yet he finds himself lost.
His heart overflows with generosity but often resides in greed.
He can give a piece of his heart to everyone he meets without missing
a piece, yet he invades and occupies it all for himself.

He possesses the strength to carry burdens even mountains would
refuse and a will that can move mountains if he so chooses,
yet he often sees himself as useless.

He can encompass the entire universe within the pupil of his eye
without making the universe smaller or his pupil larger,
yet he acts as if he has no eyesight.

He asks for help but often fails to help others.
He desires triumph but occasionally revels in others' defeat.
He craves more but fails to appreciate what he receives.

He cannot deceive himself into believing that
footsteps in the snow appear on their own,
yet he takes great pride in believing that

the universe came into existence on its own.

He possesses the potential for salvation
but often dooms himself
and places blame on everyone but himself.

The Enigma of Human Suffering

Suffering is the thread that binds us all, regardless of our background or beliefs. It is as universal as the air we breathe yet as misunderstood.

Have you ever pondered the enigma of human suffering? As my Nana once told me, "My son, if you ever find out why most people struggle to be happy, let me know." Her words have since been etched in my mind, unwittingly setting me on a lifelong quest to understand the nature of human suffering. This quest has become a lens through which I see the world.

Perhaps that is why I am drawn to individuals with heavy hearts, regardless of their age. In their presence, I feel deeply privileged, as though I've lived countless lifetimes through the lens of their pain. It feels as though a sacred duty has been entrusted to me: to share the invaluable wisdom gained from these profound experiences.

What exactly is human suffering? Is it the pain itself, or is it our inability to comprehend and make sense of it? Together, let us explore this question.

Life is inherently dualistic: a dynamic interplay of paradoxes that shapes both our inner worlds and the vast landscape around us. These contradictions, woven into the fabric of human experience, invite us to delve deeper into their mysteries. Each paradox, like a knot waiting to be untied, holds profound lessons that resonate with the essence of our humanity. By unraveling these knots, we uncover the hidden roots of our suffering. Yet, this transformative journey requires more than mere intellectual curiosity. It calls for the bravery to question our deepest assumptions, to embrace the discomfort of unlearning, and to step boldly into the process of relearning.

Are you prepared to question everything you believe? Are you ready to challenge your perceptions, expand your horizons, and explore the depths of your own truth?

Understanding the depths of human misery not only clarifies the struggles we endure but also sets the stage for discovering our true purpose—why we endure, what we strive for, and how we find meaning in the journey ahead.

2: The Purpose

The Light Found in Darkness

Have you ever stopped to wonder, 'Why am I here?' This timeless question has echoed through the ages, whispered by philosophers, seekers, and dreamers alike. It is not merely a query but a call, a pull on the threads of our existence that weaves through the fabric of our lives. The search for purpose begins the moment we dare to question the world around us. It speaks to us in our highest joys, reminding us of life's potential, and lingers in our darkest moments, urging us to find meaning in the shadows. Once awakened, this question becomes a companion we cannot ignore, guiding and challenging us on the path to self-discovery.

One heavy-hearted night, I found myself on my prayer mat on the balcony, gazing up at the vast night sky. Even the air felt heavy, or perhaps it was the weight of my prayers. Each whispered word was a plea for guidance, a desperate call for clarity amidst the uncertainties surrounding me. I felt as though I was drowning in turbulent waters, questioning whether my difficulties were a divine test or a consequence of my own decisions. Deep within, I knew that God, in His infinite power, could change my circumstances in an instant. Yet the question lingered: *Why hasn't He?* It hung in the cool breeze, silently echoing the tension between faith and human understanding.

In my confusion, I wrestled with why God had chosen such a difficult path for me. As I sought the strength to overcome my trials, each effort seemed only to pull me deeper into despair. It felt as though the ground itself was disintegrating beneath my feet. I longed for stability, a solid foundation upon which to build a life for myself and my family. Yet instead of providing this stability, God seemed to shake the very foundation He had once established, leaving me unsettled and uncertain. The pillars of security I had relied on crumbled, forcing me to confront the stark reality of an unpredictable world that had once felt comfortable.

Ironically, people often rush to support those who seem least in need, yet vanish when genuine help is required. I came to realize that many in my circle weren't truly there for me; they were there for what I represented to them. To some, I was a financial opportunity, and to others, I was simply good company when it suited them. They remained by my side when it was favorable for them, but as soon as they saw no benefit, they faded into the background, leaving me feeling isolated and deserted. The phone calls stopped, perhaps to avoid any situation where they might have to offer support. Even though they knew asking for help would be my absolute last resort, it seems the mere possibility was enough to keep them away. What hurt the most was that I had never once asked them for anything. On the contrary, I had always given freely, sharing generously without hesitation. By God's grace, my hands have never been outstretched in desperation to others—they've always reached upward to Him. I prayed for companionship and understanding, but God had different plans.

He taught me a painful yet valuable truth: sometimes, you need to stand alone to see people and situations clearly, without the distortion of misplaced expectations. It's in solitude that you learn who truly values you—not for what you have or what you offer, but for who you are.

In my solitude, I yearned for love—a connection to fill the emptiness. Yet, God allowed me to experience profound loneliness instead of offering comfort. In those moments, I began to understand that love isn't solely found in the embrace of others; it must first be nurtured within oneself.

I pleaded for joy, for respite from the burdens that weighed heavily on me. Yet, at every turn, new reasons for tears seemed to arise. I questioned why I faced these challenges and why happiness seemed so elusive. However, as I journeyed through the darkness, I came to realize that joy is not a destination—it is a mindset. It can be found in the smallest moments, even amid tears.

God placed before me the most challenging trials to deepen my faith. It felt as though the universe conspired against me, testing my resilience and pushing me to my limits. And yet, with each trial, my faith grew stronger. I learned that faith is not about having all the answers; it is about trusting the process and believing in a higher purpose for every challenge. As I reflect on the past, I discover not just a glimmer of light within myself, but a profound strength that comes from beyond me. This realization has brought comfort, gratitude, and joy, reminding me that we are never truly alone.

Ultimately, I understood that God's ways are mysterious and often beyond our understanding. While I prayed for specific outcomes, God had His own plans, and His ways are best. Through the darkness, I discovered my strength, resilience, and capacity for growth. Sometimes, we must lose our way to find our true path. I cherish the lessons gleaned from these challenging times. I cling to faith, not just emotionally, but intellectually. I welcome the darkness, for it is in those moments that the light shines brightest. Most importantly, I am grateful for everything, because it is through these trials that I have become who I am today.

God truly guides whom He wills in His own unique way. His methods may diverge from our expectations, but His wisdom is boundless, and His love unwavering. By surrendering to His plan, we find the strength to overcome, the resilience to endure, and the faith to trust that brighter days lie ahead. My trials and pains were not a punishment, but a gift, one meant to be shared.

This is the power of vibration. We have both manifested this moment in the past, and therefore, we are connected on the same frequency in this present. This book has found its way to you for a reason; you did not find me by accident. I was searching for you, just as you were searching for me. Let's discover why together. As we begin to grasp our purpose, we find ourselves at the threshold of a deeper mystery: the secrets of our very existence and the fundamental truths that shape our lives, ready to be unlocked in the next chapter.

Exercise: Reflect on a moment of hardship in your life. Write down what you learned from it, how it shaped you, and how it could guide your future choices. End by identifying one positive action you can take inspired by this experience.

3: Unlock the Secret

The Purpose of Our Existence

Before we embark on this enlightening journey together, let's begin with a profound question that lies at the core of human misery: *What is the purpose of our existence?*

This question isn't merely about collecting knowledge; it demands a profound exploration into the core of human nature, the purpose of existence, and the origins of the universe. As we delve into it, we encounter a cascade of other essential questions: *Who are we? How did we come to exist? What is the ultimate purpose of life? What lies beyond death? Does God exist?* These questions lie at the heart of human experience, each interwoven with the others, reflecting the deep and intricate complexities of life itself.

If we focus only on the superficial layers of suffering, we will never unveil the true roots of human misery. It's like trying to understand an entire ecosystem by only examining the role of bees.

Imagine participating in a game without knowing your role or the objective. How long would you stay engaged? Likely not very long. The truth is, everything in our existence—from the sun and moon to the rain and sky—serves a purpose, without exception. I invite you to challenge this perspective by identifying anything in existence that lacks purpose.

Our actions, too, must have purpose; otherwise, they feel meaningless. And yet, many believe that humans—arguably the most intelligent species in the Milky Way—lack purpose. This notion is staggering. Why do we shy away from these fundamental questions? Perhaps it's because we have been conditioned to think that the answers are elusive or unnecessary. Society urges us to focus on health, wealth, and happiness, as if these pursuits are incompatible with a deeper understanding of life. As a result, we often find ourselves playing the game of life without ever grasping our true role or understanding its broader significance.

In this book, my goal is to provide different perspectives and unpack the complexities of human misery. Together, we will explore these foundational questions one step at a time. I promise you this: you will begin to see life through a new lens. Our typical perception of life as a linear progression—past, present, and future—can be limiting. We are conditioned to focus on what has been or what might be, but I encourage you to delve deeper, to embrace a more expansive understanding of existence. If life is not merely a straight line from past through present to future, you must be thinking, what other options can there be? Let's uncover the answers in the chapter ahead.

4: Life Is an Upward Spiral

The Spiral of Existence

Our perspective on life is foundational to understanding human suffering because it shapes how we interpret our experiences. Biologically, we are conditioned to solve problems, seeing them as disruptions to order. Restoring order provides a sense of accomplishment, reinforcing our desire for control and perfection. This inclination drives our obsession with straight lines, as if they symbolize clarity and progress, while anything curved or non-linear feels chaotic.

Yet, nothing in the universe truly moves in straight lines. Energy flows in vortices, waves, and spirals, curving and evolving in harmony with natural laws. From the orbits of planets to the patterns of our fingerprints, nature itself operates in spirals and cycles. If nothing in the natural world adheres to a straight line, why do we insist on seeing life that way?

This linear perspective traps us in a damaging mindset. Viewing life as a straight timeline causes us to carry the weight of the past into the present, leaving us exhausted and anxious about the future. We're wired for progress, and anything that feels like regression triggers frustration. When unresolved wounds from the past linger in our present, we often interpret it as a lack of growth. This inability to let go of the past is one of the root causes of human misery.

Life, however, is not linear. It is cyclical. It revolves around recurring experiences I call the "human package": emotions like joy, surprise, sadness, fear, anger, and more. These universal emotions bring us back to familiar places, but each time we encounter them, we do so from a higher plane of awareness, ascending like a spiral of consciousness.

Every facet of existence traces a spiral, from the intricate design of our DNA to the golden spirals found in nature, the swirling galaxies in space, and the vastness of the universe itself. What if we've been viewing life from the wrong perspective?

Life unfolds as an upward spiral, continuously rising from birth until our departure from this realm: a transition to the next stage of existence. The past lies below, and the future rises above, but they converge only in the present moment.

The Illusion of Time

Our relationship with time is another fascinating aspect of existence. We perceive time as divided into past, present, and future, but from God's view, only the present exists. Time is not an absolute reality but a tool we use to navigate our experiences. With each encounter, whether we label it "good" or "bad"—we ascend the spiral, revisiting familiar challenges from a higher level of consciousness.

Consider this: imagine a child working on a jigsaw puzzle. Frustrated, they search for the final piece, believing it is "missing" and that finding it belongs to some future moment. From their perspective, the solution lies ahead. Yet, as an observer standing above, you see the piece right behind the box. For you, the solution exists in the present—you already know where it is and how close they are to completion.

From the child's perspective, the missing piece belongs to their future. But from your elevated vantage point, the entire situation—the search, the discovery, and the completion—exists simultaneously in your "now." This illustrates how time and perception are relative, shifting depending on the perspective from which we view existence.

Now, imagine if the child gives up, frustrated and disheartened. They might abandon the puzzle, concluding that the missing piece was simply "not part of their present reality." Yet, the truth remains: the piece was always there, just out of view. This serves as a profound reminder that while our struggles and longings may feel endless, from a higher perspective, the answers are often much closer than we think. Perseverance is the bridge between what feels unattainable and what is already prepared for us.

God's Eternal Perspective

From God's perspective, there is no past or future—there is only the eternal now. What we perceive as a journey of waiting, searching, and longing is, in His view, a single, complete moment. He sees the entirety of our lives—the challenges, the lessons, the victories—as one interconnected whole. Trusting in this divine perspective can help us endure moments when we cannot yet see the full picture unfolding.

Embracing the Spiral

The key to navigating life is not avoiding challenges or pain but understanding and accepting the evolving nature of our experiences. Healing from past pain is not the ultimate goal; rather, embracing our scars and accepting our wounds is the true essence of life. It is human to feel sadness, to be triggered by past hurts. Real strength lies not in denying this pain but in refusing to identify with it.

Past pain is not a burden; it is a foundation of wisdom. Each scar is a reminder of a lesson learned, and every wound you've embraced becomes part of the strength that propels you upward. Life's upward spiral invites us to revisit the same emotions and challenges, but each time from a greater height, with deeper wisdom and broader understanding.

When we begin to see life as an upward spiral, our relationship with challenges, time, and pain transforms. Challenges turn into gateways for growth, time shifts from a constraint to a companion, and pain becomes the soil from which wisdom blooms. Through this lens, life reveals itself as a continuous ascent toward deeper understanding, naturally us to the most essential question of all: *Can we truly change?* That's the question I look forward to exploring with you next.

Exercise: Visualize your life as a spiral. Sketch or describe key moments where you revisited the same challenges or emotions but from a higher level of awareness. Identify where you are currently on this spiral and what the next upward step might look like.

5: We Don't Change

Do People Really Change?

I once believed that people could transform completely — that we could shed our patterns as easily as old skin. But with time, I've come to see that true change runs deeper. We are not meant to erase our essence, but to refine it. What we call change is really awakening — the unfolding of awareness that allows us to meet the same storms with wiser eyes. The blueprint within us — our inherited patterns, even our DNA — may set the stage, but it does not define the play. It is the soul that chooses how to dance with what it has been given. And in that dance, we ascend.

The phrase "I want to change" or "you need to change" is often used in relation to actions. Yet actions are rooted in perspectives, and perspectives are shaped by our experiences — and how intelligently we interpret our reality. If anything needs to evolve, it is our thoughts. But here lies the paradox: the experiences that shape our thoughts — beginning from birth — are largely outside our control.

We don't choose the struggles our parents face, the wounds they unintentionally pass down, the people who influence us, or the environment in which we grow up. Our DNA adds another layer of complexity — an inherited wiring system from our ancestors that shapes not only our physical form and health, but even some of our instincts, behaviors, and fears. If DNA cannot be changed, then neither can the "starting package" we are born with.

What we *can* do, however, is elevate our thinking and deepen our understanding of the reality we live in. Through awareness, we learn to make better choices. But does this mean our nature truly changes? Not entirely. The impulses, habits, and instincts ingrained within us still rise to the surface — the difference is that we learn to meet them consciously.

True growth lies not in erasing these patterns, but in mastering them.

Let me share a personal example. I've always struggled with my temper. My siblings used to say, "You remind us of our father," and I hated that comparison. For years, I tried to eliminate my temper completely, only to fail time and again. It wasn't until I shifted my perspective that I discovered something profound: my temper wasn't the problem — my lack of control was.

Without my temper, I would lose my spark. Without my spark, I would lose my passion. Without my passion, I would lose my joy. The temper wasn't something to destroy; it was something to understand and channel. As much as we are capable of love, we are capable of anger. As much as we despise lies, we defend truth with the same fire. As much as we hate injustice, we pursue justice with equal intensity. These dualities live within us all, powered by the same inner flame.

Perhaps this is why life is an upward spiral. We keep returning to our inner challenges — but from higher planes, with greater awareness and compassion each time. The fight never truly ends because we do not fundamentally change — our understanding does. And from that understanding, our actions evolve.

Our actions are not permanent reflections of who we are, but of our current state of mind — and that can always grow. This is why true change is not about becoming someone else; it is about becoming more conscious of who we already are. Before we can rise, we must first understand what holds us down. This is the purpose of awareness — to illuminate what hides beneath the surface, to bring shadow into light.

In Japanese aesthetics, *wabi-sabi* teaches that beauty is found in imperfection — in what is flawed, transient, and incomplete. Likewise, personal growth begins not by rejecting our imperfections, but by embracing them. When we accept that we are both light and shadow, we stop chasing perfection and start pursuing truth.

Only by recognizing and appreciating the beauty in our flaws can we align our goals with an authentic understanding of ourselves. For how can we aim to change if we do not first understand what truly needs to change?

Awareness, then, is not the opposite of imperfection — it is its refinement. And through that refinement, we spiral upward — wiser, humbler, and closer to the essence of who we were always meant to be.

6: The Five Knots

The journey ahead unfolds through what I call *The Five Knots* — sacred threads that bind the story of our existence. Each knot is both a question and a key, waiting to be untied with patience and sincerity. As you move through them, you do not merely read lessons; you revisit yourself. Every return reveals a higher rhythm in the same melody, guiding you gently upward along the spiral of your becoming.

To truly understand the root causes of human suffering, we must embrace a holistic approach, one that explores life's deepest questions through a human-centric lens, grounded in the totality of human nature. This journey unfolds across five comprehensive parts:

Knot 1: The Vessel

This knot reminds us that our physical form is only the vessel through which we experience life. It challenges the illusions we inherited from society—about beauty, worth, and success—and invites us to unlearn what dims our spirit. True fulfillment begins not with how we appear, but with how we *are* within.

Knot 2: Our True Being

Here, we journey inward to rediscover the essence buried beneath expectations, labels, and the need for validation. This knot calls us to peel back the layers that hide our authenticity, reconnecting us with the self that existed before the world told us who to be.

Knot 3: The Truth of Life

This knot reveals life as an upward spiral—where our outer reality mirrors our inner state. It teaches us to align our ambitions with our deepest values, finding lasting fulfillment not in possessions or status, but in gratitude, purpose, and the relationships that anchor us.

Knot 4: Interpersonal Connection

Here, we explore the architecture of love, trust, and human bonds. This knot refines how we relate to those around us—helping us break unhealthy patterns, heal emotional wounds, and deepen the connections that shape our lives.

Knot 5: The Great Orchestra

The final knot invites us to contemplate our place in the grand design—whether we call it God, the Divine, or a universal force. It harmonizes faith and intellect, encouraging a spiritual understanding that honors both reason and revelation, both searching and surrender.

Together, these knots form a single, interconnected framework—a map of the human journey from the question *"Who am I?"* to the ultimate realization of the One who created us.

To Transcend the Paradox of Human Misery

To truly understand and address the complexity of human misery, we must recognize the inseparable nature of our existence's various facets. Our lives consist of interconnected threads: our physical form, our inner essence, our relationships, and our spiritual connections, which together shape our experience. To seek solutions in isolation is to miss the tapestry of life. Instead, we must embark on a comprehensive journey, integrating all aspects of our being to uncover holistic insights.

Embracing life's entirety allows us to break free from misery's grip. This book does not promise the eradication of pain; rather, it acknowledges suffering as an inevitable, although misunderstood, companion. Through the lessons shared, you will learn to view misery through a lens of harmony and understanding, distinguishing this approach from typical self-help narratives that often promise unrealistic elimination of suffering.

Our path of self-discovery involves nurturing our physical selves with love, reconnecting with our true identities, forging meaningful relationships, and pursuing spiritual depth. This holistic approach reveals that true fulfillment and lasting joy do not stem from external achievements but from the harmonious integration of all life's elements.

Reflecting on my own journey toward enlightenment, this book is woven with the invaluable lessons gleaned from the darkest moments of hardship—stranded, homeless in an unfamiliar city, with empty pockets and not a bite to eat. During those times, I carried the weight of my struggle in silence, determined to shield my family from despair. To them, I was still the pillar, the unbreakable light, even as I fought to keep that spark alive within myself.

As you engage with this book, imagine re-experiencing life anew, this time with a conscious and awakened mind. View your journey from a higher perspective, and approach each lesson with the depth of reflection it deserves. The insights woven into these pages have the potential to reach far beyond their surface, serving as a gateway to profound layers of wisdom for those who take the time to pause, reflect, and explore more deeply.

The Vessel

Unlearn to Relearn

A Journey to Self-Understanding

Unraveling the mystery of human suffering begins with recognizing our deep connection to our body—which I refer to as the physical form—and how it interacts with our environment. Therefore, it is crucial to explore the complex relationship between our physical existence and our pursuit of self-awareness.

When our journey begins, we are shaped by nature's own hands and given a name by our parents. This name echoes through time and becomes a symbol of our identity. With our first breath, our birthplace marks us. This place of origin becomes our passport to the world, defining our initial connection to it.

Before we fully understand our physical form, we are already deeply intertwined with it, closely identifying with its contours and constraints. It becomes our constant companion, though it's never formally introduced to us. Essentially, we occupy our bodies without any guidance, much like two strangers who meet and grow together, gradually developing such a deep bond that they merge into one. In a similar way, we integrate with our bodies, becoming a unified entity.

To decipher the enigma of human suffering, we must trace our origins—not only from a physiological standpoint but through an intellectual lens that extends beyond traditional learning. This exploration requires questioning our current beliefs, opening us to the profound wisdom that lies in wait.

At our core, we recognize that our physical vessel merely houses our true essence. This recognition is echoed in the phrases "my body," "my heart," and "my mind." Intuitively, we sense that we are more than these components. Yet, we frequently neglect this deeper truth, limiting ourselves to our physical existence. Our senses plunge us so deeply into each moment of life that our physical form seems inseparable from who we are, profoundly influencing our self-perception and overall well-being.

Our bodies serve as canvases for self-esteem and self-image, molded by societal norms, cultural expectations, and media portrayals. We navigate a complex landscape of self-perception, choosing either to embrace our physical forms or wrestle with dissatisfaction. This attachment to our appearance significantly contributes to human suffering, often restricting us from exploring our deeper selves and confining our focus to the physical.

The common advice to unconditionally love our physical selves is often promoted as the first step toward enlightenment. However, the nature and achievement of such self-love are elusive, with many battling varying degrees of self-esteem issues, making the journey to the next step seem far-off. It may be time to reevaluate what truly constitutes the initial step toward enlightenment and to consider alternative paths or perspectives.

The initial step may seem small, yet its significance becomes clear when we understand that our physical existence is deeply intertwined with our self-esteem, woven into a larger tapestry that connects mind, body, and soul. Remarkably, each cell in our body responds to our thoughts and beliefs, revealing the profound interconnection between mind and body, even as they remain distinct entities. Our understanding of the human form continues to evolve, but true enlightenment arises from within, nurtured through introspection and self-reflection.

Moreover, our physical form is shaped by social constructs like gender, race, and ability, which affect how we are perceived, treated, and valued across different societies. These constructs set societal expectations regarding our appearance, physical abilities, and health. Consequently, our relationship with our bodies orchestrates a complex interplay of personal, social, and cultural dimensions. It influences our self-perception, adds meaning to our daily experiences, and deeply impacts our lives. Embracing and understanding our physical selves are essential steps toward unlocking greater vitality and fulfillment.

Reflecting on identity, you'll come to realize that the question *Who am I?* sits at the heart of a profound dilemma. It urges you to define yourself, either through traits shaped by your environment or through an abstract self-image. This self-image remains abstract because all characteristics are inherently subjective. Qualities like kindness or open-mindedness, for instance, can appear vastly different depending on the observer's perspective, contextual comparisons, and the influences of one's environment or current mood.

A more transformative question to consider is, *What am I?* One question confines your growth, while the other opens up limitless possibilities. In this segment, which I call *the first knot*, we will unravel the preconceived notions bound to our identities, allowing us to transcend beyond them.

In this transformative journey we will tackle challenges that affect us all. We'll start by gently peeling away the layers of our physical form and exploring our attachment to it. This process may stir emotions. The decision to shed limiting beliefs and open yourself to new perspectives is yours to make. While emotions are valuable, they can sometimes obscure our view of reality. Therefore, I encourage you to temporarily put emotions aside, engage your intellectual curiosity, discover your untapped potential, and craft a life of purpose and deep significance.

What better way to begin than by correctly answering the wrong question?

7: The Wrong Question

The question *Who am I?* has fascinated human minds since the dawn of consciousness and remains one of the primary causes of suffering. It shapes our self-perception and deeply impacts our interactions with the world. Society teaches us to define ourselves with a fixed identity, providing a reassuring answer when asked, *"Who are you?"* The concept of self begins with our first conscious acknowledgment of *"I,"* which reveals itself through our desires and marks the start of self-awareness.

With that initial *"I,"* an inner whisper of *"I want"* emerges, marking the beginning of our individual journey and setting us apart from others. Like a star in the night sky, it becomes a small yet distinct light amidst the vastness of humanity. This uniqueness can be beautiful, but it also creates a sense of separation, introducing the duality that eventually becomes the root of suffering. The ego, constantly whispering for more, emerges, promising happiness if its demands are met. Yet, what brings joy can also become a source of misery if we fail to satisfy the unquenchable thirst of the ego. As we pursue these ego-driven desires, we often lose ourselves in competition, division, and superficiality.

We strive to *become* something—a particular person, a role, a fixed identity—believing that this will lead to satisfaction. Society encourages us to achieve these labels, whether defined by nationality, culture, race, or other distinctions. Unfortunately, defining ourselves in this way perpetuates division rather than fostering unity. I recall numerous dinner table conversations where my family casually discussed the behavior of other children in our neighborhood. Countless times, my mother would remind me: "You are not like them. Behave differently. I've raised you better." While these words may hold some truth, they inadvertently foster a sense of separation and discrimination, subtly implying superiority over others.

These early influences shape our sense of identity, compelling us to cling to external markers as though they possess sacred significance, thereby fostering suffering. Such seemingly simple and innocent remarks can quietly shape us in the wrong direction, underscoring the vital importance of conscious parenting.

The question *Who am I?* inherently demands a finite answer: a definition, a label. But to become something is to accept a limitation, no matter what that something is. Even if you were to become the leader of all creation, you would still be nothing compared to the Creator. The desire to become something gives rise to duality and, with it, the beginning of suffering. On the other hand, *What am I?* is a different question entirely. It opens doors to infinite possibilities and allows you to transcend these limitations. It helps you see beyond the superficial divisions of race, religion, nationality, and culture that can create barriers between us.

The paradox is that we are designed to hold on to something, leading the self to cling desperately to its own identity. Society's conditioning reinforces this attachment, perpetuating our dependence on external validation and rigid self-definitions. Perhaps this is why life is a test. Our intelligence must rise above our desires, above the conditioning that confines us. The self that desires cannot simply be killed; it must die through the gradual process of enlightenment. Bliss cannot be forced; the self must naturally diminish as wisdom grows.

Ironically, it is the journey of becoming nothing that brings true fulfillment. The goal of life is not to become something but to ultimately become nothing. To let go of self and ego is to shed the duality that separates us from the universe, and in doing so, we find our true place within it. One will never arrive, while the other has never left. It is this stage of bliss that every truth-seeking soul yearns for: a state of harmony that is both everything and nothing, like an atom that holds the paradoxical potential of both.

Although the world is designed to make you become something—a role, a title, an identity—true freedom lies in letting go of this need to become anything at all. We must unravel the preconceived notions tied to our identity and transcend the desire to fit neatly into labels. As we journey toward societal integration, most of us unwittingly fall victim to rigid categorizations, which in turn perpetuate biases, stereotypes, and a subjective understanding of life.

To spiral upward in enlightenment, we must embrace the process of unlearning and replace our old perspectives with new ones. Enlightenment does not begin with the question Who am I? because this question confines us to definitions that constantly change. To truly understand ourselves, we need to ask, What am I? A question that elevates our existence beyond ego, beyond labels, and beyond physical form. When we understand what we are, we stop struggling to become anything else. Suddenly, we are no longer wrestling with how we wish to appear; instead, we embrace who we are in our entirety, beyond the limits of our physical form.

This transformative journey takes us through the layers of our physical form and helps us understand our attachment to it. The decision to shed limiting beliefs and open yourself to new perspectives is yours alone. Engage with your intellectual curiosity, question the structures that bind your identity, and seek your untapped potential. The end of suffering begins with the end of duality, and the end of duality begins with the dissolution of the self.

On this journey, we do not aim to eliminate our physical form or ego but to understand their place in the grand design of existence. Our bodies and minds are tools, and the ego—though often misleading—is part of our navigation system. When we no longer let these aspects define who we are, we open ourselves to the possibility of being everything by becoming nothing.

...

Spiral Upward

In surrendering your ego and embracing the question What am I?, you will experience a profound shift. You will transcend the illusion of separateness, recognizing that while you are unique, you are also an inseparable part of the whole. It is this harmony that will transform your perception of identity and lead you toward a life of purpose, significance, and deep fulfillment. The wrong question has always been Who am I?

Instead, ask What am I? In doing so, you will spiral upward, evolving beyond the limitations of the self, embracing the fullness of existence, and discovering your boundless potential.

Exercise: Take a moment to reflect deeply on the question, *What am I?* Begin by listing the core qualities, values, and experiences that reflect your true essence—beyond societal labels, roles, or external expectations. Next, create a separate list of the labels you currently identify with (e.g., job titles, cultural roles, or self-imposed identities). Finally, evaluate how these labels might be shaping or limiting your perception of yourself. Are they empowering you, or are they holding you back from embracing your true potential?

8: The "Right" Skin Color

The Institutionalization of Minds

As we begin our journey toward societal integration, we often face a system that reinforces division, beginning with educational institutions that rigidly categorize students, inadvertently perpetuating institutionalization. From an early age, we are shaped by systems that reward conformity and discourage individuality. These institutions that, knowingly or not, contribute to a narrowing of our potential.

This stifling of potential was starkly illustrated in a study commissioned by NASA in 1960, where they sought to define genius and unlock human creativity. Their initial tests on five-year-olds showed that 98 percent of them qualified as creative geniuses. Yet, as the children aged, this figure plummeted: 30 percent at age ten, 12 percent at age fifteen, and just 2 percent in adulthood. This decline was attributed largely to the influence of the education system, which, rather than nurturing creativity, taught uncreative thinking. The creative spirit was dampened, the imagination curbed, and our natural, expansive way of viewing the world replaced with a rigid perspective focused on fitting in.

Educational institutions categorize, label, and place students into boxes, from nursery to university. While this system may be administratively convenient, it leads to biases and stereotypes that hinder us from achieving a more inclusive world. Such institutional indoctrination occurs gradually, so much so that we may be unaware of how deeply these labels and limitations shape our perceptions and behavior.

"Superman is white"

This system of categorization extends beyond creative potential; it reaches into the very core of identity, including the color of our skin. My own awareness of identity and difference began in a powerful way during my fourth-grade year. In an art class, we had a painting competition, which became a defining moment in my understanding of racism. Filled with excitement and creativity, I decided to paint Superman, but with a twist. I made his skin black because I had never seen a Black superhero before, and I thought it would be a powerful statement.

When I presented my artwork to the class, I watched as my teacher's expression shifted from approval to disapproval. She told me, "Superman is white," implying that my depiction was somehow incorrect. My innocent attempt to showcase diversity had ignited a controversy I couldn't fully understand at the time. I felt confused and unsettled, unsure of what I had done wrong. That day, I went home burdened with questions and asked my mother, "What is racism?"

Her answer was profound yet simple. "There are two kinds of people in the world," she said, her voice both gentle and firm. "Those who do good deeds and those who do bad deeds. People reveal their true character through their actions, not their nationality or skin color. Remember, the bad deeds of others can strengthen you, teaching you important lessons, while the good deeds can uplift you and inspire your spirit."

Her words touched me deeply, igniting in me a desire to uplift others, to be a beacon of light in their lives. Then she spoke again, her words carrying a depth that resonated with my soul, becoming the driving force that propelled me to strive for my best and persist through any obstacle.

"Life is akin to a race, my son, with everyone chasing after their dreams," she continued, her voice filled with both hope and sadness. "To achieve anything meaningful, you must run faster than anyone else. Run with unwavering determination, for there are forces that may try to diminish your accomplishments."

Intrigued, I asked, "Why must I run faster than others?" With a touch of sadness in her eyes, she replied, "Because of the unjust world we live in, where people are often judged by appearances or circumstances beyond their control." Her words carried the weight of generations of struggle: the unjust realities that some face simply because of their skin color. Yet despite the sadness, her voice radiated resilience and hope. It was a call to action, a reminder that the world may not always be fair, but we possess the power to transcend its limitations.

From that pivotal moment, I awakened to the profound reality of how my skin color shaped perceptions and invited judgment. I made a quiet but unwavering vow: to challenge the status quo, rise above prejudice, and become a force for meaningful change. My mother's words ignited a fire within me, compelling me to break down barriers, elevate those around me, and prove that our dreams are not defined by our skin color. Every step I take, every goal I pursue, is a declaration of my inner strength and resilience, and a steadfast hope for a more equitable and inclusive world.

The Root Causes of Racism and Institutionalization

Delving deeper into the complex roots of racism, I came to understand it not as a superficial notion, but as a deeply ingrained bias sustained by multiple factors, including the institutions that structure our lives. Just as our creative spirit can be diminished by categorization in educational systems, our understanding of one another is limited by the labels imposed upon us. These labels—based on skin color, nationality, or other arbitrary traits—serve only to divide and categorize, rather than uplift and inspire.

In exploring our biological sameness, I realized that, at our core, we share fundamental traits, differing only in superficial characteristics. Scientifically, there is no justification for one race to claim superiority over another. The belief that skin color determines worth is a harmful myth, propagated by those who have yet to understand the true essence of humanity.

So, what is the root cause of racism? It stems from a distorted sense of pride, often based on superficial attributes such as skin color, race, or nationality. True pride should be rooted in personal accomplishments, achieved through influence and effort. We must ask ourselves: Do we have any control over our birthplace or the color of our skin? Clearly, the answer is no. So, what truly warrants pride? It appears illogical, even absurd, to take pride in aspects of our existence that we had no role in shaping.

Unfortunately, we often prioritize feeding our egos over recognizing society's impact on us. We fail to see how its influence reshapes the most precious gift we possess: our inherent humanity. The constant flood of biased narratives, stereotypes, and distorted portrayals creates an environment ripe for ignorance, perpetuating discrimination. We become blind to the shared experiences, challenges, and aspirations that unify us as human beings.

To effectively combat racism, we must address its root causes and confront our own ingrained biases. Education is essential, but it doesn't necessarily begin in school nor end with a graduation degree. True education elevates our thinking, cultivates empathy, and broadens our understanding. By embracing the rich diversity that enriches our world, we can overcome ignorance and build a society where everyone is valued and celebrated for their unique contributions.

...

Spiral Upward

The journey of growth involves breaking free from labels, whether imposed by institutions, society, or even ourselves. Stop defining yourself or others by skin color or any other physical attribute. The color of your skin, the shape of your body, or any outward characteristic holds no inherent value; it is your actions, achievements, and character that truly reflect who you are. These qualities are not the entirety of your essence but rather the current stage of your growth. By moving beyond superficial judgments, you contribute to dismantling barriers such as racism, prejudice, and bias, paving the way for a future where love, acceptance, and equality flourish for everyone.

9: You Don't Need Validation

It is ironic that in our quest to grasp our identity, we often distance ourselves from the crowd, yet eventually define ourselves by our association with one. In our daily lives, the natural inclination to seek acceptance and validation begins within our close circle—our parents, family, and friends. Over time, this desire transforms into a deep-rooted need to belong to a group, especially during our teenage years, as we explore our boundaries and identities.

Regrettably, most of us become an extension of those who raised us, embodying both their strengths and flaws. Our perceptions of ourselves, especially of our physical form, are shaped by our environment, which is why we often find ourselves seeking validation and the urge to belong. This need for belonging can sometimes lead us to gravitate toward individuals who display negative behaviors, perhaps because they seem exciting or rebellious, yet these associations may not truly nurture our well-being.

This inclination is rooted in our fundamental social nature. We are wired for connection and interaction, naturally seeking validation to stave off loneliness, whether from loved ones or strangers. It is a normal part of the social fabric we live in. However, cultivating self-awareness before stepping into the unknown is essential. This involves understanding your values, setting boundaries, and choosing relationships and behaviors that align with who you truly are.

Let me share a personal story that greatly influenced my understanding of validation. My journey began in Quetta, a small city near the Afghan border. While my father sought opportunities in Europe to provide for us, my mother, siblings, and I lived in a modest clay house. My mother told me that my father had always wanted a son, but circumstances kept him away during my early years. When we finally reunited, my mother became pregnant with my younger brother.

I had always craved my father's attention, and despite my efforts, I found myself overshadowed. When my brother was born, my father's attention shifted entirely to him, cherishing the opportunity to be involved in his youngest son's early years. It became a competition for affection that I was destined to lose. During this time, I learned to live without the validation I so desperately sought.

When I was just eight years old, my father passed away from lung cancer (may he rest in peace). The day he died is etched deeply in my memory, particularly the image of my mother, her face streaked with tears. Turning to me, her voice heavy with sorrow, she said, "Your childhood is over, my son; you are now the man of the house." I walked over to her, hugged her tightly, and whispered in her ear, "Don't worry, Nana, from now on, only good times will come." My mother was taken aback, wondering what made an eight-year-old boy say such a thing on the day his father passed away.

Tragically, I had only three years with my father before his illness took him away. I can hardly recall moments of genuine connection; our time together was so brief. Moments later, I took my baby brother outside to the swings. He was only two years old at the time and asked me, "Where is Baba?" I looked up at the sky and told him, "Up there, in the skies." When he asked if our father would come back, I replied, "No, but don't worry, I am your Baba now, and I will protect and take care of you."

Suddenly, the responsibility of caring for our family rested on my young shoulders. With three older sisters and a younger brother depending on us, my mother urged me to fill the void my father had left. Though I was still a child, I never saw myself that way again. My childhood slipped away, replaced by the weight of responsibility. Every action in life has a cost, and for me, stepping into adulthood meant sacrificing those precious years of being a child. It was a pivotal event that shaped my understanding of independence and validation—an early realization that I would have to become my own source of strength.

I never had a father figure to validate me, to guide me on my path to becoming a decent man. I had to evolve into that role by stumbling, falling, and picking myself back up. As an Afghan child who moved to Denmark at five, I faced additional challenges in speaking and writing, which added to the emotional difficulties of my life. I struggled to communicate effectively with other kids, making me an easy target for mockery. Though I couldn't fully understand the root of my anger, I often found myself in fights at school, worsening my situation.

Football was my passion, but I found it unbearable when other kids asked why my father was never there to support me on the field. In one way or another, I always felt set apart from the crowd. Reflecting on those challenging times fills me with gratitude, for they were opportunities to cultivate resilience and inner strength.

In my teenage years, I embraced my individuality and the choices that set me apart. In a society where experimenting with substances and attending social events is considered the norm, I remained true to myself, abstaining from alcohol, drugs, and parties. At first, this made me feel like an outsider, the odd one who didn't partake in these experiences. Over time, however, people began to see it as a source of strength rather than a flaw. Standing firm in my beliefs, even in the face of pressure, demonstrated unwavering determination. Not receiving validation from my father taught me not to seek it from others, but to validate myself.

My mother often reminded me that life presents two choices: right and wrong. Choosing the right path may be challenging initially, but it leads to a rewarding end. Conversely, choosing the wrong path may offer temporary pleasure, but it never ends well. True validation lies in following the path that aligns with your heart and values, not in the fleeting approval of others.

•••

Spiral Upward

Focus on validating your thoughts rather than seeking validation for your character. To validate your thoughts means to assess whether they are rooted in truth. In contrast, seeking validation for your character from others can lead you to mold yourself to meet their expectations, rather than your own. Your thoughts are a reflection of your unique experiences, but they only shape your character if you choose to act on them. Let your actions be guided and validated by your core values, not by external expectations. Remember, while external validation may provide momentary satisfaction, adhering to your principles will bring lasting fulfillment.

10: Standing Alone Is Not a Weakness

The Power of the Mind

Realizing the power of the mind has been a profound awakening for me. A strong mind can transcend weak thoughts, while a weak mind can easily be consumed by them.

A weak mind can make even the strongest person feel powerless, while a strong mind can empower even the weakest individual. One is governed by thoughts, mistaking them for reality; the other uses thoughts to shape reality. The difference lies in the strength of will.

Thoughts are tools, not absolute representations of reality. They may reflect reality, but they originate from the mind's limitless capacity to think, imagine, and create. Whether driven by fear or excitement, thoughts can manifest into reality through the power of the mind.

The strength of our thoughts and ideas shapes our lives and influences the world around us. Society often leads us to believe that the way of the majority is always superior. Yet history consistently proves that true power does not lie in numbers but in the thoughts and ideas championed by individuals. Every significant breakthrough, invention, or societal transformation has begun in the mind of a single person. These individuals, with their unique perspectives and visions, have sparked revolutionary changes, from scientific discoveries to creative masterpieces, that have shaped humanity and impacted millions.

Standing alone can be intimidating. It requires immense courage to go against the tide, to challenge the current of popular opinion. Standing alone cannot be forced or done for its own sake; it arises from an inner conviction that something must be better. You feel it first in your heart, then you voice it, and eventually, you strive to change it with your actions. If change is not possible, you distance yourself from what cannot be transformed.

You do not choose solitude; solitude chooses you. In these moments of solitude and reflection, we find a deeper connection between our physical form and our true self. We come to realize that the strength of the body means little if the mind lacks resilience, flexibility, and the ability to cope with adversity. True strength comes from a resilient mind, one that is capable of adapting, persisting, and thriving, regardless of external circumstances.

A Strong Mind

A strong mind cannot simply conform to society, even if it wishes to; it creates its own thoughts, dreams, and aspirations, free from the expectations of others. It is driven by the desire to contribute something meaningful and original to the world, guided by its unique perspectives. Instead of harboring envy or resentment, a strong mind celebrates the successes of others. The achievements of others do not diminish our potential; rather, they inspire us to strive for greater heights. By supporting and uplifting one another, we foster a culture of collaboration, growth, and mutual empowerment.

Standing Alone in the Real World

Embracing our individuality and making choices based on our values and principles requires courage and maturity. It takes effort and depends on the strength of our thoughts. The deeper our understanding, the stronger our standpoint, and the harder it becomes for others to sway us. Life always offers at least two choices, and our paths and decisions define who we become. By standing alone when needed, we navigate life's challenges and emerge stronger, wiser, and more fulfilled.

Standing alone means rising above the allure of negativity and the fear of loneliness. It does not imply isolation from the world; rather, it signifies the courage to remain true to oneself. By walking our own path, guided by our convictions, we not only live authentically but also inspire others to do the same.

Stand Tall

Biologically, our brain is wired to protect us, shutting down when it perceives potential harm to the body. Even in moments of extreme exhaustion, our body is capable of performing far beyond what we think possible; however, the brain sets a limit to keep us safe. This means our physical potential is far greater than we realize—our mental limits are reached long before our physical ones. By cultivating a strong will and mastering our minds, we can stand firm, unafraid to embrace our uniqueness and pursue our dreams.

This inner resolve allows us to stand tall even in the face of challenges like disabilities, bias, or discrimination—obstacles that might otherwise cause us to shrink back. Our mind, however, has a natural inclination toward comfort and laziness. If we give in to this tendency, it can lead to an unwillingness to step outside our comfort zones, whether it's getting out of bed or trying something new. This resistance to change is the greatest barrier to personal growth and transformation. By mastering our minds and overcoming this resistance, we allow ourselves to evolve, rise above our limitations, and reach our true potential.

...

Spiral Upward

Strengthen your mind by cultivating and deepening your thoughts. Seek the truth within them, and let that truth be your guide. Forge your path with courage; the world will try to mold you, but true power is sculpted from within. Instead of depending on others for positivity, nurture it within yourself—remember, like the sun, your energy must come from within. When you radiate positivity from your core, like-minded individuals will naturally be drawn to you.

Stare down your fears to uncover the courage that lies beneath. Each brave step turns doubt into confidence. There is immense power in standing alone, in embracing your individuality, and in genuinely celebrating the successes of others. Do not shy away from standing alone when it fosters your growth. Confront your fears, for in doing so, you will uncover your true courage and resilience.

Embrace your authenticity and let your inner strength light the way. By facing your challenges with bravery and grace, you transform fear into confidence, standing as a testament to the power of self-belief and perseverance.

11: Becoming a Man

This life lesson is essential for both men and women, as women play a pivotal role in shaping men's upbringing, while men often face challenges in staying connected to their authentic masculine identity. Women naturally embody the qualities of exceptional leaders yet often seek guidance—not out of inability, but out of love, to nurture and elevate the masculine role in their partner. It's a gesture of trust, much like asking for help opening a jar they could easily manage themselves. On the other hand, men are inherently driven to lead but often thrive when they incorporate emotional intelligence into their leadership. Perhaps this is why the saying goes, "Behind every successful man is a strong woman." This dynamic beautifully illustrates the interdependence between masculine and feminine energies—a timeless and profound love story that reveals the power of unity, mutual respect, and support.

Among life's significant milestones, the transition from boyhood to manhood stands out, filled with excitement, confusion, and uncertainty. It is a transformative journey marked by the embrace of responsibility, the cultivation of courage, and the embodiment of integrity. Let us explore the insights that arise when we truly step into these roles, unlocking the powerful synergy between masculine and feminine forces that shape us all.

The Evolution of Manhood

The evolution of manhood is undoubtedly a complex and often controversial subject, but it is one that demands thoughtful exploration. Biologically and socially, women often exhibit qualities that naturally align with leadership—qualities that are perhaps most profoundly expressed through motherhood. In becoming mothers, women often evolve into fierce protectors and nurturing guides, channeling a unique combination of strength, empathy, and intuitive wisdom. These attributes enable them to steer their children's growth with remarkable insight, embodying the very essence of authentic and transformative leadership.

Similarly, fathers are instinctively wired to protect their families. A UK study demonstrated this dynamic through a simple experiment: When a baby cried out in distress during the night, mothers woke immediately, while fathers often slept through it. Conversely, when a rustling of leaves signaled potential danger outside the home, fathers woke instantly, but mothers remained asleep. This difference is linked to vasopressin, a hormone abundant in fathers, often called the "protective aggression hormone," which primes men to safeguard their families. These instincts highlight how deeply biological wiring shapes our roles as caregivers and protectors, underscoring the complementary relationship between the masculine and feminine.

Traits such as vision, empathy, and integrity are hallmarks of effective leadership. Impactful leaders adapt to change, make decisive choices, communicate with clarity, remain resilient in the face of setbacks, and demonstrate high emotional intelligence—understanding not only their own emotions but also those of others. They take accountability for their actions, viewing mistakes as opportunities for growth, and inspire others to excel. Interestingly, these are the very qualities mothers often display in raising their children. Yet, these traits are not exclusive to women; men also possess them, though they may manifest in different ways.

When men step into fatherhood, many naturally embrace their paternal instincts, developing a profound sense of responsibility as providers. Biologically, women may feel a stronger inclination toward nurturing and guiding the family, while men often gravitate toward roles of providing and protecting. However, being a provider is only one dimension of fatherhood, just as nurturing is only one aspect of motherhood. Many fathers embody nurturing qualities, offering emotional support and guidance, just as mothers can excel as providers. This interplay underscores the fluidity and shared responsibility of parenting roles.

The concept of manhood is multifaceted, transcending cultural, societal, and generational boundaries, making it difficult to define. To understand authentic manhood, we must examine both the biological influences that shape our roles and the personal growth that defines us as individuals. We must also question whether our understanding of manhood mirrors the behaviors of our fathers, conforms to societal expectations, or requires a transformative journey of unlearning and relearning what it truly means to be a man.

True manhood is not a fixed set of traits but an evolution—an ongoing journey that demands courage, introspection, and growth. It is about embracing authenticity, challenging outdated norms, and striving to become the best version of oneself.

Challenging Stereotypes of Masculinity

While our mothers raise us with care, our fathers often serve as our role models. Sometimes, what we are taught contradicts what we observe, and we must understand that our father's journey cannot serve as a universal blueprint for our own lives. It is important to appreciate our fathers' positive qualities while recognizing that we each have unique paths to follow. Relying solely on their examples denies us our individuality and the power of our own minds to shape our futures.

Society imposes limiting stereotypes about masculinity that we must challenge to truly understand what it means to be a man. Reevaluating these stereotypes allows us to embrace a broader and more inclusive vision of masculinity. By unlearning outdated expectations, we free ourselves to be more authentic, compassionate, and fully ourselves.

One common stereotype about men is the intense focus on physical appearance. From a young age, this expectation is ingrained in us—reinforced by action figures and media portrayals of masculine heroes with idealized bodies. This cultural narrative places an undue emphasis on physical strength and appearance rather than intellectual or emotional development. Consequently, many men grow up focusing on building their bodies rather than their minds.

However, true strength lies not solely in physical prowess but in balanced development—one that values mental and emotional growth alongside physical fitness. Men, like anyone else, benefit immensely from a more holistic approach to well-being. By nurturing all aspects of ourselves—physical, intellectual, and emotional—we challenge the narrow definitions of masculinity that prioritize appearance over deeper attributes. This approach paves the way for a more well-rounded, fulfilling, and authentic expression of manhood.

Embracing Responsibility and Courage

I vividly remember a conversation with my mother about what it means to become a man. When she told me, "It's time for you to assume the role of the man of the house," I had not yet fully grasped what it even meant to be a boy.

Seeing the worry in my eyes, she reassured me, "Being a man is not solely defined by age, but by the circumstances you face, the responsibilities you bear, and the attitude you adopt. The weight you carry can either break you or shape you—but the choice to rise above your challenges is yours."

Though fear gripped me, her words became my guiding light, teaching me the essence of true bravery. She showed me that our dreams are intertwined with our courage. Courage isn't about the absence of fear—it's about the willingness to confront and overcome it. Every step taken beyond our comfort zone, every plunge into the unknown, molds our character and propels personal growth. Along the way, mistakes and setbacks are inevitable, but it is our resilience in these moments that ignites the flame of true courage.

The Intersection of Physical and Mental Well-Being

Throughout this journey, I made countless mistakes, but my mother always encouraged me to keep moving forward. Over time, I came to understand that manhood is not about power—it is about strength. The misconception that masculinity is defined by success, wealth, or conquests often leads us astray. True strength lies in our capacity to be gentle, compassionate, and respectful. The bravest among us are those who love deeply, support others, and inspire change through empathy rather than instilling fear.

There is nothing more dangerous than a weak man spending his life compensating for his lack of true masculinity. True manhood is about upholding self-respect and integrity, even in the face of adversity. It is not about seeking validation from others, but about staying true to one's internal compass. A man's character should bring smiles to people's faces, and his honesty should provide comfort, establishing a foundation of trust and respect with others.

Misguided notions of manhood can divert us, emphasizing superficial markers of success. Being a man entails far more than material wealth, status, or the mastery of romantic pursuits. It is about leadership, compassion, and positively impacting the lives of others. Our perspective shifts when we recognize that every woman we encounter is someone's daughter, deserving of the same respect and dignity we afford our mothers and sisters. This realization deepens our empathy and respect for all women.

Becoming a man is an ongoing journey that extends beyond physical growth or the passage of time. It involves embracing responsibility, finding courage in the face of adversity, and embodying integrity. By caring for our bodies, nurturing our health, and understanding the connection between our physical and mental well-being, we foster our growth as men. True manhood is not about domination or strength for its own sake, but about the balance of gentleness with resilience, and compassion with courage.

...

Spiral Upward

Embark on the journey of becoming, supporting, or raising a man. It is a path shaped by responsibility, courage in adversity, and integrity in every action. True manhood is not about titles or appearances; it is about self-respect and the commitment to be a force for positive change. By nurturing both body and mind, you equip yourself to face challenges, lead with purpose, and rise toward your best self. Answer the call to true manhood with boldness, authenticity, and unwavering determination.

12: Lead Yourself

Embracing responsibility as a guiding force in life is essential to personal growth, as true leadership naturally emerges from taking responsibility. Therefore, understanding authentic leadership is a pivotal life lesson that each of us must learn.

Let's begin with a fundamental question: *What is leadership?* The standard definition, as per Oxford Dictionaries, describes it as "the action of leading a group of people or an organization." Yet, this definition overlooks the most crucial aspect—authentic leadership goes far beyond simply guiding others.

Authentic leadership starts with leading oneself. True leaders do not seek positions of power; instead, they are called into leadership by those around them. They understand the immense responsibility of guiding others and take on this role only for selfless reasons. The distinction between exploiting leadership for personal gain and practicing genuine leadership is significant. Those who exploit leadership manipulate others for their own benefit, whereas genuine leaders prioritize the well-being of those they serve. Unfortunately, many of today's leaders exemplify the self-serving type, focused more on personal ambition than true service.

True leadership begins with addressing and overcoming our own internal battles. How can we extend a helping hand to others if we are still struggling to stay afloat ourselves? If we are drowning in our own challenges, our desperate attempts to survive may lead to panic, clouding our judgment and unintentionally harming those around us. We cannot guide others if we have not first mastered guiding ourselves. We must navigate our own storms before we can offer steady hands and a clear direction to those who need us.

True Leadership

Your drive to lead and inspire others should not stem from personal ambition, unless it is in the service of a greater good. Your very presence should become a source of direction and motivation for others. Your actions and behavior should serve as a compass, pointing the way upward and helping others discover their own paths. Like a seasoned sailor who reads the currents, anticipates challenges, and steers toward calmer waters, a true leader guides others through life's uncertainties.

The challenges you have faced should become wisdom to uplift others, not stories to boost your ego or gain sympathy. Your energy speaks before you do, and your presence should be felt before it is seen. As a leader, you embody the role of a gardener, cultivating an environment that nurtures growth. Your presence creates fertile ground where dreams can take root and flourish. With genuine care, you offer support, encouragement, and mentorship, empowering others to express their unique leadership qualities.

In this metaphorical garden of leadership, you are both the gardener and the catalyst for growth. Through self-reflection and continuous learning, you become a transformative force, inspiring and empowering others to embark on their own leadership journeys. This remarkable transition brings you to a place where you are not a performer seeking applause, but a beacon of authenticity and inspiration.

The journey from self-discovery to leadership becomes a symphony, each note resonating with purpose and passion. Gone are the masks and costumes that once concealed your true self; in their place, you wear the cloak of vulnerability, embracing imperfections as badges of honor. You become a guiding light, illuminating the path for others.

Remember, the extraordinary journey of genuine leadership—encompassing both the spiritual and physical dimensions of your being—will not be without its challenges. Yet, with every obstacle you overcome, you become stronger and more resilient. Your authenticity becomes a compass, guiding others on their own quests for self-discovery. Leadership is not about perfection; it's about showing up with integrity, authenticity, and a commitment to serve others.

...

Spiral Upward

Leadership begins by mastering your own mind and body, and by staying true to yourself. Cast aside the masks and release the burden of external expectations. Step into the world with courage and authenticity. Let every action you take create ripples of positive change, uplifting not only yourself but also those around you. Embrace challenges, celebrate your victories with humility, and let your genuine leadership become a source of inspiration for others.

13: Visualization Is Not Enough

If you can't see it, how can you achieve it? In the labyrinth of our minds, a profound truth echoes: if you cannot control your thoughts, you are enslaved by them. Leadership is more than just authority—it is about mastering our own minds and taking dominion over our thoughts. But how do we liberate ourselves from the shackles of inherited and conditioned perspectives?

The answer lies in peeling back the layers of our thinking until we no longer identify with our thoughts but instead use them as tools to propel ourselves upward.

Delving into the Depths of Thinking

Both conscious and subconscious thinking originate from the vast realm of thought, where a delicate balance holds: we can either be dominated by our thoughts or master them. The conscious mind is where our current awareness resides, actively engaging in thoughts, decision-making, and handling tasks that require focus and logical thinking. In contrast, the subconscious mind operates below our conscious awareness, influencing our emotions, habits, and automatic responses, drawing on stored memories and past experiences.

Delving deep into these thought processes is crucial for personal growth. While we naturally aspire to achieve specific goals or crave change, merely desiring these outcomes is insufficient; success hinges on adopting the correct approach to thinking.

Imagine a toolbox filled with various tools, symbolizing your subconscious mind. When a specific need arises, you select the appropriate tools from this box, comparable to how we utilize our conscious mind. Knowing which tools to select is merely the first step; the true skill lies in effectively employing them.

Within our conscious mind, we engage in both active and passive thinking. Understanding this distinction is vital; otherwise, we risk falling into a cycle of wishful thinking, where achieving our goals seems unattainable, leading us to believe they were never within our reach.

Passive Thinking vs. Active Thinking

Passive thinking is akin to slipping into a mode of wishful contemplation, where we become mere spectators, hoping for outcomes to unfold on their own without taking concrete actions. This approach keeps us confined to daydreams, presenting endless possibilities without the empowerment to act on them.

In contrast, active thinking transforms aspirations into tangible achievements and propels us toward a fulfilling life. It involves a proactive mindset—not merely dreaming but taking meaningful action toward realizing those dreams. Active thinking immerses us in a dynamic world of possibilities, envisioning our goals as if they are already realized. This mindset instills a strong sense of responsibility for our lives, fueling the motivation and determination needed to make our dreams a reality. Active thinking is the key to converting aspirations into actionable steps and driving us toward success.

Now, try this exercise to embody active thinking: Write down one of your primary goals. Close your eyes and imagine it has already come to pass. Feel the success. Let this sensation elevate your energy from longing to having achieved. Notice how your aura glows with accomplishment. Ask yourself, "How would I behave if I achieve this goal?" Strive to match your vibration to that frequency, embodying the success as if it were your current reality.

Growth and Self-Reflection

Growth is the essence of personal evolution. Just as a delicate plant requires constant nurturing to bloom, we must actively pursue growth to prevent stagnation, for without growth, we risk losing our vitality and purpose.

By adopting the powerful perspective of active thinking, we acknowledge challenges as gateways to self-improvement. Every experience, whether it results in success or appears as a setback, serves as a valuable lesson, pushing us closer to our true potential. Growth is the life force that keeps us thriving, and active thinking helps us embrace challenges as stepping stones on our journey to personal evolution.

Circumstances and True Identity

Many believe that circumstances can change us; I believe they unveil us. Different circumstances uniquely reveal who we truly are and challenge who we thought we were. It's easy to imagine how we would like to react in a given situation, but reality often tells a different story when challenges arise.

While external circumstances can shape our experiences, they do not determine our identity. In times of difficulty, our character is tested and shaped. Instead of allowing hardships to chip away at our sense of self, we can use these trials as catalysts that reveal our finest qualities.

By embracing active thinking, we protect our authenticity and remain steadfast in our commitment to our core values, regardless of the unpredictable nature of the outside world. We harness our inner strength and resilience to navigate challenging situations, ensuring that they do not diminish our true selves but reveal our stability and integrity.

Be the Master of Your Own Narrative

People will always have opinions and judgments about us. It's natural to feel overwhelmed by this noise, whether positive or negative. However, it is crucial to remember that the opinions of others do not define who we truly are. Instead of becoming mirrors reflecting others' perceptions, we must strive to embody our authenticity.

By embracing active thinking, we nurture an unwavering sense of self and let go of the need for external validation. This liberation allows our true selves to soar freely, unhindered by others' expectations. In essence, we become the authors of our own narrative, actively shaping our story rather than passively letting others write it for us.

Letting Go of "What Ifs"

Regret and the weight of "What ifs" can burden our souls, preventing us from fully experiencing the present. When we dwell on past actions or anxiously worry about an uncertain future, we diminish our capacity for active thinking and limit our control over our lives.

We must strive to break free from these chains of uncertainty and embrace the serenity of the present. By releasing the burden of "What ifs," we liberate our spirit, empowering ourselves to shape our reality and seize the opportunities before us. In doing so, we escape the grip of regret and anxious anticipation, allowing ourselves to engage fully in the present and actively create a brighter future.

...

Spiral Upward

Embrace active thinking as the spark of your transformation—fueling growth, empowerment, and genuine fulfillment. Move beyond the passive comfort of simple visualization and step into the realm of intentional action, where change becomes real and your life begins to rise. Become the architect of your reality, navigating challenges with resilience, embodying authenticity, and infusing each moment with intention. Harness the power of active thinking, trusting in God's decree, to shape a life that reflects the best of your God-given potential.

14: The Power of Manifestation

Active thinking is a crucial step toward achieving our goals, but on its own, it is not enough. To truly harness the power of manifestation, we must understand how thought, intention, and prayer shape the course of our lives.

Every thought carries energy. Every intention is like a seed planted in the soil of reality. When nourished with action, sincerity, and trust in God, those seeds may grow into outcomes we never imagined. The Qur'an reminds us: *"Call upon Me; I will respond to you"* (40:60).

But manifestation is not magic. It is not about bending the universe to our will. It is about aligning ourselves — our thoughts, our emotions, our actions — with God's will, and trusting that He is the One who opens or closes doors.

Let's explore how embodiment and collective consciousness can elevate us to manifest our visions fully.

These are the foundational principles of the law of attraction:

The Principle of Reversibility: Just as water can transform into steam, and steam back into water, they are fundamentally the same, merely vibrating at different frequencies. Similarly, circumstances can produce feelings, and feelings can shape circumstances. Everything is energy, and energy moves in waves, just like our thoughts. By fueling our thoughts with emotions—whether love or fear—we shape our choices and actions. And when our intentions are aligned with sincerity and trust in God, He may open the doors to what we seek. What we seek is also seeking us. If it is written for us by His will.

Thoughts Become Reality: Your thoughts hold immense power to shape your reality. By consistently focusing on and believing in specific outcomes, you plant seeds that grow into tangible results. Positive thinking acts as a magnet, drawing favorable experiences, while negative thoughts often attract adverse circumstances.

The Law of Input and Output: The energy you send into the universe will be reflected back to you. This means the effort you put in directly determines the rewards you receive. Radiating positivity attracts uplifting experiences and people, while emitting negativity tends to draw similar adverse circumstances.

Harnessing Visualization and Affirmations: Visualization and affirmations are powerful tools that guide the mind toward desired outcomes. They reinforce positive beliefs, enhancing the manifestation process and solidifying your commitment to your goals.

Cultivating Gratitude and Optimism: Cultivating gratitude and maintaining an optimistic outlook amplify the law of attraction. Gratitude infuses your energy field with positivity, further aligning you with your desires.

Beyond Visualization

To manifest effectively, it's crucial to understand that the law of attraction involves more than just visualization, it requires us to immerse ourselves fully in the experience of our envisioned reality as if it has already come to pass. When we visualize our desired future, we may unintentionally signal to our mind and body that the goal is still out of reach, creating a sense of longing.

It's essential to recognize that the mind and body cannot differentiate between vividly imagined scenarios and actual experiences. The power of our visualizations can evoke physiological responses as if they were real events. Just like in dreams that feel like reality and cause our bodies to react as though they are real, we should use this phenomenon to our advantage.

True awareness lies in understanding the blurred line between what is imagined and what is real, enabling us to harness the full potential of visualization for effective manifestation. This doesn't mean we should be delusional about our reality but rather apply the foundational principles of the law of attraction to shape our desired environment, grounding our aspirations in actionable strategies.

Becoming a Reflection of Our Desires

Manifestation is not merely about wishful thinking; it is a declaration, to ourselves and to the universe, that we are ready for and deserving of our desires. The power of our thoughts profoundly shapes our perception of reality. By focusing steadfastly on our desires and maintaining a positive state of mind, we convince ourselves that our vision is achievable.

Consider the act of lying down: as you relax, each cell communicates tiredness to your mind, eventually leading you to sleep. This interconnectedness is powerful. Now, imagine being utterly exhausted but suddenly facing an emergency: instantly, your mind activates every cell in your body, flooding it with energy and alertness. This rapid response illustrates the seamless connection between mind and body and underscores the influence of our thoughts on our physical state.

The Power of Self-Talk

Consistent positive self-talk is as crucial as avoiding negative self-talk in reshaping our self-image and reinforcing our belief that we are deserving of our aspirations. Through affirmations, we not only reprogram our subconscious but also foster a mindset that aligns with our vision. It's essential to remember that the art of positive affirmation is not merely in repeating words but in visualizing the outcome. Seeing it in the mind's eye transforms abstract desires into concrete goals.

As our self-talk supports our desired reality, our behavior naturally evolves to bring us closer to our goals. Our words become a catalyst, propelling our dreams into reality. Regardless of our circumstances, the capacity of what we can achieve is remarkable, demonstrating the profound connection between our thoughts, words, and actions.

Embracing Collective Consciousness

While individual effort is crucial, the law of attraction also thrives in the collective sphere. As our vision takes root within us, it is important to share it and inspire those around us. By involving others, we plant seeds in the collective consciousness. When others believe in our vision, their energy harmonizes with ours, amplifying the manifestation process. The law of attraction becomes even more powerful through the combined intentions and actions of the community, creating opportunities beyond what we can achieve alone.

Transcending Personal Vision

As we progress on the journey of manifestation, our vision begins to expand from purely personal desires to encompass a greater purpose. The law of attraction molds our aspirations into something larger than ourselves: transforming them into a force that shapes not only our lives but also impacts and uplifts others. This expanded vision fuels a deeper sense of purpose, compelling us to continue our journey and make a positive difference in the world.

My Own Story

I've witnessed these principles in both their pain and their promise. For years, my prayers to God carried a single plea: *"Test me in anything You choose, except in two things — my wife and my brother."* They were everything to me. My wife, who is now my ex-wife. And my brother, who has always been my Achilles' heel in life. But what I feared most became the very trials I was handed. My fear became my input, and, true to the principle, it became my output. My decisions, shaped by that fear, led me to lose my wife and to be separated from my brother for years.

It shattered me. I had asked God to spare me, and yet the very thing I begged to be spared from was written for me. That's when I realized: fear itself can summon the very trial we dread. And sometimes, God does not answer our prayers by protecting us from pain, but by guiding us through it — so that we may emerge stronger.

But manifestation is not only about fear. It is also about hidden intention. When I was twenty-eight years old, I wrote something on a piece of paper: *"I will be successful and retire by the age of forty-two."* I didn't make a plan. I didn't obsess over it. I simply wrote it, folded it away, and forgot about it.

Decades later, while sifting through old papers in my factory, I came across that forgotten note. When I unfolded it and read the words, I couldn't help but smile. I had retired at exactly forty-two — not by force, not by relentless chasing, but because the seed of that intention had been carried silently through time, and God had willed it into reality.

This was especially powerful because, at the age of thirty-nine, I was homeless and drowning in a debt of 1.6 million. Today I am debt-free, with multiple businesses, and I have not "worked" or needed employment for years. The boy's words had met the man's destiny.

That scrap of paper reminded me of something profound: fear had once carved the path to my downfall, but intention, surrendered to God, had carved the path to my freedom.

...

Spiral Upward

Embrace the law of attraction and awaken your innate ability to bring your visions to life. Cultivate vivid mental states, engage in positive self-talk, and collaborate with others to unlock transformative potential. As your vision grows beyond personal desires, let it become a force that turns dreams into tangible realities, impacting countless lives. Seize your power: your vision holds the potential to make a difference. Remember, persistence and purposeful action are the keys to manifestation. Are you ready to unleash your potential and shape the reality you envision?

15: Motivation Through Action

Let's take a moment to recap and ensure we're continuing to evolve in the right direction. Our transformative journey began by challenging the limiting notions of identity, recognizing that rigid beliefs about who we are can confine our true potential. We then embraced the understanding that the physical form—its shape, color, or other attributes—holds no inherent value in the grander scope of the human experience. This realization empowers us to break free from the need for external validation, opening the door to authentic growth and self-discovery.

We moved forward by focusing on character development, exploring the true strength of standing alone and embracing the power of individuality. This exploration naturally led us to redefine masculinity, moving beyond traditional stereotypes to understand manhood in a more holistic and authentic way.

Next, we addressed the misconceptions surrounding leadership, highlighting that authentic leadership begins with self-guidance—an essential element in achieving any goal. From here, we learned that successfully pursuing our goals requires envisioning them clearly and engaging in active thinking, which revealed the transformative potential of manifestation.

The natural progression from this point is motivation. A flawed understanding can leave us stagnant, while a clear understanding propels us upward, continuing our journey toward self-mastery and personal growth.

The Fuel Behind Motivation

Motivation is a popular topic among motivational speakers, often addressed in stirring speeches. However, in my experience, it boils down to two essential questions: *What do you truly want?* and *How badly do you want it?* Trying to motivate someone who lacks desire is often futile. History teaches us that growth is an intrinsic aspect of human nature, while stagnation leaves us feeling empty and unfulfilled. Our very biology drives us to dream, grow, and evolve. Yet, we all face moments when inspiration eludes us. The challenge is not in experiencing these moments but in ensuring we don't remain in them for too long. So, how do we rekindle our motivation during such times?

A common misconception about motivation is that it must come before action—that we need motivation in order to begin. This belief often traps people in a cycle of demotivation, waiting for inspiration to strike. In truth, goals provide direction, passion is discovered along the way, and motivation is cultivated through movement, all of which require that first step. Your life's calling is ultimately about your commitment, but it all begins with action.

Advice like, "You need a reason to get out of bed," or "Focus on a goal," can inadvertently support the misconception that motivation is a prerequisite for action. The truth is, action often ignites motivation.

To better understand this, we must consider how our brain works, particularly the role of dopamine, a neurotransmitter that generates feelings of reward and drive. This reveals that motivation frequently follows action, rather than the other way around. Engaging in activities and achieving small goals trigger the release of dopamine, which reinforces behavior and enhances our drive to continue. This cycle shows us that even small steps can initiate a positive feedback loop of motivation, pushing us upward.

The key lies in taking that first step—however small—to set the cycle in motion. Action leads to progress, progress sparks motivation, and motivation sustains growth. Motivation, then, is not just a feeling to be waited for, but a process that can be cultivated by making consistent, deliberate choices to move forward.

Unleashing Motivation Through Action

For years, I was encouraged to write a book, but I kept waiting for the perfect surge of inspiration—a wave of creative energy that I believed would sweep over me and fuel my writing. That moment of motivation never came. It wasn't until I changed my approach that things began to shift. Instead of waiting, I decided to take action: I bought a camera and began sharing my thoughts across various platforms. Though I felt hesitant and uncomfortable speaking into the lens at first, I persisted. Over six months of creating and recording content, I gradually found my voice, and my creativity started to flow. To my surprise, my videos resonated with millions.

Undeterred by challenges, I committed myself to writing daily. Initially, the process felt slow and awkward, but over time, the words began to flow more naturally, evolving into life lessons that would form the foundation of this book. Years later, I completed my manuscript: a living testament to the truth that action ignites motivation. It wasn't motivation that started my journey; it was taking that first step that eventually sparked the inspiration I needed to keep going.

...

Spiral Upward

Unlock your true passions and life's calling by embracing action. Motivation isn't a mysterious force; it's something you create through your own actions and determination. Just like when you dip your finger into the ocean, no matter how vast the ocean is or how small and insignificant the act of your finger may seem, it still creates ripples that spread outward, setting movement into motion. Similarly, even the smallest action you take can spark waves of progress in your life. Seek opportunities, push your boundaries, and you'll find both inspiration and accomplishment waiting for you. Break free from the cycle of demotivation by taking that crucial first step. Action is the key to unlocking your potential; motivation is not beyond reach but within your grasp, cultivated through consistency and perseverance. Embrace action, fuel it with unwavering determination, and watch your dreams transform into reality.

16: The Fear of Missing Out

Our understanding of motivation has evolved, moving beyond fleeting sparks of inspiration to encompass the consistent actions that propel us forward. But beneath the surface lies a deeper, more complex question: *What truly drives us?* Too often, we discover that our motivations are not rooted in genuine needs but instead arise from the fear of missing out; the pervasive feeling that life's most meaningful experiences are happening elsewhere, without us.

This fear thrives on perception, as our thoughts and interpretations profoundly shape our reality. It's easy to be swept up in illusions, chasing after what appears significant while overlooking what genuinely matters. To break free from this cycle, we must peel back the layers of assumption and illusion that cloud our understanding of fulfillment. When we do, we begin to see our desires for what they truly are: reflections of how we perceive the world, not necessarily of reality itself.

One of the most revealing aspects of human desire is its paradoxical nature: *"You don't want what I have, and I don't want what you have. You want what you think I have, and I want what I think you have."* This observation highlights the role of perception and assumption in shaping our desires. Often, we are not drawn to the actual lives of others but to the curated, imagined versions we construct in our minds. The grass always seems greener because we are viewing it through a lens of comparison, not reality.

Imagine if everyone's challenges and burdens were laid bare for all to see, with each of us given the choice to select our own. How many of us would willingly reclaim what we already carry? More often than not, we would choose to stick with our own trials because, whether we realize it or not, we are uniquely equipped to handle them. They are ours for a reason, part of our individual journey and growth.

Our endless pursuit of unattainable desires often stems from the stories we tell ourselves and the assumptions we make about what others possess. We chase an elusive version of happiness, convinced it lies just beyond our reach. In doing so, we rob ourselves of the opportunity to find contentment in the present moment. The constant feeling of missing out creates a mindset that the "real" life is always happening elsewhere, leaving us disheartened and disconnected from the beauty that already surrounds us.

To shift this perspective, let's broaden our understanding of existence. We *are* not merely humans navigating the vastness of the universe; we are the universe, manifesting itself to explore the wonders of human experience. Composed of stardust and boundless cosmic energy, we are intimately connected to everything around us. Embracing this truth can lift the weight of comparison from our shoulders, helping us view life with renewed wonder. This realization reminds us that our existence is not a passive observation but an active, meaningful participation in the grand dance of the cosmos.

To fully embrace the human condition, we must accept it as a whole—joy and sorrow, success and failure, love and heartbreak. True freedom lies not in avoiding life's dualities but in embracing them. The richness of life comes not from accumulating more but from immersing ourselves in the present moment and finding beauty in every breath. This shift in perspective transforms life from a race to an unfolding journey, full of depth and meaning.

By letting go of unrealistic expectations and releasing the need for external validation, we can rediscover the joy of simply living. Fulfillment does not come from pursuing what others have; it emerges when we walk our own unique path. As we shed the weight of comparison, we open ourselves to countless possibilities, deepening our connection to our true selves and the world around us.

...

Spiral Upward

Break free from the fleeting illusions that distract you from the richness of the present moment. Life is not a relentless pursuit of more, nor is it a competition to measure up to others. Instead, it is an invitation to dance with the universe, to revel in the wonder of existence, and to find joy in simply *being*. Cast aside the burdens of comparison and recognize the profound interconnectedness that unites us all. The essence of life doesn't lie elsewhere—it dwells within you, waiting to be discovered. Embrace the present moment, honor your unique journey, and celebrate the extraordinary beauty of your existence.

17: Spend Time Alone

In the constant rush of modern life, it's all too easy to lose touch with our authentic selves amidst the noise of external pressures. How can we distinguish between our true needs and those desires fueled merely by the fear of missing out?

The key lies in cultivating mindfulness: taking the time to pause, reflect, and evaluate whether our desires align with our core values and contribute to our long-term well-being.

Spending time alone is not a luxury; it is essential for enriching our lives. It serves as a gateway to self-awareness, providing space to explore our thoughts, feelings, and interests without the interference of external distractions. In solitude, we uncover the true essence of our being, offering us the opportunity for introspection and a deeper understanding of ourselves. Such reflection is crucial for ensuring that our desires are genuinely aligned with our values. While solitude may seem daunting at first, it allows our minds the freedom to wander, to explore our desires deeply, and to gain fresh perspectives.

Perception is a powerful force; it not only shapes our experiences but also holds the key to transforming our outlook on life. By altering our perspective, we can greatly enhance our well-being and navigate life's complexities with greater clarity.

In the depths of solitude, we encounter a paradox of our nature: the delicate balance between our need for social connection and the value of spending time alone. During more than a decade spent primarily in solitude due to my circumstances, I discovered that wisdom often emerges in the darkest of times. While we certainly learn from our environment, true awareness blossoms from within.

Consider this idea: problems and their solutions are inherently connected. Embracing this duality can offer profound insights. For instance, someone who perceives themselves as introverted might find unexpected growth by embracing moments of extroversion. This principle of duality—where everything has a counterpart—offers a deep well of wisdom.

Biologically, we are wired to be social beings, our survival historically linked to interaction and collaboration within communities. This instinct helps us thrive in social settings. Yet, it is equally vital to recognize the immense benefits of solitude for personal growth and self-awareness.

I suggest setting aside at least one hour each day, free from phones and other distractions, to cultivate this practice. In these moments of intentional solitude, clarity often surfaces, fears are faced, and true passions are uncovered. This practice of solitude provides fertile soil for self-discovery, empowering us to evolve and fully embrace our individuality.

In our quest for belonging, we encounter a beautiful irony: we don't simply belong to the universe; we are an integral part of it. By nurturing our inner world and embracing our uniqueness, we create a sanctuary of comfort and strength within ourselves. Our sense of belonging, then, extends beyond human relationships to encompass the entire fabric of existence.

By accepting these contradictions, we deepen our understanding of both ourselves and the universe. True wisdom arises from recognizing and balancing these contrasting forces, finding harmony within them.

...

Spiral Upward

Ensure that your desires stem from genuine needs rather than the fear of missing out. Take time to reflect and embrace the paradoxes of life. In periods of solitude, delve deeply into your desires, fears, and motivations, unraveling the complexities of your nature. By shifting your perspective and embracing the inherent duality within yourself, you can find wisdom even in darkness and clarity within solitude. Ultimately, let your sense of belonging transcend external validations, grounding itself in your profound connection to the universe and in your acceptance of who you are.

18: Let Go of Your Worries

Upon examining human nature and observing behavior, it becomes evident that humans possess an inherent tendency toward dissatisfaction. This intrinsic desire for more than what is currently possessed often serves as the root cause of this discontentment. Consequently, being happy typically requires more effort than being sad. So, if you find that being happy requires considerable effort, rest assured that you are not alone; this challenge is an integral aspect of human nature.

Therefore, when engaging in solitary reflection, it's vital to be mindful of your thoughts. Often, when alone, our minds gravitate toward perceived deficiencies, revisiting past regrets or projecting anxieties onto the future. This focus on what might be lacking is a common response among humans. Yet, letting go of such worries and embracing life's uncertainties is essential for mental and emotional well-being. Left unchecked, worries can spiral into stress and tension, often manifesting physically. This feedback loop reinforces the worries, creating a cycle that feels difficult to break.

This life lesson explores the nature of worries and provides practical strategies to manage them. By addressing your concerns with awareness and intentionality, you can cultivate resilience and optimism, equipping yourself to navigate life's uncertainties with confidence.

Understanding the Nature of Worries

Life is inherently unpredictable, and no amount of worrying can alter its uncertain nature. Yet, it's easy to become consumed by fears about the future, second-guessing decisions, and ruminating on possible outcomes.

Worry often stems from a desire to control the uncontrollable, creating an illusion of influence over events. However, this illusion drains our energy and distracts us from meaningful actions.

It's important to distinguish between constructive concern and unproductive worry. While proactive steps can shape aspects of our circumstances, there will always be factors beyond our control. Accepting this reality is liberating. It reminds us that our energy is better spent focusing on what we can influence, rather than dwelling on hypothetical scenarios. By relinquishing the belief that worry provides control, we can redirect our mental and emotional resources toward growth and positivity.

The Role of Imagination

Imagination is a powerful force. It can ignite boundless creativity or amplify our fears. Worry thrives in the fertile soil of imagination, growing from seeds of uncertainty into elaborate worst-case scenarios.

Think of your mind as a garden where each thought is a seed. Some seeds grow into vibrant flowers of creativity and joy, while others sprout into weeds of fear and anxiety. Worry flourishes when we water these negative seeds, indulging in "What if?" narratives that spiral into increasingly unlikely and distressing possibilities.

It's crucial to recognize that worries, no matter how vivid, are products of imagination until they become reality. They are shadows cast by our fears, obscuring the present moment's beauty and potential. Just as a skilled gardener chooses which plants to nurture, we have the power to decide which thoughts to cultivate. By actively uprooting harmful thoughts and replacing them with empowering ones, we reclaim our mental landscape.

Imagine tending this mental garden with care, nurturing seeds of hope, gratitude, and mindfulness. Over time, these positive thoughts grow stronger, overshadowing the weeds of worry. This shift in perspective enables us to view worries for what they are: constructs of our imagination that we can reshape. By doing so, we reclaim our peace and create a mental space where positivity and resilience can thrive.

Embracing Life's Unknowns

Worry often stems from a misplaced belief that we can predict or control the future. We long for certainty, as though a crystal ball might reveal every outcome, offering solace and security. But life's beauty lies in its unpredictability: the twists and turns that make it a story worth experiencing.

Think of life as a compelling novel. Would you want to skip to the final chapter, knowing every detail in advance? The suspense, surprise, and wonder would be lost. Similarly, life's unknowns should not be feared but embraced. They provide opportunities for growth, discovery, and serendipity.

Imagine walking through a forest. If you fixate on what might be hidden behind every tree or lurking beyond every bend, you'll miss the journey's beauty—the rustling leaves, chirping birds, and sunlight filtering through the branches. By embracing uncertainty, you allow the experience to unfold, enriching your perspective and deepening your appreciation of the moment.

Letting go of the need for absolute certainty creates space for mental and emotional freedom. It transforms the unknown from a source of anxiety into a canvas of possibility, allowing you to fully engage with life's adventure.

Letting Go and Embracing the Adventure

Picture yourself in a small wooden boat on a vast ocean. You have two choices: exhaust yourself by rowing endlessly against the current, or hoist the sail and let the wind guide your journey. The wind represents life's uncertainties, forces beyond your control that will persist regardless of your efforts. Resisting them only leads to exhaustion. Worrying is akin to rowing against the wind. It drains your energy and obscures the present moment's beauty. Instead, consider hoisting the sail, trusting the currents to carry you toward new horizons. By letting go of the need to control every aspect of your journey, you invite wonder and spontaneity into your life. Surrendering to life's flow doesn't mean passivity; it means choosing to navigate with trust and courage rather than fear and resistance.

...

Spiral Upward

Letting go of worries is not about ignoring life's challenges but approaching them with clarity and balance. Acknowledge that worry offers no real control; it magnifies your fears through the lens of imagination. By recognizing this, you can step back, ground yourself in the present, and respond with intention. Embrace life's uncertainties as integral to its beauty. Practice patience and mindfulness, savoring each moment as it comes. Life is an unfolding journey, filled with surprises, growth, and wonder. By letting go of your worries and embracing the unknown, you open yourself to the fullness of experience, allowing your spirit to flourish in the adventure of life.

19: Detachment Is Embracing Life

Now that we have explored the nature of worrying, let us weave it together with the wisdom of detachment to understand how this philosophy can soften our fears. In this life lesson, we will clarify the common misunderstandings around detachment and uncover how it allows us to embrace life with clarity, simplicity, and beauty. You will see how detachment not only frees us from unnecessary fear but also deepens our engagement with the world in a more meaningful way.

The Misconception of Detachment

Detachment is often misunderstood as disengagement or withdrawal from life. When addressing human suffering, we frequently encounter two extremes: one that clings desperately to the material world out of fear, and another that advocates cutting all ties to worldly matters in search of spiritual bliss. Both perspectives are misguided. They are often shaped by interpretations from spiritual leaders, religious doctrines, or political ideologies — interpretations that can obscure the true essence of detachment.

True detachment is not about rejecting life's pleasures or stepping away from the world. It is about fully engaging with life while maintaining an inner independence from its outcomes. It means participating wholeheartedly without being consumed by results, holding a balanced perspective that nurtures peace and resilience.

The Pitfalls of Attachment

Attachment, when rooted in fear and insecurity, becomes a silent force that pushes us to cling tightly to whatever brings us joy. In trying to keep what we love close, we may hold on so tightly that we suffocate it — just as overprotective parenting, even when born from love, can inadvertently hinder a child's growth.

This grip, disguised as care, blinds us to the very beauty of the experience we aim to preserve. Consider the person who, terrified of losing their partner, becomes possessive and jealous. Their constant need for reassurance overwhelms the relationship, until the very love they feared losing begins to fade. Paradoxically, attachment often destroys the very thing it seeks to protect.

Beyond emotional strain, intense attachment burdens the body. The fear of loss activates the stress response system, flooding us with cortisol and adrenaline. When this becomes chronic, it weakens the immune system and drains our physical well-being. In the end, attachment born from fear does not secure love — it slowly erodes it, both in our relationships and within ourselves.

Finding Fullness Through Detachment

Detachment invites us to be fully present in each moment — to experience life with open hands rather than clenched fists. It allows us to savor beauty without being imprisoned by the fear of its passing, creating a natural harmony with the ever-changing rhythm of life.

Imagine standing on a quiet beach as the sun melts into the horizon. You are absorbed in the colors, the breeze, the soft hush of the waves. You know this moment is temporary — the sky will darken, night will rise, and a new dawn will follow. Yet this awareness does not lessen the experience; it enriches it.

In that stillness, you embrace the moment without trying to hold it in place. You appreciate its beauty while accepting its impermanence. In doing so, you embody the true spirit of detachment — present, peaceful, and free.

Embracing Detachment

Attachment is the emotional clinging that ties our happiness to people, objects, or outcomes. Detachment, by contrast, is the art of releasing that grip with grace. It is not indifference, coldness, or absence of care.

It is caring deeply without the chains of expectation — loving without possession, giving without demand, and living without relying on external circumstances for inner peace.

Life is always shifting. People grow, circumstances evolve, and everything we hold eventually changes form. Detachment frees you from the suffering that comes from trying to hold onto what cannot remain fixed. When your well-being no longer rises and falls with the external world, a quiet freedom unfolds within you.

This way of being does not ask you to withdraw from life. It asks you to walk through it with balance — to pursue your dreams wholeheartedly while remaining grounded enough not to collapse if things unfold differently than you imagined. You stay engaged, but not enslaved by expectation.

Detachment also opens the door to introspection. When your mind is no longer tangled in craving or fear of loss, you gain clarity about what truly matters — your values, your motivations, your deeper desires. This clarity enriches your experience of life itself.

And strangely, detachment does not make life feel emptier; it makes it feel more precious. You begin to see the beauty in impermanence. A sunset becomes more vivid because it fades. A friendship becomes more meaningful because it evolves. Moments of joy become sweeter because you no longer demand they stay forever.

You simply meet each moment fully, appreciate it deeply, and let it pass naturally — just as it was always meant to.

...

Spiral Upward

Embracing detachment is not a decision you make once; it is a continuous practice that requires patience and dedication. Through this commitment, you enrich every facet of your life. Its greatest reward is the ability to find contentment and joy amid life's inevitable changes.

With consistent practice, detachment makes you less vulnerable to emotional turbulence triggered by external circumstances. You begin to maintain a calm inner state, regardless of what unfolds around you.

Detachment enables you to engage fully with life while freeing yourself from unnecessary attachments. This balanced approach fosters a profound sense of freedom, allowing you to experience each moment with greater presence and clarity. Ultimately, detachment empowers you to live more fully — free from the weight of clinging and open to the beauty of life's unfolding journey.of what unfolds around you.

Detachment enables you to engage fully with life while freeing yourself from unnecessary attachments. This balanced approach fosters a profound sense of freedom, allowing you to experience each moment with greater presence and clarity. Ultimately, detachment empowers you to live more fully—free from the weight of clinging, and open to the beauty of life's unfolding journey.

20: Let Pain Pass Through You

Having explored the essence of detachment — the art of fully engaging with life without clinging to it — we now transition to our next vital life lesson: allowing pain to pass through us. Life is filled with challenges that test our resilience and shape our character.

Each obstacle offers a chance for growth and transformation, yet only a few master the skill of letting these experiences move through them without leaving permanent scars. Too often, we cling to our pains, letting them weigh down our souls with the burden of past struggles. Rather than letting challenges influence us temporarily, we mistakenly allow them to define who we are.

In this lesson, we will explore the importance of letting go. We will look at how to release the hold of past challenges and move through life with a lightness of being — enabling us to face future hurdles with greater ease and resilience.

The Burden We Bear

Life's challenges are inevitable. They touch every corner of our emotional, physical, and spiritual selves. But when we resist letting these experiences move through us, they don't simply disappear — they accumulate. Instead, they form *patches* over our souls, each one covering a part of who we truly are. Layer by layer, these patches hide our essence, making it harder for us to show up authentically in the world.

Over time, when people meet us, they no longer see *us* — they see the patches: the disappointments we never released, the heartbreaks we never healed, the anger we never expressed, the fears we never faced. Our true being remains underneath, but hidden, muted, and weighed down by everything we've carried for far too long.

Picture yourself driving down your street. The radio plays softly. The sky is a gentle blue. People walk the sidewalks, birds fill the air with song, and children laugh as they run and play. You take it all in — every sound, every color, every breath of life around you. And yet, none of it clings to you. These moments flow through you as naturally as you move through them.

Then suddenly, a song comes on the radio. Within seconds, it opens a door to old memories — love, loss, heartbreak. A familiar heaviness settles on your chest. Your breath shifts. The vibrant world around you grows distant. The blue sky, the passerby, the birds, the laughter — everything fades as the past floods your present.

This moment reveals a deeper truth: we often do not struggle with life itself, but with our inability to let past experiences pass through us. Instead, we hold them, replay them, and allow them to overshadow what is happening right now.

When we release the grip of yesterday's pain — when we let experiences move through us instead of letting them define us — our present becomes lighter, clearer, and more open. In that openness, we regain the ability to truly engage with life as it unfolds.

Passing Through, Not Holding On

To navigate life's challenges with strength and clarity, we must adopt a mindset of detachment. This does not mean ignoring our pain or pretending it doesn't exist — it means allowing it to flow through us rather than letting it take root within us.

Detachment begins with the recognition that challenges are temporary experiences, not permanent definitions of who we are. Pain, adversity, heartbreak — these are moments along the path, not the path itself. When we stop identifying with our struggles and start seeing them as passing events, we reclaim our power.

By understanding that what we feel is not who we are, we free ourselves from the weight of yesterday's wounds. And in that freedom, we create the space to rise — to spiral upward — unburdened by the stories that once held us down.

Traveling Light

Imagine life as a grand adventure, where every challenge is a mile-stone on your journey of growth and self-discovery. Just as a seasoned traveler packs only what is essential, we too must learn to carry only what truly serves us. Move through life lightly — unburdened by the emotional "luggage" that slows your steps and clouds your vision.

Holding onto grudges, regrets, or past pains does not protect us; it limits us. These burdens weigh down the spirit, making even the simplest moments feel heavy. But when we release what no longer belongs to us, we create space for joy, clarity, love, and new beginnings.

Letting go is not forgetting — it is freeing. It is choosing to step forward without dragging yesterday's shadows into today's light. When we travel with a lighter heart, we experience life with greater openness and grace. To fully embrace the present, we must loosen our grip on the past. Only then can we walk our path with ease, presence, and a spirit unbound.

Embracing Transformation

When we master the art of letting experiences move through us instead of anchoring within us, we open the door to genuine transformation. Challenges no longer appear as punishments or obstacles, but as catalysts — each one inviting us to rise, adapt, and evolve.

By choosing to see difficulties as stepping stones rather than dead ends, we tap into a reservoir of resilience and inner strength. We begin to shape our lives intentionally, becoming the architects of our own growth rather than mere reactors to circumstance. Our future becomes something we design with clarity, rather than something dictated by past wounds.

In this light, transformation stops feeling heavy or intimidating. It becomes a liberating force — one that lifts us rather than drags us, one that propels us upward rather than holds us down. Embracing change with an open heart turns life's challenges into momentum, allowing us to spiral upward with purpose, wisdom, and grace.

...

Spiral Upward

Life's challenges are part of the human experience, and how you approach them shapes your path. Some pains wound the body, while others reach deep into the soul. By learning the art of letting pain pass through you as you pass through life, you release the burdens of past sorrows and rediscover freedom in the present moment.

When you stop clinging to pain, you reconnect with the essence of life within you. Travel through life with a light heart, carrying only what is essential, and let the winds of change guide you toward a brighter and more fulfilling future.

21: Let the Unknown Unfold

Life's most profound lessons often reveal themselves through surrender — through the quiet courage of releasing our need to control the path ahead. When we embrace the unseen and trust life to unfold in its own divine timing, we begin to learn the art of allowing.

In this state, we are no longer held captive by passing worries; we move with a steadiness rooted in trust — trust in the process, trust in life's rhythm, and trust in our ability to meet whatever comes.

Letting go becomes a bridge between who we were and who we are becoming. It allows us to observe the past with acceptance, just as we watch clouds drift across the sky. We may hope for the clouds to part and reveal a clear blue horizon — but we cannot command them. We can only acknowledge their presence and let them pass. This is the essence of non-resistance: welcoming life as it arrives, without forcing it into shapes of our own choosing.

And when we reach the highest plane of contentment, even the grey clouds cease to trouble us. Their presence no longer steals our peace, because we understand that the sky — vast, constant, and untouched — remains behind them.

The future, wide and unwritten, invites us to dream boldly and walk forward with faith. Yet we often become caught between the pull of fear and the pull of hope — imagining what could go wrong while longing for what could go right. In that inner struggle, the present moment — the only place where life truly lives — slips by unseen.

But when we surrender the illusion of control and return to the now, we reclaim the purest joy: the serenity of simply being.

The Hidden Truth of Tomorrow

Human curiosity often pushes us toward the unseen, urging us to search for certainty in fortune tellers, astrologers, or anything that promises a glimpse of what lies ahead. Yet in reaching for these illusions of control, we risk overlooking the quiet beauty of life's unfolding — the unexpected moments that shape us, strengthen us, and reveal who we are becoming.

The desire to know the future does not empower us; it quietly weakens us. When we place our faith in predictions, we hand over the authorship of our lives to assumption rather than intention. This disconnects us from the present moment — the only place where real clarity, growth, and transformation happen.

Yet in focusing too intensely on imagined outcomes, we may unintentionally breathe life into them. Our thoughts, attention, and energy begin to shape our reality, drawing us toward the very future we feared or fantasized about. In trying to eliminate uncertainty, we manifest it. True strength comes not from predicting the future, but from trusting ourselves to meet it with presence, wisdom, and grace.

Consider this: a fully predictable future would feel like merely reliving the past — safe, perhaps, but stripped of wonder. What brings life its electricity is the unexpected: risk, possibility, the chance of failure, and the hope of becoming someone more evolved. Uncertainty is not an enemy; it is the birthplace of growth.

Even something as fundamental as your breath is not entirely under your control, yet it sustains every step you take into the future. Life is shaped by forces beyond our understanding.

Plans, Purpose, and a Greater Design

So what does this realization mean for us? Should we abandon planning altogether? Absolutely not.

Plan for the future as if time were abundant — but surrender the illusion that you control every outcome. Yield to the greater forces that shape existence: the unseen currents guiding your path, the divine order orchestrating what lies beyond your sight, and the quiet rhythm of your own heartbeat reminding you of life's fragility and depth.

Take comfort in knowing that your plans do not stand alone; they are woven into a vast design, intricate and mysterious, yet purposeful. Your role may appear small from where you stand, but it carries a significance far beyond what you can perceive.

Think of the bee — moving from flower to flower, simply fulfilling its nature. It has no awareness of the enormous impact its actions have on forests, harvests, and entire ecosystems. Yet without it, life as we know it would collapse.

In the same way, you, too, are part of something far greater than you may ever comprehend. Your choices, actions, and intentions ripple outward — touching lives, shaping paths, and contributing to the unfolding tapestry of the world.

Embrace Uncertainty

Though life appears to offer us countless choices, many events unfold beyond our control. Even when our plans shift or fall apart, they still belong to a greater design — one whose wisdom is not yet visible to us. Our task is not to resist but to trust, moving forward with a calm and open heart.

Approach the unknown the way you approach the reality of death: it could arrive tomorrow, and no amount of effort can prevent it. Yet we do not live in constant fear of it. We continue loving, dreaming, building, and hoping.

This same acceptance can be applied to the uncertainties of life. When we release the burden of excessive worry, we create space to live more authentically. Let uncertainty be a teacher rather than an enemy. Let it remind you of what truly matters — and of how precious each moment is precisely because it cannot be guaranteed.

Life's greatest beauty lies in its unpredictability — in the unfolding of a story we do not fully control, but one in which we participate with intention, presence, and courage.

...

Spiral Upward

Let go of the need for absolute control and embrace the dynamic dance of life. Within the delicate balance of dreams and surrender, fears and hope, find fulfillment in experiencing each moment deeply and honestly. Welcome the future as a sacred opportunity for growth and self-discovery. Attune yourself to life's mysterious melody, find serenity in the present, and move gracefully in rhythm with the unfolding journey of existence.

22: The Power of Patience

How can we ever embrace the uncertainty of tomorrow without patience? Though essential, patience remains one of life's most overlooked virtues.

To truly understand it, we must explore it with intention and depth — there is no shortcut to appreciating its power. In a world driven by speed, deadlines, and constant ambition, we rush toward our goals believing that faster is better. We are conditioned to equate urgency with success. Yet in this relentless chase, we forget a fundamental truth: rushing clouds our clarity, blurs our judgment, and steals our peace. It replaces presence with pressure, and wisdom with worry.

This life lesson invites you to rediscover patience — not as passive waiting, but as a transformative force that enriches the journey just as deeply as the destination itself.

The Illusion of Arrival

One of the greatest misconceptions we carry is the belief in a final destination — a moment where everything falls into place, where fulfillment becomes permanent, and where life finally "arrives." We convince ourselves that once a particular goal is reached, a certain milestone is achieved, or a specific desire is fulfilled, we will at last feel complete.

But life does not work this way. Life is not a straight line leading to a finish; it is a continuous unfolding — a journey that evolves with every breath we take. The only certainty ahead of us is the eventual passing of our physical selves; everything else is fluid, shifting, and alive.

When we stop racing toward the fantasy of arrival, something remarkable happens: we begin to live. Instead of postponing joy until we reach some imagined state of perfection, we discover fulfillment in the present moment — in the steps, not just the peak; in the becoming, not only the becoming something.

Life is not about waiting for a distant future to deliver happiness. It is about being here — fully, consciously, gratefully — embracing each moment as it rises and falls like waves against the shore. When we adopt this perspective, we finally understand a deeper truth: the journey is the destination. The arrival was an illusion all along.

The Pitfalls of Rushing

Rushing toward our goals often comes with a hidden cost — the quiet erosion of our mental well-being and emotional balance. Impatience blinds us to the beauty of the journey, pushing us into impulsive choices, reactive decisions, and emotions that flare and fade without substance. In this hurried state, stress, frustration, and anxiety start to feel normal, as if they are the price we must pay for progress.

But in our haste, we unintentionally strip ourselves of clarity. We lose the space needed for thoughtful decisions, meaningful reflection, and intentional action — the very ingredients that lead to genuine fulfillment and inner peace. We may reach our destination faster, but we arrive depleted, confused, and disconnected from ourselves.

A steady pace, however, allows life to breathe. It gives us room to think, to feel, and to grow. Slowing down helps us notice the beauty we would have otherwise allowed to slip past unnoticed — the lessons, the signs, the subtle shifts that guide us toward deeper purpose.

By choosing presence over haste, we rediscover joy in the process and cultivate a richer sense of meaning. Patience does not delay success; it strengthens the foundation on which success is built.

The Power of Slow Growth

Contrary to popular belief, the path to genuine growth and meaningful accomplishment requires us to slow down. It has taken an entire lifetime to become who we are today — so it is unrealistic to expect deep transformation to happen overnight. Patience sharpens our clarity, steadies our judgment, and allows us to approach challenges with calm intention rather than emotional impulse.

Just as a tree needs years to take root, grow tall, and bear fruit, our own development demands time, care, and consistent nurturing. Nothing truly lasting is built in haste. When we embrace the power of slow, intentional growth, we create a solid foundation for success — one that can withstand life's inevitable storms.

By honoring the pace at which real transformation unfolds, we allow ourselves to fully appreciate the beauty of the journey rather than rushing blindly toward an imagined destination.

Conscious Action

In pursuing our goals, cultivating a conscious and present state of mind is essential. When we are fully aware and grounded in the moment, our choices become deliberate, and our actions carry intention. The most meaningful deeds rarely arise from haste; they are born from clarity, reflection, and thoughtful planning.

Though these actions may be fewer in number, their impact is far greater. They shape our lives with purpose and influence the lives of those around us in ways that endure. Acting with presence ensures that every step we take moves us not only forward, but forward in the right direction.

Divine Timing

The ultimate lesson in patience lies in understanding the nature and limits of our own capacity. Perhaps this is why God says, "If you walk toward Me, I will run toward you." It reflects His boundless ability, not ours. We take one small step — He responds with a stride beyond measure.

Embracing patience means surrendering to the natural rhythm of life, trusting that everything unfolds in its appointed time, and believing that divine wisdom is at work even when we cannot see it. When we align ourselves with this understanding, we no longer fight the pace of life — we flow with it.

Patience becomes an act of faith: a quiet confidence that what is meant for us will arrive, and what is not meant for us will gently fall away. By living with this trust, we find solace in the journey and open ourselves to the miracles that reveal themselves along the way — not rushed, not forced, but perfectly timed.

...

Spiral Upward

In a world that prioritizes instant gratification and constant hustle, the power of patience is often overlooked. Rushing toward your goals may feel productive, but it silently strips away clarity, calm, and emotional balance — replacing them with stress, frustration, and restlessness.

True growth doesn't happen in restless motion; it emerges through slowness, intentionality, and trust. Patience is not passive waiting — it is the quiet discipline of holding your inner peace while time unfolds.

Let life's tapestry unravel at its natural pace. When you surrender the impulse to force outcomes, you make room for clarity to rise, for wisdom to settle, and for your actions to come from a place of strength rather than desperation.

Embrace the power of patience, and you will rediscover a profound sense of peace, purpose, and presence. By allowing life to flow organically — without resistance, without haste — you create the space needed for intentional living, deeper understanding, and the quiet, steady beauty of becoming who you were meant to be.

23: The Translation of Sensations

Finding Freedom in Impermanence

Life unfolds within a delicate space: the reality we encounter and the meaning we assign to it. This narrow gap shapes the entire fabric of our existence. When our interpretation of sensations and emotions becomes distorted, our understanding of reality follows—and we may find ourselves walking paths that pull us away from who we truly are.

Every moment offers us a stream of sensations — joy, anger, love, sorrow — each one an invitation to meet life as it is. Yet their fleeting nature often becomes a source of tension. We cling to happiness, hoping to trap it in place, or we resist pain, wishing it away. Both impulses arise from misunderstanding life's inherent impermanence.

This lesson invites us to examine how the way we interpret our emotions determines how we experience the world. Misinterpretation fogs our clarity, drives impulsive reactions, and creates layers of unnecessary suffering. But when we understand the transient nature of our inner experiences, something shifts. We learn to respond rather than react — to observe rather than be overwhelmed.

By cultivating mindful awareness and seeing sensations for what they are — momentary visitors rather than permanent truths — we free ourselves from these traps. In doing so, we align our actions with deeper wisdom and move through life with greater clarity, presence, and purpose.

The Paradox of Permanence

We often cling to happiness as if it were a treasure to protect, and treat pain as an unwelcome guest we must expel. But life is neither a quest for eternal joy nor a war against suffering — it is a dance of constant change. Ironically, the harder we chase happiness, the further it slips from our grasp. And the more we resist pain, the deeper its roots grow.

It is like trying to hold a flame in your hand: the tighter your grip, the more it burns. Life, with all its shifting sensations, invites us to soften our hold — not to suppress or deny what we feel, but to meet each emotion with presence and understanding.

This misunderstanding of our inner landscape gives rise to two major pitfalls:

1. Clinging to joy, believing that tightening our grip will make it stay.

2. Suppressing pain, treating emotions as enemies instead of guides.

Both arise from a distorted perception of reality. When we cling to pleasure or push away discomfort, we interfere with the natural rhythm of life — trying to freeze a flowing river or trap a breeze in our hands.

These distortions, born from misinterpretation, pull us away from truth. But when we recognize emotions as temporary visitors rather than permanent residents, we begin to experience life with clarity, balance, and freedom.

The Role of Interpretation

Life's sensations exist within a narrow space — the gap between what happens and how we interpret it. When our understanding of what we feel becomes distorted, our perception of reality misaligns.

See how easily misinterpretation leads us astray:

- A brief moment of happiness may be mistaken for something we must chase endlessly, turning its natural fading into a sense of loss.

- A passing wave of sadness may be misread as a permanent state, leading to despair even though it is simply moving through us.

The emotions themselves are not the issue — our interpretation of them is. When we translate our experiences through the lens of fear, expectation, or misconception, we respond to illusions instead of truth. But when we pause and recognize sensations as they are — temporary, meaningful, and woven into the larger tapestry of our lives — we free ourselves from the urge to control them.

In that awareness, we reclaim our power. We respond with clarity instead of reacting with confusion, and we reconnect with reality as it is, not as our misinterpretations convince us it must be.

Embracing Impermanence

Human suffering often stems from resisting change. Yet it is impermanence that gives life its depth and beauty. Happiness is precious because it does not last forever. Pain is bearable because it, too, eventually fades. When we understand this truth, we shift from reacting impulsively to responding with wisdom and grace.

Hold this understanding close:

- Enjoy happiness, but release the urge to make it permanent.

- Cherish love, knowing it will evolve and transform.

- Welcome sadness, aware it is only visiting.

Instead of clinging to fleeting sensations or fearing their departure, we begin to experience them as gifts — each offering insight, each arriving with purpose. By respecting their temporary nature and interpreting them clearly, we free ourselves from expectation, illusion, and emotional distortion.

Impermanence is not a threat. It is a reminder that life is always moving, teaching, renewing. When we embrace it, we live with greater openness, humility, and peace.

...

Spiral Upward

Dear seeker, life's ever-changing nature carries a profound truth: nothing is permanent, yet everything is purposeful. When you embrace the impermanence of your sensations, you begin to interpret reality with clarity — freeing yourself from illusion and aligning more deeply with truth.

Happiness, like every emotion, is a visitor in the theater of life. Welcome it with warmth, appreciate its presence, and release it with ease. Pain, too, arrives with intention, shaping your strength and deepening your soul. Both are threads in the spiral of your becoming, guiding you toward greater awareness and fulfillment.

Life unfolds in the space between what is and how you perceive it. By refining your interpretation of each moment, you open the door to a life anchored in wisdom and inner balance. Every experience — joyful or sorrowful, brief or intense — becomes a stepping stone in your upward journey.

Live lightly, yet fully. Let each sensation touch you, but never bind you. Observe, understand, and allow. For in this practice lies your truest freedom: the freedom to meet life exactly as it is and respond with grace, purpose, and peace.

24: Trust the Process

Enjoying a sensation intensely while simultaneously letting it go requires us to trust the process: a delicate balance that is often easier said than done. How do we cultivate this trust? The key lies in understanding that our journey is both purposeful and dynamic, shaped by forces both within and beyond our control. Life unfolds within the interplay of action and surrender. Some aspects are firmly within our grasp, while others are orchestrated by a grander design, unseen but deeply interconnected. Trusting the process means acknowledging this duality: we take meaningful steps forward while embracing the mystery of the unknown.

The experiences that intrigue, challenge, or even frustrate us are not random; they are threads in a larger tapestry that we may not fully comprehend in the moment. Every step—be it a triumph or a stumble—shapes the foundation of who we are becoming. Purpose is not a static endpoint; it is an ever-evolving journey of growth, discovery, and transformation.

The Power of Transformation

Imagine a caterpillar, clinging to a branch, unaware of its extraordinary destiny. It may not comprehend the changes ahead, but it instinctively trusts the process. Through patience and surrender, it undergoes a remarkable transformation, emerging as a butterfly free to soar.

Similarly, we often fail to see the extraordinary changes awaiting us. Yet, by believing in the process and showing up each day, we allow our purpose to gradually reveal itself. Trusting the process means releasing the need for instant answers and learning to embrace uncertainty as a powerful teacher.

This trust is not passive; it is active faith. It requires us to engage with life fully, aligning our actions with our purpose while surrendering the outcomes to forces beyond our understanding.

Guided by Heart and Mind

As we heed the whispers of our hearts, it is essential to involve our minds in this journey. The heart acts as a compass, pointing us toward our true path, while the mind serves as a rational advisor, helping us navigate obstacles and opportunities.

Balancing these two forces enables us to make informed decisions, take calculated risks, and stay aligned with our purpose. When the heart and mind work in harmony, we cultivate clarity, resilience, and the courage to face uncertainty with grace.

The Unfolding of Purpose

Purpose is not always immediately clear or neatly presented; it often reveals itself in unexpected ways. By remaining open to life's unfolding possibilities, we invite opportunities that resonate deeply with who we are meant to be.

Consider this: every detour, every unexpected challenge, carries a lesson that enriches your journey. What seems like a setback may be the stepping stone to a breakthrough.

A Personal Reflection

Let me take you back to a pivotal moment in my life: a moment when trust in the process was all I had. In seventh grade, I faced an uncomfortable truth. My teacher pulled me aside, concerned about my performance. I struggled in almost every subject except one—drawing. "But drawing," she said, "won't secure your future." Her words stung, not because they were harsh, but because they echoed my own doubts. Back then, the traditional education system felt like a rigid structure where I didn't quite fit. Still, I pressed on, eventually making it to university, despite feeling like I was walking a path designed for someone else.

Everything changed one day during my second semester. Sitting in a chemistry lecture, I was consumed by a question far more urgent than any formula on the board: *How can I support my family when this path feels so misaligned with who I am?* The thought of spending four more years in a system that drained me felt unbearable.

Then, in a moment of instinct—some might call it madness—I raised my hand.

"May I leave the class?" I asked.

The professor looked confused. "Where are you going?"

"Home," I replied, my voice steady despite my trembling hands. "And I'm not coming back."

Walking out of that room felt like stepping into the unknown. I had no plan, only a fierce determination to find my own way. But the hardest part was yet to come: telling my mother.

When I called her, I could hear the worry in her voice before I even spoke. "I quit university," I said. The line went silent, then she started to cry. Once she calmed down, I nervously explained my impulsive idea: to start a business.

"With what money?" she asked, her voice sharp with skepticism. After a long pause, I blurted out, "Can we sell the house?"

The silence that followed was deafening. Then, with a click, she hung up.

I spent days drowning in uncertainty, questioning whether I had shattered everything beyond repair. Then, to my utter amazement and against all odds, she agreed. This was the kind of mother who had raised me: someone willing to take an unimaginable risk out of love and belief. Selling the house felt like an extraordinary gamble, but it became the launchpad for my first real chance to turn a daring vision into reality.

At 21, I franchised my first fashion store in Scandinavia's largest mall, becoming the youngest franchisee in the company's history and running its flagship store. By 25, I had ventured into multiple industries, each one teaching me invaluable lessons. Then came an unexpected opportunity: the chance to become CEO of a company in the graduation cap-and-gown business.

Initially, it seemed like just another business venture. But over the next decade, it became clear that this was something more. Meeting thousands of students and educators revealed the deep dissatisfaction with the traditional education system: a system that left so many feeling as lost as I once did.

This realization planted a seed: a vision to not just create an educational platform for students like me, but to revolutionize the entire system. My goal became clear: to design an approach that values diverse talents, fosters creativity, and empowers individuals to thrive in a rapidly changing world. Looking back, I see how every twist and turn in my journey prepared me for this purpose. The setbacks, doubts, and bold leaps of faith weren't distractions; they were essential steps on the path to something greater.

This journey taught me one of life's greatest truths: we live life forwards, but we only understand it in hindsight. Trusting the process isn't about having all the answers; it's about believing that every step, no matter how uncertain, is part of a larger design.

...

Spiral Upward

Some days, everything falls into place effortlessly; on others, nothing seems to work. Both kinds of days are essential. On challenging days, your task is to balance your efforts with your expectations, to trust the process even when the path ahead is unclear.

Like the caterpillar transforming into a butterfly, you, too, will rise from uncertainty to soar to new heights. Follow your heart while engaging your mind, and let your sense of purpose guide you to a life rich with meaning, fulfillment, and joy.

Take a moment to reflect on your journey and recognize the immense potential within you—ready to unfold, one step at a time. Trust the process, and allow your transformation to reveal the extraordinary destiny waiting for you.

25: Embrace Brokenness

Trusting the process to lead us to our purpose often involves embracing our brokenness rather than merely seeking to heal it. Many might ask, *Isn't healing the ultimate goal?* I propose a different perspective: the idea of complete healing, often emphasized in self-help literature and therapy, may not be the ultimate objective.

Consider this: does healing imply that once we've undergone the process, we are immune to future pain, that it will never resurface, or that we can't be triggered again? If pain can indeed be retriggered, can we truly consider ourselves healed?

As we deepen our understanding of our pain, we come to accept it. While the pain may be triggered again by memories, our increasing awareness allows us to manage it more effectively each time. This life lesson is not about eradicating pain but about embracing our brokenness. Just like a physical wound, it heals in its own time, all we can do is allow it. Forcing the process only causes further damage, delaying the natural course of recovery. And when our wounds heal, they always leave a mark: a reminder of where we've been and the lessons we've learned. These marks are not just scars; they are stories waiting to be told, symbols of resilience, growth, and the journey toward wholeness. Before we can unlock our purpose, we must understand the role of brokenness in realizing our potential. Otherwise, we might spend a lifetime trying to "fix" ourselves when, in reality, there is nothing to fix and everything to embrace. Brokenness is not merely something that happens to us; it happens for us. Our brokenness enhances our capacity to experience life fully, serving a purpose, not as a punishment.

During my darkest moments, when shadows were my only companions, faith became the light that guided me forward. Even when my struggles felt senseless and overwhelming, a quiet voice within—my intuition—reassured me that a higher purpose was unfolding. Brought to my knees, I found solace in prayer, as if guided by a divine hand gently urging me to surrender to the wisdom and compassion of an all-knowing Creator. In accepting my flaws and embracing my vulnerabilities, I uncovered a profound source of strength: a wellspring of motivation that carried me toward healing and growth.

Motivation drives us to pursue goals and overcome obstacles. Yet, there are times when we feel utterly broken and devoid of motivation. This life lesson explores what it truly means to be broken and how it can catalyze growth and transformation.

Brokenness is a universal experience, not a personal failing. Challenges and hardships often serve as divine guidance, prompting us to pause, reflect, and elevate to higher levels of understanding in our life's journey. Brokenness does not necessitate endless suffering; it offers a choice. Much like the physics of a bow and arrow, the more we are pulled back by life's challenges, the more potent our trajectory can be when released, propelling us toward our intended targets.

Be Broken

Let's be broken like the clouds that release rain, blessing the earth below. When they shed their burden, the earth receives nourishment, giving life to all it touches. In a similar way, embracing our brokenness can lead to positive transformations. Through our own wounds, we cultivate empathy and compassion, understanding the suffering of others and enhancing our ability to uplift those around us.

Let's be broken like the soil, inherently imperfect, yet perfect in its purpose. Its cracks allow for growth, becoming fertile ground where seeds take root and flourish. Our pain creates gaps from which we can grow, shedding old patterns, limiting beliefs, and self-imposed boundaries to invite transformation.

Or let's be broken like seeds, each break in their shell giving rise to new life. In our brokenness, we too can catalyze growth and transformation, not just for ourselves but also for the world around us. Being broken is not a prelude to suffering; it's the beginning of evolution, a powerful journey where each experience molds us, leaving lasting imprints on our hearts and souls.

From brokenness, we discover our true strength and wisdom. We realize that what breaks never heals the same; it grows in unique and transformative ways, revealing new depths of resilience and courage. At the pivotal moment of brokenness, we face a choice: remain tethered to the past or seize the opportunity for growth and renewal.

For instance, when faced with setbacks and failures in my career, I chose not to surrender to despair. Instead, I embraced my vulnerabilities and delved into introspection, which not only built my resilience but also ignited a passion for writing.

If you ever wonder, *Am I broken enough?* and find the answer is yes, consider it a cause for celebration. You are on the brink of something greater. Embrace brokenness as a transformative force that molds you into the person you are meant to be. Your journey of acceptance and growth starts now, and within this brokenness lies immense power—the power to rise and inspire others with your resilience.

In this context, healing involves letting the wound heal naturally and accepting the scar, akin to how nature effortlessly mends itself. Just as an earthquake releases what needs to come to the surface, our pain cracks open the heart, allowing buried emotions to rise and be acknowledged. These fractures don't seal immediately; they remain as openings for new beginnings. By embracing our brokenness, we create space for healing to unfold in its own time. There's no need to force the process—healing will happen as it must, revealing the beauty of transformation.

In reconstructing ourselves, we don't return to our former selves but evolve into something stronger and more profound. These cracks become the marks of our journey, reminding us of our resilience. We become living embodiments of the indomitable human spirit and its vast potential for growth and renewal. Embrace your brokenness; it carries the power to propel you toward becoming the best version of yourself.

...

Spiral Upward

Being broken doesn't mean you're destined to suffer; instead, it is an opportunity to evolve and transform. Imagine being trapped in darkness, and then suddenly a crack appears, allowing light to seep in—how could that ever be seen as negative?

Embrace your brokenness as nature does: the clouds releasing rain, the soil nurturing seeds, the crops growing from that very nourishment—all agents of positive change. You stand on the threshold of something extraordinary. By accepting your brokenness, you open the door to a realm of limitless possibilities, where transformation and growth become inevitable.

26: You Are Not Your Wounds

Being broken does not condemn us to a life of suffering; in many ways, it is what sets us free. Life will inevitably bring moments of physical pain and emotional upheaval, leaving behind scars — some visible, others hidden deep within. These marks aren't flaws; they are evidence. Evidence that you endured what *could* have broken you, and emerged with a strength that can no longer be denied.

What if your wounds were not symbols of shame, but badges of honor? Your scars — both emotional and physical — are not obstacles to joy. They are milestones of growth, testimonies to the resilience that has carried you forward. You are more complete not despite *your* struggles, but *because* of them.

Think of lightning streaking across the sky — brilliant, brief, yet breathtaking. Or the lone tree standing steadfast in a vast forest: solitary, perhaps, but majestic in its endurance. We do not judge the lightning for its short-lived glow, nor pity the tree for its isolation. We marvel at their raw beauty and singular presence. Imagine offering yourself that same grace.

Your wounds are not defects; they are brushstrokes that give texture and depth to the masterpiece of your life. They do not imprison you — they shape you, refine you, and open you to transformation. When you shift your perspective, brokenness no longer appears as weakness but as the foundation upon which strength, wisdom, and inner freedom are built.

You are not your wounds. You are the strength that grew from them.

Breaking Free from the Chains of Victimhood

We are not defined by what hurt us. Healing begins the moment we stop seeking sympathy and step away from the narrative that binds us to our past. When we cling to our wounds — retelling them, reliving them, and identifying with them — we unknowingly imprison ourselves in a story that no longer serves us. The more we see ourselves as victims, the more we reinforce a cycle that keeps us tied to yesterday's pain. But your identity is not rooted in what broke you.

Your wounds are past events, not permanent labels. They may have shaped you, but they do not have to govern you. The power to choose what influences your present — and what no longer does — rests in your hands. When you release the narratives that keep you small, you create space for a new chapter to unfold — one written not from pain, but from intention, strength, and self-awareness. You are more than what hurt you. You are who you choose to become.

Embracing Life's Unfairness

Life is inherently filled with challenges and hardships that test and shape us. These struggles are not unique burdens placed upon certain individuals — they are part of the universal human story. Every person you meet carries their own trials, their own hidden storms.

When we take life's difficulties personally, we shrink our world and magnify our suffering. But when we accept that hardship is a natural part of existence, something shifts. We stop asking, *"Why me?"* and begin to ask, *"What is this teaching me?"*

Life's challenges are not punishments; they are invitations — calling us to rise, to grow, and to uncover the reservoir of strength that has always lived within us. By embracing this truth, we move from resistance to resilience, from self-pity to self-power. Within every difficulty lies potential for transformation; within every challenge, a doorway into who we are becoming.

Observing Life through a Wider Lens

Nature teaches us balance. It shows us that challenges are not interruptions to life — they *are* life. Every struggle in the natural world serves a purpose: storms strengthen roots, harsh seasons build resilience, and obstacles ensure growth and renewal.

Similarly, when we widen our perspective, we begin to see our own challenges differently. Instead of viewing hardships as injustices directed solely at us, we recognize them as essential threads woven into the larger tapestry of existence. They are part of a universal rhythm, not isolated misfortunes.

By shifting from a narrow, self-focused lens to a broader, more expansive one, we discover a deeper truth: life's difficulties are not meant to break us, but to shape us. They deepen our character, expand our capacity, and prepare us for the chapters ahead. When we stop fixating on *"Why me?"* and begin embracing *"What is this teaching me?"*, we align ourselves with the natural order of growth — just as nature intended.

Transcending Trauma and Seeking Wisdom

We hold the power to transform even our deepest wounds into catalysts for strength and wisdom. When we choose to accept our past rather than resist or deny it, something profound happens: our pain becomes a source of insight instead of limitation.

By turning inward — with honesty and compassion — we uncover the meaning hidden within our struggles. This inner work empowers us not only to rise above our own challenges but to uplift others through theirs.

Embracing resilience allows us to reclaim our agency. We become defined not by what happened to us, but by how we rise in response. Through understanding and self-compassion, we rebuild a life anchored in clarity, strength, and purpose — a life shaped not by the wounds we endured, but by the courage with which we heal.

Liberating Yourself from the Past

The past cannot be rewritten, but its power over you can. When we cling to old wounds, we carry them like heavy chains — restricting our movement, dimming our spirit, and holding us back from the life unfolding before us. These invisible restraints anchor us to moments long gone, preventing us from stepping fully into the present.

Letting go does not mean forgetting. Nor does it diminish what you endured. It simply means choosing freedom over imprisonment. It is the conscious release of what no longer serves your growth. Imagine those old wounds as literal chains wrapped around you — cold, heavy, limiting. Each time you replay the past, the chains tighten. But each act of letting go loosens them, link by link, until they eventually fall away.

By releasing your attachment to past trauma, you create space for renewal: for joy, for clarity, for healing, for purpose. Letting go is not abandoning your story. It is reclaiming your power to write the next chapter.

...

Spiral Upward

Deep within you lies a vast reservoir of strength — far greater than you may yet realize. To live a life of meaning, you must release the grip of victimhood and step fully into your power. Life's challenges, though painful, are not meant to imprison you; they are meant to shape you.

Your wounds are not burdens — they are teachers offering the lessons you need to evolve. What holds you back is not the wound itself, but the misunderstanding around it.

Give yourself permission to sit with your pain. Ask the difficult questions. Do the inner work that illuminates the darkness within. When you lean into discomfort instead of fleeing from it, something profound begins to happen: the shadows dissolve, and what once felt heavy becomes light. In that release, freedom is born.

Letting go of victimhood opens the door to clarity, resilience, and renewed purpose. Each insight becomes a stepping stone that elevates you beyond the confines of your past. With every step forward, you reclaim more of your power — moving toward a life defined not by wounds, but by growth, truth, and limitless potential.

27: The Power of Forgiveness

Welcome to the concluding life lesson of the first human knot, where we've journeyed through unlearning, relearning, and reconnecting with the deeper truths of our existence. This pivotal lesson explores forgiveness—not just as an action, but as a profound liberation that unlocks the door to your true essence.

Forgiveness is often misunderstood. It is not simply uttering, "I forgive you," nor is it about forgetting the harm done. True forgiveness requires a shift in perspective, a willingness to release the past, and an authentic transformation of the heart. Without forgiveness, we remain bound to the limitations of our physical form, trapped in resentment, and unable to embrace the freedom of our true essence.

This life lesson invites you to take forgiveness as the final step before stepping into the second knot. Forgiveness frees the tethered soul, allowing it to ascend, unburdened, into the next step of self-discovery and enlightenment. Through forgiveness, we unlock the door to healing, reclaim our inner peace, and prepare to embrace the vast potential of our existence.

Transcending the *How* Mindset

When it comes to forgiveness, our natural inclination is often to ask, *How do I forgive?* However, focusing solely on the "how" can inadvertently fuel a desire for retribution, trapping us in a cycle of negativity and prolonging our suffering. Instead, it becomes crucial to shift our focus to a more meaningful question: *Why should we forgive?*

Forgiveness is deeply rooted in compassion and love. When we understand that all harmful actions arise from some form of pain, we can see that holding onto anger only continues our own suffering. Embracing the "why" of forgiveness opens our hearts to a deeper understanding of human nature and the complexities of our emotions, allowing us to move beyond resentment. By shifting our mindset to focus on *why* we forgive, we pave the way for genuine liberation, ultimately finding peace and freedom in letting go.

Forgiveness as True Liberation

Genuine forgiveness comes from the heart; it is an act driven not by obligation but by a profound desire to liberate oneself. Holding onto grudges and resentment keeps us trapped in a cycle of suffering, limiting our growth and potential. Only through forgiveness can we break the chains that bind us, unlocking the freedom to live authentically.

At its core, forgiveness is an act of love—a conscious choice to let go of hatred and anger and instead embrace compassion, understanding, and acceptance. Love holds the power to illuminate even the darkest corners of our lives, enabling true understanding and transformation. By choosing forgiveness, we tap into the incredible power of love, transcending the destructive forces of anger and resentment. In doing so, we open ourselves to profound healing, paving the way for inner peace and growth.

The High Cost of Not Forgiving

Refusing to forgive comes at a significant cost. Holding onto grudges consumes our energy, diminishes our spirit, and keeps us bound to those who have wronged us. This emotional imprisonment, fueled by an unwillingness to forgive, prevents us from moving forward and severely limits our capacity for growth and joy. Only by releasing resentment can we free ourselves from this burden, opening the door to acceptance and reclaiming our inner peace.

A Precious Gift to Ourselves

Keep in mind that forgiveness isn't merely a favor bestowed upon others; it's a priceless gift we give ourselves. It requires inner fortitude, bravery, and a deep understanding of the human condition. When we choose to forgive, we liberate ourselves from the burdens of pain and bitterness, allowing acceptance and love to flourish. Release the chains that bind you, and embrace forgiveness; do not allow those who have hurt you to continue wielding power over your life. Indeed, forgiveness is a deeply personal journey that often demands time, effort, and introspection. Yet, it is essential. Holding onto resentment drains you, limits you, diminishes you, and prevents you from being your true self. Therefore, reflect on the reasons to forgive rather than hold onto grudges.

I recommend that you speak and listen to those who have hurt you; get it out of your chest before you start reading the second human knot. May the power of forgiveness guide you to a more profound connection with your true being and pave the way for a more fulfilling life.

...

Spiral Upward

Every pain holds at least two stories: one from the person who caused it and one from the person who endured it. At different points in life, we have all played both roles. Sharing these stories with honesty fosters understanding—not to justify, but to illuminate. As understanding grows, pain begins to dissolve, and forgiveness arises naturally.

Break the chains of past grievances with the key of love. Choose compassion and transform your future. Forgiveness is your bridge to freedom—cross it and spiral upward to a life of peace, purpose, and joy. By choosing love over resentment, you embrace the essence of who you truly are: a being capable of infinite compassion and transformation. Step into the next chapter with an unburdened heart, ready to uncover the boundless possibilities that await. Forgiveness sets you free, allowing you to heal, grow, and ascend toward the life you were meant to live. Let love be your guide and transformation your destination.

Our True Being

The Inner Journey

The Essence of Life

From Form to Essence

Every vessel has a purpose — but the purpose is never the vessel itself. The body, the name, the story — these are forms we wear, not the truth of who we are. Life begins to change the moment we stop identifying with the surface and start listening to what moves beneath it.

The storms we once feared were never meant to break us; they were meant to awaken us — to reveal what the vessel was carrying all along. What you are about to discover is not the world outside you, but the one within — the part of you that was never touched by circumstance, yet shaped by every experience. The next Knot begins where appearance ends — where the vessel meets its soul.

The second knot invites us on an inner journey to connect with the essence of life: the soul. Throughout history, the essence of life has whispered not only into our ears but also into the depths of our thoughts, beckoning us to unveil its mysteries. With every breath, we feel its pull—invisible yet profoundly present. When the soul inhabits a vessel, the body comes alive; when it departs, the body turns cold and lifeless, much like everything in nature—the leaves, the flowers, even the forest—growing rigid and losing their vibrant colors in the absence of life. This raises an essential question: If our true essence is the soul, why do we spend our lives identifying so closely with the body?

To explore this question, we must delve deep into the core of our existence, confronting eternal questions of self-love, identity, and the nature of our true being and its entanglement with the physical world. This journey requires moments of solitude, as we venture into the hidden depths of our souls, stripping away the layers that conceal our authentic selves.

We are challenged to transcend the physical persona we assume and shed the roles, masks, and identities that obscure our essence. Interestingly, the word "person" comes from "persona," a term used for the masks worn by actors in ancient theaters. This origin serves as a reminder that, much like actors, we often wear facades that hide our true nature.

Throughout history, those who have undertaken this inner journey have reached similar revelations: the unity of all life and the interconnectedness of our existence. Fundamentally, we all originate from the same source, transcending nationality, culture, and temporal boundaries.

Impermanence and change constantly remind us of life's fleeting nature, urging us to ponder deeper questions, including those about what lies beyond death. Engaging with these questions deepens our connection to our authentic selves. Personal growth and transformation are essential for understanding the essence of life, guiding us toward enlightenment and the realization of our true selves. Through continual self-reflection and introspection, we partake in a dynamic process of growth: shedding limiting beliefs and tapping into our inherent potential.

As you explore various cultural and spiritual perspectives, you will find that, while the paths may differ, they ultimately lead us to the same truth: understanding our true essence, the very core of life itself. It is time to untie the second knot, unraveling the deeper truths of our existence.

28: Self-Love Is Self-Acceptance

Let's begin the first life lesson of the second knot with a fundamental question: *Do you love yourself?* Many argue that a fulfilled life starts with self-love—the cornerstone that enables others to love us as well. While this idea appears logical, it leads us on a journey with an unclear destination. This prompts a challenging question that sends us down a rabbit hole: *What truly defines us?* Is it the societal perceptions we adopt? The expectations set by our surroundings? The limitations of our physical form? Or is it the essence of the soul that resides within us?

In a world thirsty for spiritual enlightenment, the concept of self-love takes center stage. Like many others, I embarked on this journey, seeking the elusive key to contentment and fulfillment. What I discovered led me to deep self-reflection.

Self-love, often simplified to "Love yourself first," sounds straightforward, but there's no manual. *Have you ever really considered what it means to love yourself?* What is the first step toward this elusive goal? If it were so simple, theoretically, couldn't we learn to love just about anyone?

Yet, the deeper I delved into self-love, the more elusive it became—like something intangible, slipping through my fingers like water. I felt the need to define myself in concrete terms to truly grasp the concept of self-love. To do so, I began listing traits I believed defined me. The first word I wrote was *kindness.* However, upon closer reflection, even this felt ambiguous. *Kind compared to whom?* After all, not everyone who has encountered me would describe me as kind. This realization struck me: kindness is not a fixed trait. Instead, it is a conscious choice—a deliberate alignment with our core values. It is not an inherent quality that defines us but rather an aspiration we actively strive to embody.

While many claim that our actions define us, I find this perspective limiting. *If this were true, wouldn't everyone be labeled a liar since, at some point, we all lie?* This broad labeling seems unfair. Instead, I believe our actions reflect our current state of mind and that we can evolve continuously, aligning our actions more closely with our values over time.

Defining myself became a struggle, casting doubt on my ability to genuinely love myself when I could barely articulate my own identity. This prompted me to question the very nature of love. *Is it familial love, romantic love, or the idealized love we all dream about?* It appears that happiness is often seen as a consequence of self-love, prompting us to construct a facade of 'self' to ward off feelings of unhappiness or being lost.

Yet, the harder I pursued self-love, the more elusive it felt. This led me to wonder: *What if loving ourselves isn't necessary?* Perhaps love is not just a feeling; it might be what you do despite your feelings. If perfection is an illusion, can we accept our physical form, even if we wish it were different? As long as we focus solely on our physical selves, transcending to a higher level of consciousness seems unattainable.

Love must go beyond fleeting emotions; otherwise, it's unsustainable. Anything based solely on emotions is bound to change. Love should evolve into a conscious commitment, unaffected by momentary feelings: a commitment that involves purposeful actions aligned with our genuine values and aspirations. It encompasses embracing ourselves and extending that acceptance to others and the world at large.

True love is not found in the physical but within the depths of our being. All you must do is look deep enough; then loving yourself becomes the inevitable choice. You see beyond the physical form to a manifestation of the divine.

Loving oneself means forging a connection with the source of all existence. This connection allows us to transcend the ego, embody selflessness, and fully embrace our physical form. It represents the tangible manifestation of our being, as pure souls invariably find a way to touch our hearts. *Instead of striving to love yourself, embody love itself and watch the magic unfold.*

...

Spiral Upward

Explore the art of acceptance, revel in the beauty of embracing imperfections, and celebrate the joy of recognizing your unique yet flawed physical self. This doesn't mean simply lounging around all day; actively strive to be the best version of yourself. *Prioritize eating well, staying active, and getting quality sleep as essential forms of self-care.* Focus on improving what is within your control and learn to accept what is not.

Through this transformative lens, understand that self-love is not a destination, but a continuous journey of growth and self-care. While no one can ever completely love their physical form, we can all learn to love our true essence. *By adopting this mindset, you can genuinely achieve greater fulfillment and extend love toward yourself and others.*

29: You Are Not Your Thoughts

Self-love blossoms from the fertile ground of self-acceptance, arising from a deep connection with our true essence, which defines our uniqueness. While our bodies are vessels that require care, true love emerges when we honor our true selves. Now, as we strive to uncover our authentic identities grounded in tangible evidence rather than just spiritual or intangible connections, I present a crucial question: Do you recognize the presence of a voice in your mind, constantly offering opinions on every facet of your existence?

I once grappled with the fear of losing my sanity, but I soon realized there's no need to panic; having an inner voice is a universal human experience. However, it can be disconcerting when we don't fully understand its role and origins. Merely coexisting with this voice or identifying too closely with it can have destructive consequences. Let me explain why.

Acknowledging the inner voice is crucial, as it has been a lifelong narrator of our experiences, continuously offering perspectives and judgments on everything we encounter. For example, while engaging with this book, take a moment to pause and reflect: ask yourself, *How can I quickly increase my income?* Allow your thoughts to flow freely. You'll soon notice the voice suggesting various solutions, some of which may not align with your core values. Remember, just because these thoughts arise does not mean they define who you are. This simple exercise demonstrates the mind's ability to present diverse options. Ultimately, choosing the right option is your decision, showcasing your agency, while the generation of options is merely a function of the mind.

As we become aware of our inner voice, we also become aware of the listener within us. Just as there cannot be a buyer without a seller, there can be no voice without its audience. This realization leads us to ask: Who is the listener, and who is the speaker? This awareness reveals the duality within us, highlighting that we cannot simultaneously be both the listener and the speaker. The speaker is the voice of our mind, producing a continuous stream of thoughts that seem to arise autonomously—this is an unconscious function, a perpetual chatter that we can control only when we are fully aware.

As we continue to explore this concept, we come to understand that the speaker cannot define our true identity. Consider this exercise: Imagine your mind suggesting something as outlandish as robbing a bank to quickly gain wealth, and you momentarily entertain the thought. If you find yourself laughing at the absurdity of this suggestion, it highlights your recognition that you are not the speaker. Identifying solely with the mind can trap us in the whims and fancies of our thoughts. Rather, our true essence lies in the listener: the one who attentively hears the voice, observes the thoughts, and wields the remarkable power of free will.

The voice in our minds thrives on narratives shaped by past experiences, ambitions, and fears about the future. It dwells on memories and projects into an uncertain future, often leading to distress, anxiety, and discontent. In contrast, the listener exists solely in the present moment, the only realm where true life unfolds. Here, in the now, we can fully experience the richness of existence, where each breath offers opportunities for growth, joy, and fulfillment. By anchoring ourselves in the present, we detach from the mind's relentless instabilities and discover peace in the stillness within.

It's important to recognize that staying in the present moment isn't a constant state. Our minds naturally tend to drift back to the past or wander into the future. However, by actively cultivating the ability to remain present and aware, we strengthen our connection with our true self: the listener. This practice helps us anchor more deeply in the reality of the now, enhancing our capacity for mindfulness and self-awareness.

Through this connection, we tap into our innate wisdom and intuition, transcending the mind's limitations. The listener wields the power of free will: a remarkable tool that enables us to make conscious choices aligned with our deepest passions and values. This power allows us to face life's challenges with clarity, compassion, and authenticity. By identifying ourselves as the listeners, we access unbelievable inner strength, resilience, and peace. We become empowered, with the ultimate decisions resting in our hands, regardless of the mind's wanderings.

...

Spiral Upward

Recognize yourself as the listener, not merely an echo of the voice within. Understanding that the voice is an expression of the mind and the listener is your true essence empowers you to make decisions with clarity. This awareness helps you harmonize these aspects, transcending the mind's limitations and tapping into your vast potential. As you master this, you'll become more present and attentive. You'll view the inner voice as a tool, approaching it with curiosity and compassion. By embracing your role as the listener, you free yourself from the constraints of your thoughts, opening up to the endless possibilities of the now. This shift enhances your life, allowing you to live with greater freedom and purpose.

30: Identity Is an Illusion

We've now come to understand that the listener is the essence of who we truly are, while the speaker—the mind—constantly urges us to construct a concrete identity to define ourselves. This realization leads us to our next life lesson: the nature of identity itself. Have you ever stopped to question what "identity" really is—what truly defines you?

So often, what we accept as identity is nothing more than a delicate illusion: a mask shaped by ego, conditioned by our past, and molded to meet the expectations of society. Roles shift, labels fade, appearances change, and social images crumble. Yet beneath all these layers lies the unchanging core—the soul breathed into us by God—enduring far beyond any temporary roles or outward disguises.

Let me share a personal story that might resonate with you. Years ago, I found myself entangled in the illusion of identity. I convinced myself that I wasn't materialistic. Even as I indulged in excessive spending, I rationalized it, claiming I simply liked the items I bought—not the brands themselves.

But that illusion shattered the day I lost everything. Suddenly homeless and drowning in $1.6 million of debt—a moment we will explore more deeply later in this book—I felt the ground beneath my identity collapse. With everything stripped away, I found myself clinging desperately to the image people once held of me. Without my watches, my tailored suits, and my polished lifestyle, I felt as though my entire aura had disappeared.

I withdrew from people out of shame—not because they rejected me, but because I no longer recognized myself. The greatest shock was not the financial loss, but the realization that I was not the man I believed myself to be. It is easy to project confidence, generosity, and strength when life is abundant. But when everything vanished, so did the identity I had unconsciously built around those conditions.

This crisis forced me to confront the truth: my essence had nothing to do with the labels I wore or the persona I presented. Identity created through externals is fragile. It dissolves the moment those externals are removed.

Society pressures us to define ourselves by clear labels—career titles, personality traits, social roles—yet true identity cannot be confined to any of these. It is far deeper, broader, and more fluid than we often allow ourselves to see.

Real identity emerges when we strip away the illusions and embrace the fullness of our lived experience: the love we give, the lessons we learn, the values we uphold, and the soul that remains steady beneath life's constant changes.

Breaking Free from Society's Mold

The search for identity runs deep in a world captivated by titles, hierarchies, and labels. We are conditioned—almost from birth—to find a box that defines us, to choose a role and cling to it as if our worth depends on how neatly we fit inside it. The pressure to conform has become so normalized that we rarely pause to question whether these identities truly serve us... or whether they quietly confine us.

Let me reveal a "box" you may have felt but never fully named: We live in a society that teaches us to make a living, not a life. And the consequences are profound. Making a living is driven by survival. It can drain your energy, tether your joy, and leave you feeling hollow—even when you appear successful on the outside. Making a life, on the other hand, is driven by passion. It ignites purpose, nourishes the soul, and infuses every action with meaning.

Yet we are taught to build a life that looks good, not one that feels true. As a result, millions spend their lives chasing an identity that was never theirs to begin with—an identity built on expectations, fear, and comparison. This creates a paradox: everyone is searching for themselves, yet no one feels truly found.Pause for a moment. Close your eyes.

Say to yourself:

I don't need an identity that confines me.
I don't need to fit into anyone's box.
I will grow through what I go through.

This shift in perspective aligns you with your true essence. Your deepest nature is not a label, not a job title, not a personality type—it is energy. And energy is formless, limitless, and incapable of being trapped by definitions. You were never created to be contained within an identity. You were created to evolve.

When you release the need to be a fixed "something," you open yourself to becoming everything you're meant to be—fluid, expansive, and free. Identity is not your home; it is only a resting place on your journey. Your true nature is movement, transformation, unfolding. It's time to stop sculpting yourself to fit society's mold. Instead, let yourself grow beyond it.

Embracing Formlessness: Unleashing Infinite Potential

When people ask, "Who are you?" we instinctively answer with "I am…"—and in that moment, we shrink ourselves into a box of words. These two simple words often trap us, not because they are wrong, but because we attach them to labels that limit our becoming.

Instead of saying, "I am a doctor," try saying, "I work as a doctor." One confines you to a narrow identity. The other frees you to be more than any role you play. The phrase "I am" often tricks us into adopting a rigid self-image shaped by past experiences and imagined expectations. Without realizing it, we begin to believe that our identity is fixed, defined by what we've done rather than by who we are becoming. But you are far more expansive than any label.

Your mind generates thousands of thoughts each day, but you are not the sum of those thoughts. You are not your job title, your personality traits, or the stories you've told about yourself. Your true self transcends every physical form and mental construct—it is awareness, presence, and limitless potential.

A fixed identity may feel safe, but safety can become a silent prison. Growth requires spaciousness, openness, and the willingness to evolve. When you embrace your formless nature, you stay receptive to transformation. You become a fluid expression of life itself—capable of learning, shedding, expanding, and rising.

True meaning is found not in defining yourself, but in allowing yourself to unfold. Not in holding tightly to who you think you are, but in becoming who you are meant to be. When you release the need for a rigid identity, you reclaim your freedom—and step into the boundless terrain of your truest self.

Connecting with the Essence of Existence

Imagine shedding the limitations of identity—free from labels, roles, and societal expectations. In this state of formlessness, we open ourselves to endless possibilities for growth and transformation. To truly grasp our essence, we must move beyond the confines of identity, diving deep into our being and transcending external constructs. By embracing formlessness, we unlock access to the energy within us, connecting to the core essence of existence itself.

...

Spiral Upward

Break free from the illusion of identity. Let go of the chains of expectation, both from society and from yourself. You are not fixed, but fluid; not a label, but a living presence, forever unfolding within the vast mosaic of life. Flow, adapt, and grow—unbound by definitions—and taste the freedom of your ever-changing nature.

Identity is but a sandcastle on the shore of existence. You shape it with care, knowing the tide will come. And when it does, meet its dissolving not with sorrow, but with joy, for the beauty was never in its permanence, but in the building itself. Those who cling are not spared the tide; they are only shattered by it.

31: Living Life Is an Inside Job

After the previous lesson, doesn't it feel liberating to embrace the idea of formlessness?

Every transformation is not just a movement toward something new, but also a release from something that no longer serves you. Each phase becomes a stepping stone on the spiral of growth. Now let's explore a truth that bridges the outer world and the inner one: Living is an inside job.

Have you ever felt that magnetic pull—the deep curiosity urging you to explore the world, to uncover its mysteries, to chase the feeling of "more"?

This outward pull can be intoxicating. It convinces us that life is out there, waiting to be conquered. We chase adventure, new experiences, and definitions of success shaped by the external world. But beneath that excitement lies a profound truth: The essence of life is not found outside of you. It unfolds within you.

Life takes shape in the delicate space between reality and your interpretation of it. When you recognize that living is fundamentally an internal process, your entire perspective shifts. You begin to move through the world with deeper clarity, resilience, and purpose. This inward focus allows you to reclaim your experience, align with your core values, and cultivate fulfillment that is independent of circumstance.

The Internal Perspective

What if life is not something you live outwardly, but something you craft inwardly?

Your thoughts, emotions, and perceptions frame every experience you have. When you anchor your awareness internally, you tap into the ability to influence your reality from within. Challenges stop defining you and instead become opportunities—filtered through the choices you make and the mindset you carry.

Living from within invites you to examine your inner landscape with honesty and curiosity. By reflecting on your beliefs, values, and desires, you discover what truly matters. When your actions align with this inner truth, life takes on a sense of direction and integrity.

Your inner world and outer environment are always in conversation. Mastering this relationship empowers you to become the active architect of your life, rather than a passive receiver of circumstances.

A Real-Life Illustration

Here's how this plays out in my own life:

Internal World: Personal development has always been at the core of who I am. Despite being naturally sociable, I learned early that solitude—writing, reflecting, thinking—is essential to my growth. I realized I had a gift for simplifying complex ideas in a way others found helpful, and I felt called to develop this ability.

External Environment: But the external world constantly calls. Invitations to gatherings, new business opportunities, and the fast pace of life often pull me away from the discipline that fuels my personal development.

Choice and Action: Recognizing this tension, I intentionally limit social engagements and evaluate new opportunities with care. This deliberate discipline allows me to stay aligned with my purpose and dedicate time to transcending my own spiral—so I can share the insights that emerge from it.

This is what it means to live from within:to respond consciously rather than react impulsively, and to remain faithful to what matters most.

The Inner Journey of Transformation

When we see life as an inside job, everything changes. Life becomes a canvas where you blend internal wisdom with external experiences. Fulfillment stops depending on what you can control externally and begins to grow from how you respond internally.

This journey asks you to confront your ingrained beliefs, question subconscious patterns, and shed the conditioning that limits you. As you peel back these layers, life becomes richer and more textured. Colors feel deeper. Moments feel fuller. Even challenges carry meaning.

Living from within transforms obstacles into stepping stones and setbacks into teachers. With this shift, you assume responsibility for your joy, your peace, and your purpose. You become a conscious co-creator of a life rooted in meaning.

Living Inside Out

Living life as an inside job deepens your connection to intuition—the quiet voice that rises not from the mind, but from the heart. This inner compass guides you toward what is true, even when logic cannot explain it.

When you tune into this voice, you begin to feel the interconnectedness of all things. External events become mirrors reflecting your internal state, offering insights rather than threats. With this awareness, adversity becomes a catalyst—not an enemy—inviting you to grow into the person you were meant to become. This inner alignment requires courage, honesty, and self-awareness. But the reward is clarity, freedom, and a sense of purpose that no external circumstance can shake.

...

Spiral Upward

Break free from the illusion that life is lived only in the world outside of you. Life unfolds in the meeting point between reality and your interpretation of it—and everything depends on how you navigate that inner space.

What appears "good" may hold hidden lessons. What feels "bad" may carry unexpected gifts. Claim your life by experiencing it fully from within. This inward shift cultivates resilience, gratitude, authenticity, and wisdom. It turns challenges into opportunities and setbacks into guidance. When you live from within, less becomes more. Moments become deeper. Experiences grow richer. Life becomes yours again.

Embrace this inward path—and watch your existence transform into a vibrant, meaningful journey shaped by your inner wisdom and guided by your truest values.

32: The Intelligence of the Heart

In the relentless whirlwind of modern life, we often find ourselves on a quest for meaning and enlightenment in the external world. We dive into books, seek the counsel of gurus, and gaze at the stars, hoping to unlock the secrets of existence. But what if the ultimate key to our true potential isn't hidden in the cosmos or someone else's teachings, but lies within us—buried deep in the rhythm of our own being?

As we journey toward a fulfilling life, it becomes clear that the essence of living truly comes from within. To unlock this truth, we must shift our focus inward and explore the intricate universe of our own biology—a realm teeming with wisdom and self-discovery.

Redefining Intelligence

Intelligence is often confined to the workings of the brain, celebrated for its ability to analyze, recall, and reason. But what if intelligence is much broader? Consider memory: without it, intelligence would falter. Memory doesn't just live in the mind—it exists at a cellular level, as seen in the astonishing capabilities of DNA.

DNA, the keeper of our genetic code, stores and transmits vast amounts of information, carrying the wisdom of countless generations within each cell. This remarkable capability suggests that intelligence is not solely a cognitive function; it is embedded within the very fabric of our being.

This realization expands our understanding of intelligence. Every cell in our body harbors a form of wisdom, a quiet intelligence that works in harmony with our conscious mind. This duality—the interplay of conscious and unconscious intelligence—reshapes how we perceive our capacity to understand and grow.

The Heart's Role

Delving deeper into our biology, we encounter the heart: a symbol of life, emotion, and interconnectedness. Nearly every cell in our body, except those in the cornea, is connected through a vast network of blood vessels that converge at the heart. This intricate connection raises profound questions: Is the heart merely a pump, or does it hold a deeper role in our lives?

Have you ever felt your heart tugging in one direction while your mind pulls you in another? Why does the heart, a physical organ, seem to have such a profound say in our decisions and emotions? Perhaps it's because the heart remains unblemished by ego, offering guidance rooted in purity and truth.

Interestingly, when the physical heart is unfolded, it reveals a spiral shape—an elegant reminder that the heart's wisdom mirrors the upward spiral of growth we experience in life. This spiral, both physical and symbolic, serves as a profound metaphor for the layers of understanding and transformation the heart facilitates.

A Personal Experience

Years after my divorce, I naturally started to feel a deep longing to re-marry and start a family. At the same time, I recognized the importance of spending time alone, reflecting, and rediscovering myself. It was a delicate balance—nurturing my inner growth while navigating the heartfelt yearning to create a family of my own.

The Mind's Voice: My mind, influenced by fears of aging alone and unfulfilled dreams of fatherhood, urged me to settle. I had everything else—success, security—but no one to share it with. The logical choice seemed to be compromise.

The Heart's Wisdom: My heart resisted. It reminded me of my core values, urging me not to disrupt someone else's life simply to fill a void in mine. I realized that a fulfilling life didn't require me to be a biological father. My role as a father figure to my nieces and nephews was enough. The heart's wisdom whispered that a year with the wrong person could drag on endlessly, while a decade with the right person would feel fleeting and full.

Unfolding the Spiral: Reflecting further, I saw how my heart's guidance wasn't a single moment of clarity, but a layered, spiral-like unfolding of deeper truths about patience, alignment, and trust. Each insight built upon the last, helping me navigate with integrity and purpose.

The Resolution: I chose to trust my heart and wait for the right person, confident that our paths would cross when the time was right. This decision demonstrated the delicate balance between the mind's logic and the heart's instinct—a reminder that true alignment comes from listening to both, with the heart leading the way.

The Heart's Unique Message

The heart communicates in ways the mind cannot fully grasp. Its rhythm, as unique as a fingerprint, speaks a language of intuition and emotion. A quickened heartbeat might signal caution, while its steady rhythm might offer reassurance.

When we lose someone dear, the mind struggles to rationalize the pain, but the heart feels it deeply, reminding us of the depth of our connections. These signals are not random; they are the heart's way of guiding us toward understanding and healing, even when logic falls short.

And just like its physical form, the heart's wisdom unfolds in spirals, revealing deeper truths with each turn. It is through these spirals that we align with the rhythm of life itself, embracing both its challenges and its beauty.

The Mind and the Heart

The heart shines brightest when the mind is ensnared by doubt or confusion. It acts as a beacon, cutting through the noise with its simple, profound wisdom. In these moments, the intelligence of the heart leads us toward clarity, reminding us that we are more than our thoughts—we are a symphony of interconnected cells, emotions, and instincts, each contributing to our journey.

...

Spiral Upward

Reflect deeply on the multifaceted nature of intelligence. Beyond the confines of the mind lies a treasure trove of wisdom encoded in your DNA and the intricate network of your cells. The heart, at the center of this symphony, serves as a conduit for the deep, unconscious intelligence that often escapes the mind's grasp.

When you truly listen to your heart, you uncover its spirals—intricate layers of wisdom woven through your experiences, each one guiding you toward profound truths. Every beat carries more than just life; it holds a message, inviting you to attune to its rhythm and unlock the boundless potential that lies within.

Tune into the heart's pulse and let its intelligence lead you. By trusting its quiet wisdom and embracing the spiral of growth it reveals, you unlock the boundless capacity for transformation, love, and purpose. Life becomes not just an existence but an art, lived from the inside out.

33: The Opposites
Are the Same

Having grasped that intelligence extends beyond the mind and that the heart plays a vital role in comprehending the totality of our existence, this life lesson explores the unity of two extremes and how this principle influences our emotions, motivations, and actions.

The concept of polarity implies that opposites are two separate extremes, but within this apparent contradiction lies a deep truth—opposites are essentially the same in nature. We can perceive the underlying oneness that unifies them by integrating opposing forces. Reflecting on our past, we may realize that what once seemed like punishment was crucial in bringing unforeseen blessings. This principle is why we can revisit our past and transform the bad into good and the good into bad, depending on our current state of mind, revealing the fluidity and interconnectedness of life's experiences.

Hence, we must be cautious with quick conclusions, as misinterpreting our feelings and intentions can lead us off course, just as a misdiagnosis can lead to misguided treatment.

So, what do I mean by misdiagnosing our feelings and intentions? Consider this scenario: Your dream job awaits you in Paris, and you excitedly prepare for an interview. You book your plane ticket and rush to the airport with an overwhelming feeling of being the luckiest person alive. However, an unforeseen delay in traffic causes you to miss your flight by a few minutes. You find yourself standing at the gate, the plane before you, but you are unable to board. Overwhelmed with disappointment, you burst into tears, feeling like the unluckiest person, convinced that you've lost the golden opportunity.

Upon returning home, the unexpected unfolds. You receive news of a tragic accident—the very plane you were meant to be on has crashed, and there are no survivors. How do you feel?

The paradox of feeling both fortunate and unfortunate arises from the same emotional wellspring, separated only by circumstance. This highlights that our perception of adversity can, in fact, be a facet of something positive. To navigate this delicate balance, we must relinquish resistance and embrace tomorrow's uncertainty. Choosing to interpret every emotion through the lens of acceptance becomes the key, ultimately eradicating the pain of suffering.

At the heart of comprehending our existence lies the principle of duality—the notion that everything possesses two poles and a pair of opposites. Contrary to the idea of these opposites as isolated entities, they are interconnected and form a continuous spectrum.

The dance of opposites reveals that seemingly contradictory aspects are, in fact, two extremes of the same essence, distinguished only by varying degrees.

If you keep walking steadfastly north, you will eventually be walking south. This illustrates how opposites are intricately connected, presenting themselves as extremes with various degrees in between. This illustrates a fundamental aspect of life—the dance of opposites. Let's explore this dance of opposites further in various aspects of human experience.

Love and Hate

Human emotions serve as a vivid example of duality. According to the principle of polarity, there is no absolute love or hate—these are simply terms for different ends of the same spectrum. As we move up this scale, we experience increasing love and decreasing hate, and vice versa as we move down. Love and hate exist in degrees, and there is a midpoint where feelings of like and dislike are so subtle that they are almost indistinguishable.

This explains why people we love deeply can sometimes become the targets of our strongest hatred, and why those we initially dislike can stir feelings of love. This paradox highlights that love and hate are interconnected, and it is through their interaction that we come to understand the complexities of our relationships.

Tears and Laughter

Life's encompass moments of both sorrow and joy, often intertwined in mysterious ways. Tears can give way to laughter, and laughter can dissolve into tears. This phenomenon emphasizes the interconnected nature of even the most contrasting human emotions. By embracing this connection, we find solace and a deeper appreciation for the unity inherent in life's diverse experiences.

Perspective and Mindset

Life's paradoxes extend beyond emotions and experiences; they also encompass our perspectives and mindsets, shaping our understanding and interpretation of the world. What may be seen as hardship by one person can be viewed as an opportunity for growth and learning by another. By shifting our mindset, we can transform the ordinary into the extraordinary. Recognizing the inherent duality in life allows us to redefine our own version of wealth and abundance.

...

Spiral Upward

In the magnificent orchestra of existence, opposites dance gracefully together, showcasing the delicate interplay between light and darkness, joy and sorrow, love and hate. Embracing these paradoxes enriches your understanding of the interconnectedness that weaves through every facet of your being. As you traverse the dynamic landscapes of life, keep in mind that a simple shift in perspective can unveil the limitless potentials nestled within the harmony of opposites. By acknowledging the intricate dance of contrasts within yourself and the vast expanse of the world, you invite growth, wisdom, and a deeper immersion in the beauty of life.

34: All Is From One

Here I am, speaking to you. But what is *here*?

Here, within the universe — yet the universe itself rests within time, space, and matter. And who brought these into being? They could not arise on their own. From nothing, nothing comes.

So if I exist, I must have come from a Source. And if every finite thing points back to something else, then the chain must end with an Origin unlike all else: eternal, unlimited, without beginning or end. The Qur'an calls Him *al-Awwal wa'l-Ākhir* — the First and the Last.

I am fleeting; He is Everlasting. I am dependent; He is Self-Sufficient. So again — what is *here*?

God is closer to me than my jugular vein, yet He is not me. He is above His creation, unlike His creation, sustaining all by His knowledge, power, and mercy. The moment we imagine there is a space beyond Him, we fall into contradiction, for all that exists is under His command and will.

Perhaps then, this life is like a canvas, and we — each stroke, each shade, each line — are placed with purpose. But the vision belongs to the Artist, not the paint. The Qur'an reminds us: *"We did not create the heavens and the earth and all between them in play."*

So what is the purpose? That I awaken to the truth that while I am distinct from you, we both return to the same Source. We are not fragments of God, but servants of God, and in serving Him, we discover our unity as His creation.

Much like cells in a body, each of us plays a role. Alone we are fragile; together we form a whole. Yet the body itself is not the soul: and creation itself is not the Creator. The harmony we sense between the inner and outer worlds is a sign (*āyah*) pointing us back to Him.

And if I wrong you, do I not wrong myself? Every kindness I show, do I not see it again in my own life? "Whoever does an atom's weight of good will see it, and whoever does an atom's weight of evil will see it." This is the essence of justice: our deeds return to us.

So when I speak to you, in truth I speak also to myself — for we are both standing before the same Lord, drawing from the same Source, and destined to return to Him.

The Principle of Duality and Correspondence

When we notice duality in the world, we are led to a deeper law: correspondence, the way things mirror and relate to one another. In the vast choreography of existence a truth appears: all created things are connected, because all are brought into being by one Creator. This connection does not make creation divine; it reveals a single Author behind the many pages.

The image of yin and yang — darkness and light, passivity and activity — illustrates how opposites can harmonize. This image is useful if we remember that the Artist and the painting are not the same. Yin and yang remind us that balance is maintained by complementary forces: night returns the world to rest so day can renew it; stillness readies us for motion; receptivity prepares us for action. Each pole is necessary, each has its purpose, and together they sustain the whole. In Islamic language, these patterns are signs of God's wisdom and design.

Imagine yin as receptive, inward strength and yang as outward striving and effort. Neither is superior in absolute terms; both are modes through which creation fulfills its role under Divine ordinance. Like instruments in an orchestra, each voice contributes to the symphony—not by becoming the composer, but by playing its appointed part so the music can be heard.

This wisdom invites humility. It shows that despite our differences we share a single origin and a single Sustainer. Differences point the mind back to the Maker; they do not dissolve the boundary between the created and the Creator.

The Illusion of Separation

To explore the essence of our true being — the soul — we must see life both as individuals and as part of a greater whole. Science cannot fully grasp the soul, but we still sense its presence, as undeniable as gravity.

There is no *I* without *you*; our lives are interwoven. No white without black, no life without death — contrasts give meaning. The oxygen that sustains a tree, and the tree that returns it in breath, remind us that existence is a web of giving and receiving. This interdependence does not confuse our created nature with God's nature; it is fellowship among created beings under Divine governance.

Consider the human body: though hair and nails differ in form and function, both spring from the same DNA, making them integral to a single, remarkable entity. In the same way, our cultural, personal, and spiritual differences are diverse expressions of one human reality. When this truth is remembered, prejudice, arrogance, and hatred begin to crumble.

To embrace the unity of creation — without confusing creation with the Creator — is to shatter the false walls of separation. It aligns the mind with the heart, joining reason to mercy. True efforts against ignorance must heal rather than harden, building bridges of understanding instead of trenches of division.

The Ripple Effect of Unity

If we accept that all things are connected by Divine design, then we must also accept the moral consequence: our deeds ripple. The principle of correspondence reminds us that our choices are never isolated; they reverberate across the wider web of life. Small acts of care, small acts of harm — both set in motion chains we may never see.

To value diversity is not to erase difference, but to dignify it. In doing so we cultivate empathy, build institutions of mercy, and protect the weak. A single kindness becomes a current that touches countless lives; a single cruelty becomes poison that spreads far beyond the first wound.

In practical terms: speak gently, act justly, forgive when possible, and stand firm in your responsibilities. These are ways to embody the balance the world longs for. In the Islamic moral frame, servanthood to God and service to His creation are bound together: obedience to Him includes compassion for His creatures.

As we embrace the complementary forces of life — receptivity and effort, giving and receiving, inward reflection and outward action — we rise in character and understanding. This ascent is not into unity with God's essence, but into nearness to Him through right conduct and by recognizing our complete dependence on Him.

My Own Moment of Awakening

Let me share an unforgettable moment that changed me forever.

One afternoon, I was walking in Dubai Mall with my friend and business partner from Denmark, Per. We were talking casually when suddenly, I felt a strange pull in my body — a sharp intuition. Per noticed right away.

"Are you okay?" he asked.

"I don't know," I replied. *"Something feels off. Let's just walk this way."*

Every time we reached a crossroad, I stopped and followed the same unexplainable pull. Per kept asking where we were going, and all I could say was, *"I don't know. Just follow me."*

Moments later, we found ourselves near the Dubai Fountain just as the show was about to begin. The crowd rushed toward the water to catch the performance. Per joined them, but I held back. And then I heard it — a scream that cut through everything.

A mother's cry: *"My baby! Please, help my baby!"* No one else heard her. Everyone's eyes were fixed on the dancing fountain. But I ran toward the sound and saw her little girl. She had struck her head on the bridge and fallen into the water. The father stood frozen, paralyzed by shock.

I didn't think. I just jumped — suit, phone, wallet and all. The water swallowed me. At the bottom, her tiny body lay still. For a split second, the world went silent. Then instinct took over. I grabbed her, lifted her small frame, and pushed her belly above the surface. Suddenly she coughed, then screamed — and in that cry, life returned.

When I climbed out, people were crying, hugging me, reaching out to touch the little girl. The mother collapsed into my arms, sobbing, gasping, whispering prayers between her tears. Per stood there with tears streaming down his face.

On the drive home, the car was heavy with silence. Per stared out the window, crying quietly. I was drenched, my suit sticking to me, my mind spinning. When I finally stepped into the shower, still fully clothed, the image of that little girl lying motionless at the bottom of the water hit me all at once — and I broke.

In that instant, I realized: I was connected to her. No race, no title, no history. Just soul to soul. In that moment, I was her father, her brother, her everything. And she was my daughter, my little sister, my reminder. She showed me that unity is not something we invent. It is our natural state. Division is learned; oneness is remembered.

...

Spiral Upward

Remember: you are not a lone spark adrift; you are a vital note in a divinely composed melody. Your life leaves an imprint — unique, necessary, and accountable. Free yourself from the false comfort of division; celebrate the unity of humanity as creation oriented toward its Creator.

When you look into another's eyes, you will see a reflection — not because you are the same being, but because you share the same origin, the same breath of life, and the same destiny before God. Look past the illusions of separation and false superiority. Our true dignity is that of servants who recognize their duties and their dependence.

In the end, when I speak to you I also speak to myself — for we both stand before the same Lord, bound by the same responsibilities, drawn from the same Source, and destined to return. We are one in our origin and one in our accountability; let that truth raise your heart and steady your steps.

35: Beauty of Death

We've reached the final life lesson in this section of the book. Before we delve into its depths, let's briefly revisit our journey to maintain continuity and focus. We began by questioning the very essence of who we are, challenging the notion of self-love and recognizing its vital role in human growth. From there, we embraced our physical bodies as vessels while acknowledging the boundless potential for transformation and expansion within us.

As we journeyed further inward, we uncovered the distinction between the voice in our head and our true selves—the silent observer, the listener. By dismantling the illusion of identity shaped by external labels, we liberated ourselves from imposed limitations, opening the door to infinite possibilities and a deeper connection with our true essence.

Furthermore, we delved into society's conditioning, which suggests that one must seek their identity externally, fostering a dangerous life perspective. Many of us perceive living life as an external journey, necessitating the clarification that true living emanates from within. As we explored our inner universe, we reevaluated the role of the heart and its intelligence, recognizing that peace remains elusive without it. Understanding the inherent connection between peace and chaos led us to the realization that opposites, though extremes, are inherently intertwined, requiring us to embrace both equally. How to embrace duality took us to the next life lesson: all is one; embracement arrives after grasping the unity of everything.

With the understanding that all is one, let's delve into the mysterious concept of death. Death embodies a captivating yet elusive essence—a paradox of existence. It is a gift but perceived as a penalty. It is the beginning but embraced as the end.

You may be wondering how death can be perceived as a gift. Though death often stirs fear, sorrow, and uncertainty, delving into its transformative potential unveils deep insights into our true essence and purpose. By embracing death as a gift, we unlock a deeper appreciation for the preciousness of every moment and the interconnected existence that binds us all together. The idea that everything can be over in a snap of a moment makes us humble and appreciative. Knowing that we will all die makes us question the beginning and the hereafter. What if I revealed that another awakening awaits you as you close your eyes for the final time? How would this revelation reshape the fabric of your existence? Would you reconsider your actions? Would you cherish the lives of others as much as you cherish your own?

The odds of your existence are an astonishing one in 400 trillion—a probability so slim it borders on the impossible, yet here you are. You entered this world from a state of sleep, but that doesn't mean you are meant to drift through it without awakening to its deeper truths. Isn't it our disbelief in awakening again after the final sleep that truly holds us back?

Think about it: before birth, we were asleep in our mother's womb, unaware of the life waiting for us beyond. Yet we woke, transitioning seamlessly from one realm to another. Life gives rise to life, suggesting that the source of our existence is not void or death, but life itself. Death, after all, is merely a transformation extracted from living; yet living can never be extracted from death. Life is the origin, the thread that continues, while death is but a fleeting moment in its eternal rhythm.

Yet, many hesitate to embrace the possibility of another awakening after death, perhaps because they cherish life so deeply. Yet consider this: with all the knowledge and experiences you now hold, would you willingly return to your mother's womb if that environment could be recreated? Likely not—despite the fact that your arrival into this world was marked by tears. The difference lies in our unawareness of the life that awaited us beyond the womb, just as we now grapple with uncertainty about what lies beyond this existence.

We are beings of energy, bound by the unchanging laws of the universe: energy cannot be created or destroyed; it merely transforms.

This fundamental principle leads to a profound question: if energy only transitions, where did it originate? Exploring this mystery is an invitation to delve into the intricacies of life's design, a journey that continues as we unravel the fifth knot.

Existence seems to operate in rhythmic cycles, governed by an unseen algorithm where patterns repeat and life flows in endless circles. Everything returns to its source, as if guided by an intrinsic pull. Perhaps this universal rhythm is not merely a coincidence but a cosmic call, drawing us back to the ultimate origin—our Creator.

When we die, three things follow us to our grave: our family, our wealth, and our deeds. Yet only one stays—our deeds, which accompany us to our new home. While our physical form is prepared for its final rest, this preparation does not extend to our souls. Are we truly ready for what awaits beyond?

Do not live as if death will never visit you. Just as birth was not the conclusion but the beginning of our earthly journey, death is not the end—it is the commencement of the hereafter. Our souls, woven from the eternal fabric of energy, abide by the universal law: energy cannot be destroyed, only transformed.

The concept of awakening after death challenges our deeply rooted perceptions of mortality. It invites us to confront profound questions about the essence of our existence and the legacy we will leave behind. Imagine living each day as if it were a prelude to a new awakening. How might this perspective change the way we treat one another? How much more intentional and meaningful would our actions become?

Perhaps, then, the fear of death would no longer paralyze us but serve as a powerful motivator—to live more authentically, love more deeply, and act with greater consciousness. Embracing death as a transition rather than an end liberates us to honor the life we have and the lives we touch, leaving behind a legacy of compassion and purpose.

Spiral Upward

Embrace the enigma of death, recognizing it not as an endpoint but as a passage. Life is real, but death is not; the grave cradles your body, not your essence. While awaiting the dawn of a new awakening, endeavor to make your earthly visit a testament to love, kindness, and the pursuit of truth. Just as every facet of existence serves a purpose, our deeds in this realm echo into the beyond.

The Truth of Life

Life Is an Upward Spiral

Life from a Different Perspective

From Awareness to Understanding

Awareness is the light that awakens the soul, but understanding is the path that gives that light direction. In discovering who we are, we uncover truth — yet truth alone is not enough. It must be lived, not just known.

The next step of the spiral calls us to apply our awareness — to meet life as both teacher and mirror, to find meaning not in what happens to us, but in how we choose to respond.

Every challenge becomes an invitation to rise higher. Every moment, a chance to walk the truth we once only understood in thought. For wisdom without action is only potential — and life, in its divine design, was never meant to remain unlived.

As we delve into the enigma of human suffering through the lens of life as an upward spiral, we begin to see that the journey is both repetitive and progressive. We all face similar challenges, though they manifest in different forms and intensities. To make sense of this, we must explore the intricate dynamics of our connection to the physical self while venturing deep into our inner being. Through the lessons life offers, we revisit what we thought we understood, uncovering deeper truths along the way.

Now, we arrive at the third knot. If the first two knots remain tied, our ability to fully untie this one is limited. The third knot invites us to grasp the deeper truths of life and confront the external influences that shape our perceptions. Often, what we perceive is a reflection of what we seek, and a misguided perspective can lead to flawed conclusions. Sometimes, stepping back or elevating our thinking beyond the surface is necessary to discern the true patterns underlying existence.

Objective observation suggests that life follows a spiral pattern, which may explain why challenges seem to recur in cycles. Just as we reach a level of contentment, new challenges often arise to test us. If we view life as linear, this repetitive nature can become a source of despair, as old pains resurface and seem to define our trajectory. However, when we see life as an upward spiral, we understand that we revisit these challenges from a higher vantage point. The past no longer restricts us—it becomes the foundation that propels us to greater heights.

As we ascend this spiral, we gain the tools to more effectively navigate the ebbs and flows of emotion at each new level. The essence of life is not about escaping difficult times—there is no escape. Our only path forward is to embrace these difficulties as opportunities for growth, allowing us to transcend to the next stage of our evolution. With this understanding, we must reevaluate our concept of happiness before pursuing it as life's ultimate mission.

During the third knot, we will explore how our perceptions of life shape our experiences. Together, we will learn to navigate the turbulent tides of emotion that influence our relationships with others and the world. Additionally, we will critically examine the role of wealth in mental well-being, recognizing its status as a societal benchmark for success while questioning its true impact on fulfillment.

Life, in its essence, is a gift. Yet, why does it sometimes feel like a burden? This fundamental question sets the stage for transformative lessons that will guide us to a deeper understanding. By the end of part three, I promise you will see life through an entirely new perspective—one that transforms challenges into stepping stones and suffering into a catalyst for growth.

36: Happiness Does Not Exist

I have seen people leave everything for nothing,
just because nothing seemed like everything in the beginning.

I have seen happy souls searching for joy where sad ones dwell,
drawn by distant laughter, nothing but a deceptive spell.

I have seen persistent people ask for directions
and lost people pointing the way.

Then, I have seen lost people acting like happy people
as if they finally found the way.

I have seen good people change their personalities
as if it was a disease in their brains that gave them that ability.

But the emptiness in their eyes is impossible to hide
even though they act satisfied.
They behave like blind people, but they have eyes to see.
Blindness has taken over their hearts, so it must be hard to see.

They try to fulfill what's missing inside
by chasing deceptive pleasures from the outside.

Pride covers the surface of their masks
but cracks every time the mirror asks.

They're the architects of the web that is weaved in shame.
But to live with themselves, they find someone else to blame.

They must confront the reality found within the pupil of their eyes,
for only then can the healing journey demolish the disguise.

I have seen it all in the reflection of my own eyes.

Stop Chasing and Start Embracing

In a world overflowing with dreams and inspiration, it's easy to be swept away by societal norms. The relentless pace of life pushes us forward, leaving little time to pause and reflect. Slowly, our personal beliefs dissolve into collective opinions, transforming us from mindful observers into performers in life's grand spectacle. We find ourselves chasing happiness as if it were something tangible—something we could grasp and hold onto forever. But is happiness truly a constant state of mind? By its very nature, nothing in life is permanent.

It's time to rewire our perceptions and break free from the chains of conditioning. Let us pause to reassess and realign our core values—before inadvertently passing on misguided ideals to the next generation.

Allow me to share a personal lesson from my journey. I have always approached life with a positive mindset; people often say my energy precedes me. On the surface, it seemed as though everything in my external world effortlessly fell into place. Yet, upon deeper reflection, I realized that true contentment had eluded my internal world, despite appearing to "have it all." This realization made me understand what it truly means to be poor while possessing everything.

Even amid a joyous marriage to an extraordinary woman—who was both my greatest strength and my greatest weakness—I sensed a void in my pursuit of happiness, a void that had nothing to do with her and everything to do with me. With her by my side, I felt invincible. My goals expanded, my accomplishments multiplied, and I seemed to conquer the world. And yet, in the process, I lost everything that mattered most at home. This painful realization taught me that having the right person by your side means nothing if you are not the right version of yourself.

I will never forget our last conversation before our divorce. With a tenderness that cut deeper than words, my ex-wife gently touched my face and said, "I love you, and I know you love me, too, but you will never change unless I leave." She was right, and her departure became her greatest gift to me—a gift for which I will always be profoundly grateful. She was a blessing during our marriage and a lesson after it; no man could ask for more.

You might wonder where I went wrong. I made the common mistake of chasing what seemed essential while neglecting what truly mattered. My journey was fueled by the illusion that happiness could be found externally. In my relentless pursuit of success, I overlooked the genuine joys I already had, mistakenly believing that happiness was tied to possessions, achievements, and the approval of others. Ultimately, I learned that material gains and societal accolades, while momentarily satisfying, are fleeting and hollow.

These experiences have imparted invaluable lessons about the nature of happiness. True fulfillment isn't found in external possessions or validation; it resides within us, waiting to be recognized and embraced. Happiness is not a destination but a cultivated state of being, emerging from gratitude for life's blessings and authentic connections—with ourselves and others.

Authenticity is the key to unlocking genuine contentment. By embracing our vulnerabilities and true selves, we lay a solid foundation for lasting joy.

I must admit, I never imagined my ex-wife would leave. She was my best friend, my partner in everything. Looking back, it's clear that my biggest mistake was seeing everything subjectively—through the lens of my desires and ambitions. She warned me several times, but I didn't listen. I pushed her closer to the edge until, one day, she gathered the strength to jump. And when I came home to an empty house, I was forced to confront the truth: I had sacrificed what truly mattered for the illusion of success.

...

Spiral Upward

Resist the seductive pull of external validation and instead delve deeply into the core of your being. Embrace the abundance already present in your life. Cultivate meaningful connections, foster a spirit of gratitude, and savor the richness of the present moment. True happiness isn't found in chasing fleeting fantasies but in appreciating the blessings that surround you. Be wary of sacrificing today's joys for the uncertain promises of tomorrow—for in doing so, you risk losing both the pleasures of the present and the possibilities of the future.

37: The Illusion of Bad

In a world shaped by our experiences, our outlook profoundly influences our ability to discover joy. This life lesson delves into the nature of "good" and "bad," offering insights on how a shift in perspective can lead to a more fulfilling existence. Would you believe in the idea that both the good and the bad serve a purpose in your growth? If so, how can something that ultimately serves you truly be considered bad?

Consider this: earthquakes, often viewed as terrible disasters, play a vital role in facilitating the flow of underground water, oil, natural gas, and mineral resources to the surface, which is crucial for our ecosystem. Similarly, forest fires, perceived as destructive events, are nature's way of boosting survival. Fires aid in decomposition, returning nutrients to the soil and helping plants germinate; otherwise, the forest would get old and die.

These examples challenge the simplistic notions of what is universally good or bad, highlighting the complexity of our judgments. In other words, good and bad are merely a subjective perspective based on our current knowledge. By elevating our mind, we understand that good and bad are interconnected elements and equally a part of our ecosystem as earthquakes. What seems bad on one plane is good on another plane, therefore can you trust that everything "bad" in your life serves something good?

We often come across the concepts of good and bad when we pursue our life's key objectives or the quest for happiness. Many of us tether our self-worth to the attainment of our life goals, assuming it to be the gateway to happiness. This perspective suggests that success is synonymous with good, while falling short of our objectives is deemed bad. It frames happiness as a future destination rather than a present reality. I aim to present an alternative viewpoint, providing a nuanced breakdown, with the objective of fostering a deeper understanding of these notions and their intricate roles in shaping our lives.

Life's Key Objectives

How often have you found that not reaching your previous goals has turned out to be a positive outcome?

In some magical way, life always seems to make sense when we recall the past and little sense in the present, while the future always remains mysterious. In other words, what doesn't make sense now will eventually make sense; the art is not to lose ourselves in the process.

Why do we often lose ourselves in this process? So many of us get caught in the web of others' perceptions, molding ourselves to fit their expectations instead of embracing who we truly are. In doing so, we lose sight of our own path—not living for fulfillment, but for approval. The pressure to appear successful becomes a heavy weight, and the constant chase for validation drains our energy, making us forget who we really are.

Ask yourself: how often do you measure your worth against the carefully curated highlights of others?

Happiness and Sadness

Another aspect worth considering is the prevailing belief that happiness is inherently good while sadness is undesirable. This perspective is flawed and contributes to human misery. It's essential to recognize that sadness is as valuable as happiness; one cannot exist without the other, and both play crucial roles in shaping our human experience.

Happiness is a fickle creature, zipping in and out of our lives, gracing some with its presence frequently while remaining elusive to others. I have often found myself chasing after it, desperately seeking its warmth and comfort, only to have it slip through my fingers. And when it disappears, sadness accompanies me, leading to endless talks about how much I miss happiness, which makes sadness feel purposeless.

But one day, I took my time and spoke with sadness about my sadness, and it made me understand happiness better. Only then did I realize that happiness cannot be grasped but only seen and felt; it reveals itself in fleeting moments so that we can also give love to sadness and learn from it.

Strangely, happiness seems more readily experienced by those not actively searching for it. It shies away from those who pursue it relentlessly as if it prefers to be discovered through quiet observation. While pursuing happiness seems essential, finding contentment in sadness is equally important because you can't have one without the other. This balance allows us to appreciate happiness without grasping at it desperately.

...

Spiral Upward

Your perspective shapes the way you see yourself and the world around you. Letting go of the need to label every experience as "good" or "bad" opens the door to embracing life's rich complexity. Consider something as simple as eating an avocado—what nourishes one person may not benefit another. This serves as a reminder that your journey of growth is uniquely your own. What serves you well today may no longer do so tomorrow, and that's okay. Keep moving upward, trusting that everything will align in its own time. Resist the urge to judge, for our vision is limited, and our understanding finite. True wisdom rests with the divine.

38: Each Day Is a Precious Gift

Life unfolds in multiple dimensions, yet we perceive it primarily through the three dimensions of height, width, and depth. This limitation is a product of how our eyes and brain are designed to process information, allowing us to navigate and interact with our environment effectively. While scientific theories suggest the existence of additional dimensions, our everyday experiences and biological constraints keep us anchored in the three-dimensional world.

However, life is far more complex than what meets the human eye. Similarly, our awareness can expand to new planes, enabling us to derive deeper wisdom from the same reality. This shift in perspective is why we react differently to life's challenges. By elevating our awareness, we unlock new ways to understand and engage with the world.

Let's clarify this perspective further. It's important to acknowledge that I am not denying the existence of good and evil. Instead, I propose that both serve a purpose that, when understood, can positively contribute to our growth.

Imagine asking a seal what is evil in its world. It might answer, "the great white shark." Yet the seal is unaware that the great white shark plays a vital role in maintaining balance within the ecosystem. Similarly, good and evil coexist as necessary counterparts, balancing our existence. This doesn't mean that being evil is the same as being good; rather, goodness cannot exist without the contrast of evil. Can we apply the same understanding to the challenges in our lives? Can we view "setbacks" not as punishments but as essential lessons within a greater system? After all, we are part of an interconnected ecosystem.

Favorable and Challenging Days

Life is marked by two distinct kinds of days: those that feel like they're working for us and those that feel like they're working against us. Each type of day carries its unique purpose, offering valuable lessons within the intricate dance of existence.

Favorable Days: When life's tides flow in our favor, they reveal our humility and authenticity. These moments test how grounded we remain amid abundance. Favorable days can tempt us toward arrogance or self-centeredness, but true humility lies in recognizing that these blessings are not solely the result of our actions. They emerge from a complex interplay of causes and effects, woven into the broader tapestry of existence—a concept we'll explore further in part five of this book.

Challenging Days: Conversely, challenging days test our resilience and patience. These moments reveal the depth of our inner strength and the extent of our endurance. Setbacks are not punishments but opportunities for personal growth and self-discovery. They highlight the gap between where we are and where we aspire to be. Through these trials, we uncover hidden reserves of courage and determination, accessing inner strengths we may not have realized we possessed.

Shifting Perspective

Both favorable and challenging days are essential threads in the fabric of our lives. Only by embracing and learning from both can we evolve. Success teaches gratitude and humility, while adversity shapes resilience and grit. Together, they mold us into stronger, more insightful individuals.

Consider this: a challenging day is not inherently "bad." Instead, it reflects life's way of guiding us toward growth. These days mirror the distance between our current state and our potential, urging us to rise above limitations. By shifting our perspective, we see that every experience serves a greater purpose, revealing the richness of life's complexities.

...

Spiral Upward

Life choreographs a delicate dance between moments of triumph and challenges. Embrace the sunny days with gratitude and humility, recognizing the blessings they bring. Just as importantly, welcome the stormy days as opportunities to grow, learning the invaluable lessons they offer. By accepting life's unpredictable nature, you embark on a journey of continuous evolution, moving closer to your aspirational self.

Each day, whether filled with light or shadow, is a vital part of the rich tapestry of existence. Together, they weave the narrative of your life, making it the precious gift that it truly is.

Exercise: I invite you to reflect on your day so far—whether it has brought joy or challenges. How did you respond? Did you express gratitude for a favorable day? Or, during difficult moments, did your reactions align with your ideal self? These reflections reveal your current level of awareness and help illuminate the path forward.

39: Life Is a Roller Coaster

The human mind is a captivating marvel, capable of navigating a vast spectrum of emotions and enabling us to experience wealth without possessions and depth without extensive knowledge—all through the power of perspective.

Living in a state of heightened awareness is a priceless gift. As our consciousness elevates, the beauty of life becomes more apparent, and the barriers that once separated us dissolve, revealing the unity in all things. By recognizing the interconnectedness of existence, we come to understand that goodness and challenges are not opposing forces but intertwined elements, coexisting in harmony.

Achieving mental clarity doesn't mean controlling our emotions entirely. It's more like watching a movie: we know it's not real, yet we still feel the emotions it evokes. However, the impact is temporary. Fulfillment doesn't depend on maintaining a constant state of positivity but on understanding life's processes with clarity.

Many people confuse fulfillment with happiness, believing the two are synonymous. Yet one can be fulfilled while still experiencing moments of sadness. I, too, struggled with this perspective until I began seeing life as a roller coaster ride. The question then becomes: Do we approach it with fear, or do we embrace it as an exhilarating adventure?

Imagine life as a thrilling roller coaster. We stand in line, eager for our turn, knowing challenges await yet excited by the ride's promise. Resisting these challenges won't make them disappear. Instead, we must choose to engage fully, accepting that the ride includes both highs and lows. It's in these contrasts that we truly feel alive.

Our hearts race, our senses sharpen—without this contrast, the ride would feel dull. The uncertainty fuels excitement, keeping us engaged and adding an element of adventure.

Some people push themselves to the limit because they understand that the ride is temporary. Venturing outside our comfort zones, especially on the toughest rides, builds resilience and reveals our true potential. Enjoying the roller coaster requires detachment—not in avoidance, but in seeing both discomfort and pleasure as integral parts of the experience. The ups and downs enrich our journey, adding depth and meaning.

What if we applied this mindset to life? The art of living isn't about clinging to one ride or moment; it's about having the courage to move forward, seeking new experiences without taking anything personally. Life, like an amusement park, offers endless opportunities to explore, grow, and learn.

As we navigate life's roller coaster, remember it isn't meant to be endured passively. It's an invitation to engage fully—savoring the highs, learning from the lows, and embracing the ride as a whole. So, fasten your seatbelt, hold on tight, and let the journey unfold. The next ride promises new adventures, growth, and memories to cherish.

...

Spiral Upward

Life's ultimate purpose isn't just to survive its twists and turns but to grow through them, rising stronger and more self-aware with each experience. Like a spiral ascending endlessly, every loop, no matter how disorienting, pulls us higher, offering a broader view of our potential.

The unexpected dips and sudden accelerations of life are not setbacks: they are opportunities for transformation. Each turn holds a lesson, each loop an invitation to expand your capacity for courage, wisdom, and joy. By embracing the ride fully, you discover that the path upward isn't linear; it's a dynamic, ever-evolving process of becoming.

Spiraling upward means meeting uncertainty with curiosity and discomfort with determination. Life's momentum will always push you forward; your task is to steer it upward, transforming every obstacle into a stepping stone for growth. This is the art of living: to take the highs and lows and weave them into a journey of continuous growth. It's choosing not to define yourself by a single moment, whether triumph or trial, but by the resolve to keep moving forward. Spiral upward, always. Let each loop strengthen your resolve, each climb expand your vision, and each descent prepare you for what's next. The ride may challenge you, but it also shapes you into the person you're meant to be.

40: Time Is Nothing

The human mind operates on many levels, with awakening representing its highest form. Awakening is more than simply being conscious of the present moment—it's about deeply understanding it. This begins with an awareness of your mental state, observing your thoughts and emotions fully and without judgment. Only then can you truly connect with the present.

Among the many paths to this heightened state, walking holds a special place. Its simplicity and accessibility make it a profound practice for mindfulness and awareness. The most meaningful walks are those taken without a destination in mind. These walks quiet the mind, heighten the senses, and reveal life's deeper rhythms.

When we walk, we are often moving toward something or away from something, both literally and metaphorically. Yet, the act of walking is far more than physical movement; it is a powerful metaphor for our passage through time. Each step can serve as a meditation on the interplay between the past, present, and future—and our eventual encounter with death. To fully understand time and existence, we must first confront and make peace with our mortality.

The Significance of Pace

Every walk allows us to choose our pace, and each pace carries its own meaning. Walking slowly invites reflection on the past, encouraging deliberate contemplation of the experiences that shaped us. Walking briskly draws our focus forward, urging us to think of future possibilities and what lies ahead. A moderate pace, however, strikes a balance, blending the past, present, and future into a single harmonious moment. It is at this pace that we begin to understand the essence of time and our fleeting place within it.

Grasping the Nature of Time

With every step, we move away from the past, pass through the present, and approach the future. Yet, when we examine time closely, we realize its temporary nature. We recognize that the past doesn't exist; it has existed, but it doesn't exist anymore; the future doesn't exist; it might exist, but it doesn't exist; and the present moment vanishes the instant it appears. If time were to be broken down mathematically, we'd be dividing nothingness into smaller fractions of nothingness.

This paradox highlights a profound truth: time, as we perceive it, is an illusion. It is within this interplay of existence and non-existence that we discover who we are. The key is not to hold onto the fleeting nature of time but to embrace it as a teacher, urging us to live fully in the now.

Walking Toward Death

As we reflect on time, we inevitably confront our own mortality. Life is a journey in which we walk both toward and away from death. This realization, while unsettling, can also be liberating. When viewed partially, death feels terrifying—a loss of the life we cling to. But when seen in its totality, death emerges as a natural transition, as beautiful and inevitable as birth.

The opposite of life is not death, but non-existence. Life is energy, and energy cannot die—it can only transform. Death, then, is not an end but a shift, a transition from one state to another. Just as the energy within us emerged at birth, it will continue to exist in a new form after death.

Much like our time in the womb, where we transitioned into this world, death is another gateway into something new. If it happened once, it is logical to believe it could happen again.

However, if death is feared, we will always find ourselves running from it. This fear keeps us in a state of constant alertness, waiting for an unknown that could arrive at any moment. Such a mindset robs us of contentment, chaining us to anxiety and preventing us from fully living. By making peace with death, we free ourselves to experience life with a calm and open heart.

Rather than fearing death, we can trust the same force that brought us into life to guide us through this transition. Seen this way, death becomes less a source of dread and more a reason to live with intention and grace.

Embracing the Smiles of Death

Stoic philosopher Seneca reminds us: "Death smiles at us all; all we can do is smile back." This wisdom encourages us to accept the inevitability of death as a part of life's natural cycle. It teaches us that our impermanence is what makes life precious.

By acknowledging life's fleeting nature, we gain the courage to live fully. Each moment becomes a gift, urging us to let go of what we cannot hold onto and to find joy in the here and now. Time is not something to conquer or cling to—it is a gentle reminder to savor every step of the journey.

...

Spiral Upward

As you walk, let each step be a reflection of your passage through time and existence. Walk slowly to honor your past, stride confidently toward the future, and find balance in the present. Each day is a fleeting gift—appreciate its beauty, yet remain detached.

Let the inevitability of death inspire you to live purposefully, to embrace the unknown, and to smile back at life's mysteries. With every mindful step, move forward—not just through time, but toward a deeper understanding of yourself. Let your path be a testament to a life well-lived, rich in presence, growth, and meaning.

41: Live Now

Having explored the essence of time, let's now delve into why we often postpone living to an uncertain future that may never arrive.

Many of us frequently use phrases like "I really look forward to...," "It will all be better when...," or "Once I reach my goal, everything will change." These statements condition our minds to postpone contentment, pushing it further from our present reality. By constantly telling ourselves that life isn't good enough right now, we risk rewiring our brains into a perpetual state of dissatisfaction. Imagine the impact of repeating these thoughts several times each day on your long-term mental health.

Why do we persistently believe that true satisfaction lies in the future when everything we currently have was once a dream we aspired to achieve? We even rationalize present hardships as necessary sacrifices for future gains, but this acceptance of unhappiness as a stepping stone toward our goals might explain why many lose the spark of life in their eyes.

As we delve deeper, we explore the deceptive allure of tomorrow's contentment and the transformative power of embracing today. We often find ourselves caught in a cycle of anticipation, believing that true happiness awaits us just beyond our current reach, contingent on achieving certain milestones or acquiring specific things. This hopeful vision of a better tomorrow obstructs our ability to fully experience and appreciate the abundant beauty of life surrounding us.

But why do we fall into this trap repeatedly? Why do we willingly exchange the richness of the present moment for the elusive promise of future satisfaction? These questions unravel the essence of our existence, prompting us to question whether we are truly living or merely surviving on the hope that tomorrow will fulfill what today did not.

Pause for a moment and reflect on your aspirations. What do you believe will bring you deep fulfillment? The truth is that deep within, you already possess the essence of what you seek. The challenge is uncovering it. The answer lies in the exclusion method: systematically evaluating and setting aside the distractions and misconceptions life offers. Though it might sound daunting, it's a rewarding journey. Let's embark on this together now.

Contemplating the pursuit of material possessions, societal praise, and external validation reveals a pattern of transient gratifications, ultimately leaving you with a lingering sense of emptiness due to their inherently abstract nature.

To illustrate, consider the scenario of an influencer evaluating content based on its traction. Success is often measured in likes and views, and herein lies a potential pitfall: if you surpass your usual metrics, it becomes the new baseline; conversely, maintaining the status quo offers diminishing satisfaction compared to the initial joy experienced when reaching those milestones. This cycle poses a risk of diminishing returns and highlights the ephemeral nature of relying on external markers for fulfillment.

By the exclusion method, we conclude that postponing living to the future due to external factors is not the answer. This leaves you with the internal world, where you already possess the essence of what you seek. The big question is, what do we all seek? Now that you know where to look, I want you to reflect on that. We will revisit this question in part five of the book.

It's time to liberate ourselves from the chains of delay, to stop delaying the experience of living for the sake of material achievements or social standing. Envision a day when you look back and realize that all the moments you disregarded as mere stepping stones were, in fact, the very essence of living. You were already living, but you just never lived.

Placing our hope in the future, expecting it to resolve our discontentment, is a fallacy we must acknowledge. Time, as it ceaselessly marches forward, does not hold the key to "eternal" contentment. The answer lies within us, in our ability to shift our perspective and wholeheartedly embrace the present moment.

Grasping the true nature of our existence unlocks this potential. When we awaken to the beauty of each new day and the infinite possibilities that lie ahead, we gain the power to live each moment as if it were our last. By savoring the simplicity and grandeur of life, we can cultivate a sense of contentment that transcends the need for future achievements or external validation.

Imagine the serenity of looking back on a well-lived life, free from regrets or unfulfilled desires. Acknowledging the impermanence of our existence allows us to find solace in the present moment and embrace the journey, knowing that genuine contentment resides within ourselves, not in the external world.

...

Spiral Upward

Embrace the present, for it is the only reality you can truly experience. Let go of the illusion of future fulfillment and open yourself to a life brimming with joy, satisfaction, and a sense of purpose. Understanding the true nature of your existence in the morning enables you to end the day with a heart full of contentment. The choice is yours: release the pursuit of a utopian future and immerse yourself in the rich beauty of the present moment.

42: Nothing Really *Is*

The concept of the widely recognized and embraced Power of Now, popularized by Eckhart Tolle, advocates for staying present in the moment—a principle I've emphasized in previous life lessons due to its significance. However, even though now is the only reality, this reality is not without its mysteries. Allow me to introduce a thought that I find truly mind-blowing.

What does *now* truly mean? I have spent considerable time trying to grasp what it means to be in the now. To define the present moment, we must first define what *is*, and when we delve into what *is*, we inevitably encounter the concept of matter. Matter, the fundamental substance that composes our reality, adds a fascinating layer of complexity to the concept of the now.

99.99 percent of matter is empty space; the rest is in constant motion, undergoing transformation and change. In essence, nothing truly *is*; nothing is static. This is a scientific observation grounded in the principle of vibration, which asserts that nothing rests; everything moves and vibrates. This law of reality indicates that everything is perpetually in motion, always returning to its natural state due to its inherent properties.

Everything in the universe is in a state of perpetual change: it is born, it grows, it decays. The moment something reaches its peak, its decline begins. Now, how does this relate to the concept of the now? If nothing truly *is* in a static sense, what does it mean to chase this moment? Does the realization of the constantly changing nature of the present make us breathe, or does it make us feel breathless?

To truly be in the here and now requires effort and intention. Many say that you shouldn't have desires, just be. Yet, the act of not desiring is a desire in itself, which paradoxically brings us back to square one, much like a dog chasing its own tail.

The primary reason for embracing the power of now is to alleviate human suffering. Yet, this idea appears to contradict the very fabric of human nature. We cannot eradicate suffering entirely; deep down, we may not truly wish to. Without suffering, pleasure would lose its meaning. The issue with suffering is not that it is part of our past, present, or future; the real challenge is our lack of understanding of it. Consider this alternative perspective: There are no problems in essence; the only issue with problems is our failure to understand them.

By reframing our approach to life's challenges, we can begin to see them not as obstacles, but as opportunities for growth and understanding.

Let's explore this perspective: You might carry years of resentment toward your mother for what you saw as her shortcomings—until one day, you sit with her, really listen, and hear the story behind her silence, her choices, her pain. As she opens up about her struggles, your anger softens. You still might not agree with everything she did, but now... you understand. And that understanding changes everything. Because the truth is, everyone has a story—we're just too often too busy, too hurt, or too proud to truly listen.

On one level, matter seems tangible; yet as we delve deeper, it transforms—molecules become atoms, atoms split into protons, electrons, and neutrons, and even further exploration reveals these too dissolve into nothing, much like our problems.

The essence of our existence lies not in clinging to anything but rather in our ability to adapt and let go. In reality, there is nothing substantial to hold onto, not even the now itself, because by the time we grasp the essence of the present moment, it has already passed.

This realization invites us to embrace impermanence and cultivate a sense of presence. Imagine savoring the taste of a ripe fruit, fully aware it won't last forever, or cherishing the warmth of a loved one's embrace, understanding its fleeting nature. By finding solace in the transient nature of experiences, we discover that each moment offers unique lessons and gifts.

This understanding frees us from the burden of trying to hold onto what is inherently fleeting. We become free to immerse ourselves fully in the ebb and flow of life, appreciating the continuous cycle of creation and dissolution. Like graceful dancers, we move in harmony with the ever-shifting rhythms of the universe.

...

Spiral Upward

Your mind's capacity to traverse the past and future is a gift, not a burden; it's your perspective that can transform it into a self-imposed punishment. While your body can only exist in the present, aligning your mind with your body in the now enhances your life experience. However, rather than trying to possess or cling to the present moment, embrace the eternal dance of existence. Flow gracefully with the currents of change. By doing so, you'll discover the joy of being fully present, moment by moment, as life unveils its ever-changing tapestry before your eyes.

43: Embrace Paradoxes

How Strange and Contradictory Human Nature Is.
We sacrifice our health to gain wealth,
only to spend that wealth trying to recover our health.

We ruin our present by worrying about the future,
only to weep in the future as we long for the past.

We live as though death will never come,
yet die as if we had never truly lived.

We exist, yet fail to embrace existence.
By the time we realize our existence,
there is no time left to truly live.

We were meant to savor life,
yet we spend our days running from death.
When we embrace death,
we finally begin to taste life.

We strive to build a name for ourselves,
only to lose who we truly are.
To rediscover ourselves,
we must dismantle the name we once sought to create.

We chase the light,
yet lose our way in the darkness.
But when we accept the dark, we become the light.

We live without questioning our beginning,
yet question it deeply as we near the end.

We are born as strangers,
spending a lifetime seeking to belong,
only to realize we were alone all along.

And in the end,
we leave as strangers, who didn't belong.

Life's Full Spectrum

If nothing truly *is*, and our problems feel real only because they remain unresolved, then why do we resist embracing life in its entirety? Why do we cling to pleasure yet reject pain, savor the highs while neglecting the lessons buried in our lows? What are we so afraid to feel?

To truly appreciate life's highs and lows, we must learn to recognize the wisdom woven into its contradictions. What often seems like conflict is, in truth, the delicate pattern of existence unfolding. When we step back from our narrow perspectives and view life through a wider, more objective lens, the paradoxes begin to make sense—revealing the deeper lessons hidden within the full spectrum of our experience.

Life is a delicate dance between opposites—desire and consequence, light and darkness, beginnings and endings. Within these contradictions lie invaluable insights that shape our journeys. Let's delve into some of the most profound paradoxes that define the human experience, offering a deeper understanding of ourselves and our place in the world.

Balancing Health and Wealth

One of life's most striking paradoxes is our relentless pursuit of wealth, often at the expense of health. Many of us have sacrificed well-being in the name of success, chasing material prosperity without realizing the cost. Yet, when illness strikes, we willingly part with our hard-earned wealth to restore the health we once took for granted.

This paradox teaches a vital truth: true wealth lies in the balance between physical and mental well-being. Without health, nothing else matters. Think of how a severe headache can overshadow every other joy in life. Health isn't just a condition for happiness; it's the foundation upon which all meaningful pursuits are built.

Navigating the Past and Future

Another paradox emerges from our relationship with time. We waste the present worrying about future uncertainties or dwelling on past regrets. Ironically, this fixation on what's behind or ahead prevents us from fully embracing the now.

Yet, the ability to think in time—reflecting on the past and planning for the future—is not a curse but a blessing. Just as our hands are a gift we use consciously to create and shape our world, our thoughts are tools to enhance our experience of life. The key lies in learning to use them intentionally.By reflecting on the past, we gain wisdom from our experiences. By envisioning the future, we set goals and foster hope. Both are essential, but they must be balanced with presence. This paradox reminds us that while we should strive to live in the moment, we can also embrace our ability to think in time as a powerful tool for growth and purpose.

Embracing Existence and Time

Life's fleeting nature reveals one of its deepest paradoxes. We live as though death is a distant event, taking our days for granted. Yet, when confronted with the reality of death, we become profoundly aware of life's fragility and treasure it more deeply than ever before. This paradox invites us to embrace life's brevity not with fear but with gratitude. When we acknowledge that every moment is a gift, we begin to live with greater intention, cherishing life as the precious, temporary experience it is.

Discovering Purpose

The paradox of identity and purpose is one of humanity's greatest challenges. Many of us seek external validation, believing that societal approval defines our worth. Yet, in this pursuit, we often lose sight of who we truly are. True purpose emerges when we strip away these external layers and let go of societal expectations. Like a leaf carried by the wind, we align with the universe only when we stop resisting and allow ourselves to flow naturally. This paradox encourages introspection and the courage to rediscover our authentic selves.

Revealing the Path of Self-Discovery

Within the paradox of light and darkness lies a transformative truth: our greatest growth often comes from our darkest moments. While we instinctively seek light and clarity, it is in times of struggle and uncertainty that we uncover our inner strength. By embracing life's darkness, we learn to become our own source of light. This paradox reminds us that the challenges we face are not obstacles but opportunities to reveal the resilience and brilliance within us.

Finding Meaning in Beginnings and Endings

The paradox of beginnings and endings invites us to confront the transient nature of life. Everything we begin is destined to end—yet it is precisely within this impermanence that meaning takes root. This paradox teaches us to focus on the journey rather than the destination, to find value in the present moment, and to cherish the connections we form along the way. In accepting that nothing lasts forever, we learn to appreciate life's beauty all the more deeply.

...

Spiral Upward

Life's mysteries often hide within its paradoxes. Just as a snake's venom contains the antidote to its own bite, the resolution to human suffering lies in understanding and embracing suffering itself. Your ability to reflect on the past and anticipate the future isn't a flaw—it's a unique and powerful gift. Think of your thoughts as tools, much like your hands, that allow you to consciously shape your life and the world around you. The key lies in learning to use these tools wisely: balancing presence in the moment with intentional reflection.

By accepting the contradictions that life presents, you can unlock profound insights about yourself and the world. These paradoxes are invitations to live fully, to embrace life's complexities, and to grow through every challenge. When you welcome life's full spectrum—the highs, lows, and everything in between—you transform each moment into an opportunity for growth, connection, and discovery.

44: Transcending Knowledge

Having recognized the pitfalls of surrendering to paradoxes and learning to navigate them with greater awareness, our journey now turns toward the pursuit of wisdom. But before we can rise into this realm, we must clarify a distinction that is often blurred: the difference between knowledge and wisdom. These two concepts are frequently discussed interchangeably, yet they shape our perception of life—and our suffering—in profoundly different ways.

Knowledge is the accumulation of information: theories, principles, interpretations, and ideas. But information alone does not grant truth. There was a time when humanity "knew" the Earth was flat—an accepted certainty until it wasn't. Knowledge evolves; what we believe today may be disproven tomorrow. It can enlighten, but it can also mislead. Wisdom, however, stands apart.

Wisdom is not concerned with accumulating facts. It is rooted in insight, discernment, and lived experience. While knowledge shifts with new discoveries, wisdom remains steady—guiding us not just in what to think, but in how to relate to what we know.

Before moving deeper, ask yourself: Have you ever truly examined the source of your suffering?

We are taught that misery arises from tangible losses—death, separation, financial hardship, illness. These moments undoubtedly bring sorrow, yet what if these events are not the true roots of our despair? What if the greatest source of human suffering is our unrelenting desire to eliminate suffering altogether?

Trying to eradicate suffering is like trying to forbid the rain from falling. It is impossible, because suffering is woven into the natural rhythm of life. A more sensible approach is to acknowledge its inevitability, to accept its presence, and to walk forward anyway. Just as it is futile to change the weather, it is futile to attempt a life sheltered from all pain. Our longing for endless joy is driven by preconceived ideas—information we've absorbed about how life "should" feel. But wisdom knows the deeper truth: joy and sorrow are inseparable, each giving shape and meaning to the other.

Life's adversities—loss, instability, illness, emotional upheaval—are not aberrations, but intrinsic elements of the human experience. Knowledge may mislead us into viewing the universe as hostile or unjust, but wisdom gently corrects this misperception. It teaches us to regard hardship as a fundamental part of existence. To resist suffering is to battle a storm we cannot control; to acknowledge it is to reclaim our power.

And this truth extends far beyond humanity. Every life form, from the smallest insect to the grandest creature, endures struggle as part of its survival. Pain is not a punishment uniquely reserved for us; it is part of life's universal law.

Transformation begins when we stop resisting reality. When we allow ourselves to accept life's heaviness—not as defeat, but as truth—we open the door to growth. This shift marks the defining difference between knowledge and wisdom: knowledge informs, but wisdom transforms. Knowledge describes what is. Wisdom teaches us how to live with it.

The Essence of Wisdom

Wisdom transcends knowledge. It perceives deeper truths—about human nature, relationships, ethics, and the workings of the universe. It enables us to see beneath surface appearances, revealing patterns, meanings, and principles that guide sound judgment. Wisdom aligns us not only with our personal well-being but with the well-being of others, with long-term consequences, and with the timeless laws that govern life.

In today's world, information is abundant. Ignorance, more than ever, becomes a choice. Yet despite the wealth of knowledge available to us, few ascend to wisdom. Why? Because our interpretations are shaped more by emotion and personal bias than by objective truth.

When plunged into darkness, we see only the dark. But wisdom widens our perspective, revealing that even the deepest night carries the promise of dawn. Wisdom teaches us interconnectedness—reminding us that everything influences everything, that nothing exists in isolation. It becomes the antidote to human misery. While self-pity deepens our wounds, wisdom guides us toward clarity, acceptance, and inner expansion..

The Interconnectedness of All Things

To decode life's mysteries, we must understand our existence in relation to others. Imagine life as a two-sided coin. One side depicts isolation: the feeling that suffering singles us out. The other reveals our profound interconnectedness: that our joys and sorrows are shared threads in a much larger tapestry.

Knowledge may tempt us into believing we stand apart from life's challenges. Wisdom reveals that these challenges are part of the universal rhythm of existence.

Left unexamined, knowledge can trap us in narrow perceptions—beliefs passed down through generations, absorbed without scrutiny. These inherited views often imprison us in unconscious resentment and suffering. Breaking free requires deliberate introspection. It requires us to be the generation that seeks higher understanding, questions old patterns, and opens new doors.

Curiosity and empathy become essential companions on this path. They broaden our awareness, deepen our understanding, and reveal the unity beneath life's contradictions. Through introspection, we arrive at truths not as abstract ideas but as awakenings that resonate from within. Wisdom is not merely learned—it is realized. It connects us to the essence of existence.

Living with Wisdom

As we ascend the path of wisdom, we awaken to our limitless potential. Life transforms from a battleground into a tapestry woven with meaning and purpose. With wisdom, we navigate challenges with clarity and depth, recognizing that every moment—however difficult—holds a lesson.

Wisdom is not reached through intellectual study alone. It is cultivated through practice: through reflection, humility, compassion, and the willingness to confront life honestly. It is a way of seeing, a way of being, and ultimately—a way of loving the world as it is.

On this path, you become a beacon. Not through perfection, but through awareness. Not through superiority, but through understanding. The pursuit of wisdom is not a destination; it is a lifelong unfolding. It empowers you to face adversity with insight, to live with depth and courage, and to inspire others through your clarity.

...

Spiral Upward

Embrace the intricate web of interconnectedness that binds all things. Rise beyond the limitations of mere information, allowing wisdom to illuminate your path. Through introspection, empathy, and a sincere pursuit of truth, begin unraveling the mysteries that quietly shape your existence.

This journey cultivates a purpose that transcends the ordinary—one rooted not in achievement, but in awareness. Let wisdom be your compass: helping you find solace amid hardship, meaning in uncertainty, and profound connection with yourself and the universe. For in the tireless pursuit of wisdom, we draw closest to the essence of what it means to be human.

45: The Role of Emotional Intelligence

When the mind listens to the heart, wisdom replaces noise, and connection replaces control.

In a world shaped by logic, efficiency, and constant analysis, we have learned to sharpen the mind—often at the expense of the heart. Emotional intelligence is not a skill we acquire; it is an awareness we remember.

It is the quiet capacity to recognize what moves within us, to sense what lives within others, and to respond with understanding rather than reaction. Its value lies not in managing emotions, but in listening to them and allowing them to guide how we relate to ourselves, to others, and to life itself.

Yet emotional intelligence is rarely cultivated. It is often dismissed as secondary, overlooked in our upbringing, and absent from the systems meant to prepare us for life. This absence is striking, for it shapes how we love, how we listen, and how deeply we connect. When emotional awareness is missing, relationships suffer — not because people lack good intentions, but because they lack understanding.

Therefore, it is time to dive into this lesson. Not to learn something new, but to awaken what already exists within us. The tools we need are not external; they are woven into our biology, our nervous system, and our innate capacity for connection. Emotional intelligence is not unnatural to us—forgetting it is.

Emotional intelligence is the bridge between knowing and being. Between thought and presence. Between the mind's logic and the heart's wisdom.

The Erosion of Emotional Connection

Modern life moves quickly—often too quickly for emotional presence to keep pace. Relationships that once unfolded with patience now rush toward convenience. Conversations skim the surface, vulnerability feels unsafe, and depth is replaced by efficiency. Over time, we arrive at a troubling realization: hurting one another has become a conscious part of human connection.

To protect ourselves, we build invisible walls and call them boundaries, detachment, or independence. We convince ourselves they keep us safe, forgetting that walls block wisdom and blessing as much as they block pain. When we offer only fragments of ourselves, we cannot expect fullness in return. We give limited presence yet long for deep connection, and in doing so, we deprive ourselves of what nourishes the soul.

Emotional detachment is increasingly mistaken for strength. Caring less becomes armor, distance becomes power, and relationships quietly turn into competitions where the one who wounds first believes they have won. Emotional closeness no longer feels like refuge; it feels like exposure.

What we are witnessing is not cruelty, but disconnection—an inability to recognize pain, both our own and that of others. I once found myself in a moment where someone close to me lashed out unexpectedly. My instinct was to defend myself, but instead I paused and listened beyond the words. What emerged was not hostility, but hurt. Responding with understanding rather than ego softened the moment and deepened our bond. This is the quiet power of emotional intelligence.

It teaches us a quiet truth:sometimes solitude is wiser than connection —not because we fear others, but because we respect ourselves. Emotional intelligence helps us recognize when to lean in and when to step back, ensuring that the relationships we keep nourish us rather than slowly drain us.

The Rise of Emotionless Intelligence

Our culture often glorifies emotional suppression, mistaking numbness for control and detachment for strength. Casual intimacy is celebrated, while depth is quietly dismissed. Society tells us we should experience as many partners as we wish, as if connection were consequence-free. Yet this narrative ignores our biological and emotional design.

Even something as simple as a kiss leaves traces of another person within us. Sexual intimacy reaches far deeper—it is not merely physical, but an exchange of emotion, energy, and presence.

We sense this intuitively: the heaviness of a person with negative energy is felt the moment they enter a room, before a single word is spoken. Being on the same frequency alters our mood, our nervous system, and our inner state. Now imagine carrying part of that person within you.

We are not built to fragment ourselves endlessly. We are wired for meaningful connection—bonds that allow depth, continuity, and emotional coherence. When intimacy becomes scattered, it often unsettles the nervous system and weakens emotional stability. One path aligns with our nature and supports mental and emotional well-being; the other gradually erodes it. Human interactions are more than chemical reactions—they are emotional transitions that shape how we feel, remember, and relate. Without awareness, we carry more than memories.

Choosing Your Connections Wisely

Every relationship takes up space within us. Some connections lift us, bringing clarity and growth. Others slowly drain us, leaving us confused where we once felt certain. This is rarely intentional; more often, it is simply a mismatch in awareness. Emotional intelligence sharpens discernment. It helps us choose alignment over attachment, depth over dependency, and truth over illusion. Every person we allow close shapes our emotional landscape and, over time, the direction of our lives.

The Inner Dialogue We Live By

Before emotional intelligence can transform our relationships with others, it must transform the relationship we have with ourselves. We often guide others with patience and compassion, yet speak to ourselves with harshness and judgment. We use a tone inwardly that we would never use outwardly.

Emotional intelligence calls us to speak to ourselves with love grounded in objectivity, not delusion, because the mind is skilled at creating versions of reality that make it easiest to live with ourselves. True growth requires honesty. Sometimes it asks us to acknowledge our mistakes and have the humility to apologize to others. Without objectivity, the mind becomes subjective and defensive, trapping us in self-justification rather than allowing evolution. How you speak to yourself determines how deeply you are willing to grow.

Remembering What We Forgot

Many of us learned early that emotion was inconvenient. Silence was praised. Strength was mistaken for restraint. Over time, we adapted. We learned to suppress what we could not explain, and in doing so, we slowly lost fluency in our own inner world. Emotional intelligence began to feel unfamiliar—not because it was unnatural to us, but because we had learned to live without it. Yet emotional intelligence is not weakness. It is maturity. What has been learned can be unlearned. What has been forgotten can be remembered. No matter our upbringing, the capacity to reconnect with our emotional world remains within reach.

Embracing Emotional Intelligence

Emotional intelligence restores depth. It refines how we listen, how we love, and how we navigate conflict. It allows us to connect without losing ourselves and to stand alone without bitterness. Human connection is not born from words alone, but from understanding.When the mind learns to listen and the heart is allowed to guide, something within us settles into harmony.

...

Spiral Upward

Safeguarding your emotional well-being is not self-care; it is responsibility. Every interaction leaves an imprint, and every connection shapes your inner world. Choose relationships that honor your nature and seek connections rooted in truth rather than convenience. When emotional intelligence awakens, walls dissolve—not into vulnerability without wisdom, but into openness with discernment. In that balance, connection becomes nourishment rather than burden.

So ask yourself—gently, honestly: Are your relationships reflections of emotional awareness... or reflections of emotional avoidance? Your answer determines how you spiral upward. The depth of your connections will never exceed the depth of your awareness.

46: What Is Success?

Have you ever truly paused to reflect on what success means to you?

For much of my life, I chased what I believed to be success—driven by the widely accepted notion that success leads to happiness. I set goals, achieved milestones, and ticked boxes that many would consider marks of accomplishment. And yet, when I finally arrived at what I thought was "success," I found it lacked the fulfillment I had expected.

This realization didn't strike like lightning—it unfolded slowly, shaped by years of ambition and quiet introspection. I began to ask myself: Had I confused achievement with fulfillment?

This question shook the foundation of my beliefs. Society often equates success with power, wealth, and fame—standards that, while alluring, rarely bring lasting contentment. This narrow definition is not only misleading but deeply embedded in our collective psyche, leading many to chase mirages at the expense of inner peace.

And therein lies one of life's greatest ironies: success is something we all chase, but never truly catch. The moment we believe we've reached it, the goalpost shifts. Satisfaction is fleeting, and a new ambition rises in its place. We become bound to a finish line that keeps moving.

Conventional success imposes endless demands: earn more, be more, achieve more. It silently informs our self-worth and often compromises our emotional and mental well-being in the process. This life lesson invites you to challenge that narrative. It's time to redefine success in a way that honors our humanity, feeds our intellect, and enriches our lives from the inside out.

A Reflective Exercise

Take a moment to write down your deepest wish—the one you believe would bring you the greatest joy and make you feel like the fullest, happiest version of yourself.

Now, close your eyes. Picture that version of you. See it, feel it, become it—if only for a moment. Then gently open your eyes, and write down the emotions that surfaced while you were there. What did it feel like to meet the version of you who finally got what you longed for?

Did your concept of success sneak into the picture? Whether it's career achievement, financial freedom, or a picture-perfect family, this reveals how deeply societal values are rooted in us—placing happiness in the hands of money, fame, or external milestones. This awareness invites a necessary reckoning: Are your dreams truly yours—or inherited from a world that confuses success with status?

The Toothache Test

Now imagine this: you could have your greatest wish fulfilled—the one that promises to make you the happiest version of yourself—but in exchange, you'd have to live with constant tooth pain for the rest of your life. Would you still choose it?

Most people would instinctively say no. Especially anyone who's experienced the torment of real tooth pain. I remember one Saturday evening when I was struck by such unbearable pain, I irrationally tried crushing painkillers directly onto the tooth because every clinic was closed. In the end, I paid extra just to get a dentist to reopen—simply to stop the suffering.

That moment taught me something profound: we will sacrifice anything to escape pain, and health is far more valuable than we realize. So, if good health is already yours, why don't you feel like the happiest version of yourself?

The Paradox of Wishes

Herein lies the paradox: No single wish, no matter how grand, can guarantee lasting happiness. If it could, you'd already be perpetually joyful—because everything you once longed for, you likely now possess in some form. And yet, joy fades. Desires evolve. The target moves. This suggests that happiness doesn't arise from wish fulfillment alone.

Instead, it emerges from a deeper sequence—acceptance, which leads to contentment, which blossoms into gratitude. When nurtured, this progression shapes a meaningful and joyful life.

A Moment of Perspective

I remember sitting at a red light when a young boy on a public bus spotted my car and gave me a thumbs-up, his eyes full of admiration. In that brief moment, I wished he knew: the car wasn't the source of my happiness. In fact, I was wrestling with challenges he couldn't see—struggling for contentment like everyone else. But then I paused and wondered: Was that kid once me? I saw my own reflection in his eyes. Is this the rhythm of life—each generation chasing what the last one silently questioned?

It was a humbling reminder that what people admire is often not what truly sustains us. And it left me with a deeper question: How can I elevate the next generation—not by giving them more to chase, but by helping them see more clearly what truly matters?

...

Spiral Upward

To understand and achieve true success, start with what matters most: your well-being. Let happiness, health, and gratitude become the cornerstones of your journey. Success is not merely the reaching of goals, but the rising through life's spiral—learning, evolving, and growing with each experience. True success is available to anyone who dares to redefine it.

Because success is not measured by power, wealth, or fame, but by the size of your smile, the peace in your heart, and the lives you touch along the way. So choose a life aligned with your values. Choose meaning over appearance. Choose growth over perfection. Redefine success—not as the world tells you it should be, but as your soul knows it must be.

47: Money Is an Illusion

Money—so valuable, yet so unreal
Promised as the key to survival,
Yet it quietly steals the essence of life.

It builds a house, but crumbles a home.
It fuels your dreams, yet leaves you alone.
It grants you ambition, then burns your flame
A chase so endless, it forgets your name.

It whispers of a prosperous tomorrow,
While stealing the silence of today.
It dresses as joy, parades as health,
But trades your soul for hollow wealth.

And when the curtain falls, what fills your hands?
Not love, nor time, nor threads of grace
Only echoes fading in an empty space.
The weight of things that could not hold,
The cost of chasing what was never whole.

No matter how much you earn,
enough is a mirage, always out of reach.
So you justify the chase, saying,
"I'm doing it for them, my loved ones."
The ones you dream of giving more to,
the ones you vow to protect.

But money cannot buy the love they need,
the touch they missed, or the moments you failed to seed.
So all this for what?
An illusion that money equals wealth?
That possessions translate to happiness?
That it safeguards your health?

When you face reality with honesty,
Illusions fade like shadows in the sun.
And suddenly, the truth becomes clear:
Money represents wealth as much as a menu represents food.

It isn't yours until you spend it.
Yet still, we chase paper over purpose,
coins over connection,
leaving us indebted to those who love us most
The ones who only ever wanted what money could never buy.

Rediscovering Life Beyond the Pursuit of Money

In a world entranced by the glittering allure of wealth, money remains one of life's most profound paradoxes. Though vital for survival, its pursuit can easily lead us astray, blinding us to what truly holds meaning. Money can build houses of stone, yet quietly erode the bonds that make a house feel like home.

The story we tell ourselves about money is a powerful illusion—one that weaves dreams of prosperity and promises of security for those we love. Fueled by these visions, we press forward tirelessly, often unaware of the hidden costs buried beneath our ambition. And the price we pay is steep—measured not in currency, but in time, in distance, and in the quiet moments we miss with those who matter most.

We justify the sacrifice, telling ourselves, "I'm doing it for them." But money can never replace the love they crave, the presence they long for, or the memories that go unmade. Deep down, we know the truth: the treasures of connection and belonging cannot be bought.

I have personally walked these miles. I've told myself these stories: that the sacrifices were necessary, that the ends would justify the means. But I've felt the pain of this pursuit. I've endured the suffering of separation from those I hold dearest, realizing too late that time spent apart is time that can never be reclaimed.

Why, then, do we chase this shimmering mirage of materialism? Is it because we've come to believe that money equals wealth? That success ensures happiness? That financial security can protect our health? These are the illusions we must have the courage to confront, because until we do, we risk trading what is priceless for what merely appears valuable.

Reflection reveals a profound truth: money is to wealth what a map is to a destination—it can point the way, but it is not the journey itself. Its true value lies in how we use it, not simply in how much we gather. Yet far too often, we become obsessed with accumulation, mistaking the map for the meaning. In doing so, we overlook the essence of real wealth—and gradually find ourselves indebted to those who love us most, not financially, but in an emotional absence we can never repay.

Money's true worth lies not in its accumulation but in the opportunities it creates to enrich our lives and those of others. It should serve as a tool—a means to an end, not the master of our existence. By seeing beyond the fleeting allure of material wealth, we unlock the path to deeper fulfillment, prioritizing the intangible riches of love, connection, and shared memories.

...

Spiral Upward

Guard your heart against the deceptive allure of wealth. True wealth isn't measured by numbers on a screen but by the love you give, the connections you nurture, and the moments you savor. Cherish these priceless assets—they form the foundation of a meaningful life.

When you prioritize what truly matters, you transform your existence into a treasure trove of authentic wealth. Rise above the endless chase for material gain, and create a life that resonates with joy, purpose, and the richness of human connection.

48: Real Wealth

In a world mesmerized by the glittering allure of riches, we find ourselves relentlessly chasing material prosperity—a mirage that shimmers just beyond our grasp. But what if the real treasure lies not in accumulating external wealth but in embarking on a journey toward inner fulfillment?

Let me share a chapter from my life—a story of being lost in the illusion of worldly gain. In my pursuit of wealth, I drifted far from what nourished the soul. But in losing everything, I was guided back to what truly matters: a life rooted in meaning, presence, and grace.

"May everything you touch turn to gold, my son. And if ever you find yourself in a desert, may even the sand turn to treasure beneath your fingers."

These were the words my Nana spoke—soft yet powerful, echoing through the hardest days of my life. Her prayer wasn't just a wish; it was the embodiment of a mother's boundless love. It became my shield in struggle, her blessing the quiet hope I carried through every storm.

But blessings often come entwined with trials. Life's law of rhythm teaches us that everything has its tides and cycles of highs and lows. Like a pendulum, the swing to one side is inevitably matched by a swing to the other; rhythm compensates. For every hardship, a period of ease follows; for every joy, challenges inevitably await.

By the age of 34, I had achieved nearly every conventional marker of success. I had traveled the world, explored countless business ventures, and acquired almost everything I once believed would make me whole. And yet, beneath the surface of that achievement, a quiet emptiness echoed—a sense that something essential was still missing.

Convinced that a change of scenery might spark something within, I moved to the United States, hoping its vastness would reveal a deeper sense of purpose. But the landscapes, however vibrant, brought no peace to my restless soul.

This chapter of my life taught me a difficult truth: true wealth isn't found in accumulation, but in alignment—with oneself, with one's values, and with the quiet contentment that comes from within.

Before returning to Denmark, I made a brief stop in Dubai—a city bursting with ambition, prosperity, and promise. Its skyline rose like a declaration of possibility. Drawn to its energy, I felt something stir. Maybe, I thought, this was the place where everything would finally make sense.Despite my mother's hesitations, I made the decision to relocate. Her condition for giving her blessing was simple: I had to visit her every two weeks—something I gladly accepted. A mother's blessing is the foundation upon which many of life's decisions are built. With her approval, I was convinced I had found my new home.

But what awaited me was not the golden chapter I had imagined—it was a descent I never saw coming. In the land of endless opportunity, the sands seemed to dissolve everything I had built. Month after month, my fortune faded, as if life was quietly dismantling every illusion I had clung to. Still, I refused to surrender. Too many people depended on me, and giving up simply wasn't an option.

Then came June 24, 2020—the day I declared bankruptcy. Soon after, the world was plunged into the chaos of COVID-19. As if that weren't enough, on August 19, 2020, a fire destroyed everything I owned. In one night, I was reduced to a pair of shoes, a watch, and three sets of clothes. I had not only lost my possessions—I had lost my home.

In that moment of profound loss, a friend and his family opened their doors to me, offering food, shelter, and kindness when I had nothing left. Their generosity was a lifeline. And yet, inside, I wrestled with the shame of dependence. I stayed eleven days. On the twelfth, I told them I had found a place to stay, though I hadn't. I simply couldn't bear to feel like a burden any longer.

As a gesture of gratitude, I offered them the only thing I had left of value—the watch on my wrist. They hesitated, moved by the gesture, and tried to refuse. But I insisted. They had to accept it—not for the watch, but for the dignity I was trying to hold onto. And as I walked away, tears streaming down my face, one question echoed in my mind: *How did I end up here?*

Then, in a moment of realization, my perspective shifted dramatically. Instead of dwelling on the losses of recent years, I found gratitude for the decade of abundance that had preceded them. With my hands raised to the sky, I spoke to God: *I am grateful for what You have given, for what You have taken away, and for the path You have set for me.*

At that moment, a profound sense of liberation washed over me. The weight lifted from my heart, and I felt enriched, holding a water bottle with no money in my pocket. Was this the price of my awakening? To truly appreciate the small blessings, did I need to lose everything first?

Bliss cannot be forced, nor can it be reached by snapping your fingers. It is not a prize won through relentless striving. Bliss grows naturally as wisdom deepens, as your thoughts and perspectives elevate. The cure for ignorance is enlightenment, and with that enlightenment comes contentment.

This shift made me question the nature of wealth itself. Power, fame, and material possessions had been my definition of success, yet they left me hollow. Our society's obsession with "faking it till you make it" has only amplified this false ideal. We prioritize polished appearances while neglecting our mental and emotional health.

Ironically, in our pursuit of appearing happy and successful, we've become one of the saddest generations. We've mastered the art of curating perfect lives—polished, filtered, and admired—while neglecting the raw, unfiltered truth within. We control how the world sees us, but lose touch with how we truly feel. And in the process, we trade genuine joy for the illusion of success. We chase confidence and validation through the carefully crafted illusions we project—images of wealth, achievement, and perfection. But can a life built on deception ever lead to true fulfillment?

The relationship between money and true wealth is much like that between language and reality. Just as words can point to truth but never fully embody it, money can symbolize abundance without ever delivering its essence. True wealth isn't found in bank statements or possessions—it lives in the quiet, intangible spaces of contentment, peace, and purpose, far beyond the grasp of materialism.

Consider this: some people possess everything money can buy, yet remain restless and unfulfilled. Their minds are burdened with anxieties no lighter than those of someone with far less. Because real wealth has little to do with quantity—and everything to do with quality of being. It is not about what fills your home, but what fills your heart.

...

Spiral Upward

The journey to true wealth isn't about snapping your fingers or forcing bliss—it's about changing how you perceive and respond to life. The real challenge lies not in reality itself but in how you choose to view it. Genuine wealth springs from the joy found in the present moment, not from bank accounts, luxury items, or fleeting achievements. When you free yourself from the grip of superficiality, you unlock the richness of life.

True generosity doesn't count the cost. Give freely from the heart and discover the pure joy of unconditional giving. Transform your approach to existence. Let go of illusions and embrace what truly matters: love, connection, gratitude, and inner peace. These are the priceless treasures that no fire can destroy, no pandemic can take away, and no amount of money can buy. By giving selflessly and living with presence, you align with the true essence of abundance—a wealth rooted in compassion, authenticity, and a deep appreciation for the beauty of life as it is.

49: Think It All the Way Through

"Think it all the way through." A simple phrase—yet one of life's most profound reminders. It's an invitation to look beyond the surface of our ambitions and ask ourselves: *Why do I truly want this? And what will it actually bring into my life?*

Too often, we set goals—whether it's wealth, success, recognition, or status—without ever pausing to examine the motivations driving them. We chase outcomes, believing they hold the key to happiness, security, or self-worth. But when the finish line arrives, many discover that the victory feels strangely hollow.

Take the pursuit of wealth. For many, money becomes a symbol of freedom, safety, or respect. Yet countless people who reach extraordinary financial success find themselves weighed down by new anxieties, lingering emptiness, or an insatiable craving for more. If the ultimate goal was happiness or peace of mind, why does it still feel out of reach?

This paradox reveals a deeper truth: most of our goals are not ends in themselves—they are vehicles for emotional or psychological fulfillment. The real question becomes: *What am I truly searching for beneath this pursuit?*

The Illusion of More

The illusion of more whispers that nothing is ever enough. It traps us in a relentless cycle of striving—where every milestone quickly fades, replaced by the next.

Think about it: Suppose you achieve immense wealth. What changes? Will you suddenly start living in two houses at once? Drive five cars at the same time? Eat more than your body can handle—or simply eat different food?

When you strip away the glamour, the reality becomes clear: *"More" doesn't change the fundamentals of life—it only reshapes the packaging.* The question then arises: *Would having more truly bring lasting happiness? Or would it simply birth new desires, new problems, and new cravings?*

At the core, what every human seeks is universal: love, happiness, comfort, belonging, and a sense of purpose. Whether your pursuit is wealth, relationships, health, or status, it ultimately circles back to the same longing—the desire to create a life that feels meaningful, joyful, and worth living.

The Beautiful Truth

And here's the most beautiful realization: bliss exists at every level. Whether you live with everything you've ever dreamed of—or with exactly what you have right now—the capacity for joy has always been within you. It was never waiting on circumstances to change. It was waiting on you to notice.

When we pause to *think it all the way through*, we often realize that many of our aspirations are misaligned with what truly matters. And in that moment of clarity, a deeper truth emerges: contentment only exists in the now.

If you cannot find peace within your current reality, no amount of accumulation—whether money, possessions, or achievements—will ever satisfy that hunger. Because the finish line will keep moving. The antidote is simple, yet profound: gratitude. When you learn to appreciate the life you have—the breath in your lungs, the love that surrounds you, the simple joys that fill ordinary days—you unlock a kind of wealth that no money can buy. True fulfillment doesn't come from chasing more. It comes from realizing that you already hold the keys.

The Cost of Chasing Illusions

"Think it all the way through" invites us to examine not only what we're chasing, but what it's truly costing us. Pursuing wealth, success, or

recognition with a weak mindset often comes at a price far greater than we realize. The truth is—anything we pursue obsessively eventually loses its meaning. But when we pause long enough to reflect, we begin to reclaim our clarity—And recognize how deeply society has shaped the desires we once believed were ours. From that awareness, we can begin to choose differently. Not from conditioning—but from truth. Not from fear—but from purpose.

From childhood, we're taught to prepare endlessly for a future that always seems just out of reach. Study hard. Get the degree. Secure the job. Climb the ladder. *"Real life starts after this,"* they tell us—after the next achievement, the next milestone. But this perspective traps us in a quiet prison of postponement, where joy is always delayed…until later. A later that never quite arrives.

Take retirement, for example—a phase so often romanticized as the moment to finally *start living*. Yet for many, it arrives alongside declining health, isolation, and the realization that time, not money, was the most precious currency all along. It's the painful aftermath of chasing a promise that was never real.

Seeing Beyond Conditioning

When we step back and view life through a wider lens, we begin to recognize the patterns that quietly shape our pursuits—and question whether they were ever truly ours. Much of what we chase is simply a reflection of what we believe we lack.

Perhaps that's why the poor dream of riches, the rich long for peace, the famous crave privacy, and the unwell would trade it all for one more breath. It is the human condition to yearn—but even with greater awareness, feelings of dissatisfaction will still surface. Because no love can fully cure loneliness. No achievement can offer eternal fulfillment. And no destination can free us from the truth that life, by design, is an endless unfolding—an ever-evolving journey of growth, surrender, and becoming.

Yet, this very understanding holds a quiet liberation: the realization that there is no future state of happiness waiting for us. We have already arrived. Everything we need to access peace, meaning, and contentment is within reach—right here, right now.

Joy was never meant to be postponed. Life isn't something we graduate into later. It's happening now—in the breaths we take, in the love we give, in the simple act of being present to the miracle of existence. When we stop chasing an imagined future, we begin living the life we were searching for all along.

The Beauty of Uncertainty

Just as fire cannot burn itself, and water cannot drown itself, perhaps we were never meant to fully solve the mystery of existence. And therein lies its beauty. Life isn't a problem to be solved; it's an experience to be felt. The key to fulfillment is learning to dance between the known and the unknown, the tangible and the intangible—the certainty of what you hold now, and the mystery of what's still unfolding. When you *think it all the way through*, you begin to uncover something deeper: that happiness was never hiding in the distance. It was always here—woven quietly into the fabric of now.

...

Spiral Upward

When you begin to understand the deeper motivations behind your goals, something profound is revealed: what you think you want isn't always what you truly need. Real transformation doesn't come from acquiring more, but from shifting how you perceive yourself, your desires, and the meaning you assign to life. The illusion of more whispers that nothing is ever enough. But this mindset isn't a life sentence—it can be broken. Pause and reflect: *Would having more genuinely fulfill me? Or am I simply offering new fuel to the same unending hunger?*

Here's the quiet truth: bliss exists at every level. Whether it's in what you hold today or what you dream of tomorrow, the capacity for joy has never been something to chase—it has always been something to choose.

The real beauty of life lies in mastering the delicate balance between appreciating what you have and aspiring for what's next. To explore this fully, imagine your desires already fulfilled—and then ask yourself: *Am I truly happier now?* This simple act of introspection often reveals a surprising truth: the joy you seek isn't waiting at some distant finish line. It's already hidden in the fabric of this very moment. By choosing presence over illusion and gratitude over lack, you transform your life into an ever-evolving upward spiral—one of discovery, alignment, and lasting fulfillment.

50: True Support Will Find You

This life lesson is delicate—it touches the tender dynamics of our inner circle: the family and friends we hold closest to our hearts. Instinctively, it may seem natural to turn to them for encouragement and validation. After all, who better to support us than those who know us best—right?

But here's a perspective that challenges that assumption—and invites growth. Our inner circle is deeply woven into the fabric of our identity. Each person is invested in us in their own unique way. Imagine sharing a bold new dream with your closest friends. If your dream includes them, their support may come easily. But when your vision begins to take you somewhere unfamiliar—somewhere they cannot follow or do not understand—their reactions may shift.

You may encounter hesitation, skepticism, or even subtle resistance—not out of cruelty, but out of care. Not because they don't love you, but because they see the world through the lens of their own fears, limitations, and expectations. Growth can feel like a threat to those who knew you before you evolved—before your path began to outgrow their comfort zone.

I've lived this truth. Friends often told me my ambitions were unrealistic—from quitting university and starting my own businesses, to moving abroad, launching a podcast, and even writing this book. My family, too, urged me to stay on the safe path: *Don't leave school. Don't start a business. Don't move away. And why would you want to podcast?*

To this day, most of them haven't read this book. And that's okay. Because here's what I've learned: you can't take it personally.

Your inner circle may not see your vision—and they don't need to.

While they may not call to check in or cheer you on, somewhere out there are strangers who will. People who haven't met you yet, but will one day thank you for choosing yourself. People who will see your courage and feel empowered to follow their own.

It's a sobering truth: those closest to us, despite their love, can unintentionally hold us back. They know the version of us they've grown comfortable with. And change, even when it's beautiful, threatens the roles we've played in their lives. Their advice may come from a place of protection, not empowerment—anchoring us to the familiar rather than encouraging us to rise.

As we evolve, this dynamic becomes more visible. What once felt like support may begin to feel like silence. What was once encouragement may become caution. But this is not cause for resentment—it's a call for understanding.

True support doesn't always come from where you expect it. But it always finds you—when you walk boldly toward who you're becoming. So keep walking. Keep creating. Keep becoming. Those who are meant to walk with you will. And those who fall away simply made space for someone new to walk beside you—not with history, but with hope.

Family and the Comfort Zone

When it comes to family, the emotional stakes are often higher than anywhere else. Their love is usually unconditional, and their concern for our well-being is sincere. But it's precisely this depth of care that can also create quiet limitations. Guided by a desire to protect, family members often encourage choices that stay within the bounds of what feels familiar and safe.

A parent's hesitation toward a new career path may not come from a lack of belief in your abilities, but from a fear of the unknown. Their well-intentioned advice can, however subtly, tether you to a life that prioritizes security over self-discovery. Yet true growth rarely blooms within the safety of comfort.

Honoring your family's love doesn't mean living within their limits. Respect their opinions, but recognize that their idea of *what's best for you* may not reflect your purpose, your passion, or your potential. Personal evolution often calls us into unfamiliar territory—places where their protection can't follow, and their map no longer applies.

That doesn't make their love any less real. It just means that your path may lead beyond where they imagined you'd go.

Expanding Your Circle

As you seek support and validation on your journey, it's essential to distinguish between encouragement that uplifts—and advice that unintentionally holds you back. While the love of your inner circle is invaluable, it's not always the most objective or expansive source of guidance. Sometimes, the most transformative insights come not from those who know your past, but from those who believe in your future.

Seek out mentors, role models, and peers who see you not as a reflection of your past, but as a canvas of your becoming. These are the ones who will stretch your limits, challenge your assumptions, and offer guidance unshaped by the weight of shared history. Their insight widens your horizon, drawing you toward versions of yourself you have yet to imagine.

This isn't about turning away from the people who love you—it's about complementing their support with a wider circle of influence. Balance the comfort of familiarity with the clarity of fresh perspective. Surround yourself with those who hold you with love—and those who push you toward your edge. Together, they form the foundation for real, sustained growth.

...

Spiral Upward

True support often comes from the most unexpected sources. While your inner circle offers love and well-meaning advice, their perspectives are shaped by shared history and personal biases. To truly grow, you must expand your horizons and embrace guidance from those outside your familiar boundaries.

The beauty of mentorship and fresh perspectives lies in their ability to see you through a lens of potential, untethered by the roles you've played in others' lives. They offer insights rooted in who you're becoming, not who you've been. By seeking wisdom from a variety of sources, you enrich your journey and broaden your perspective. Growth isn't about leaving your inner circle behind; it's about creating a tapestry of support that empowers you to thrive. Embrace this diversity of guidance, and you'll find the strength to rise above limitations, realizing the full scope of your potential.

Interpersonal Connection

Love and Relationships

The Alchemy of Meaningful Connections

From Soul to Soul

Every truth we discover within ourselves eventually calls us toward others. For what good is wisdom if it does not touch another heart? What meaning has healing if it does not extend beyond the self?

The journey through the first three knots teaches us to understand the self — our nature, our patterns, our purpose. But now, the spiral widens. We step from solitude into connection, from knowing ourselves to understanding the mirror of those we love. Every relationship — whether brief or lifelong — becomes a reflection of our growth. Through them, we encounter the parts of ourselves still waiting to be refined. As you enter the next Knot, remember: love is not simply something you receive. It is a sacred mirror through which the soul recognizes its own reflection in another.

Every human being carries knots within—threads of pain, memory, and longing that quietly shape how we live, love, and suffer. Untangling them is not merely an act of healing; it is an act of becoming. For we rise along our personal upward spiral not defined by what we are, but by the bonds that have wounded us, the ties that have lifted us, and the connections that continue to shape our journey.

This journey into the heart of human suffering has revealed a series of profound truths, each one symbolized by a knot we have patiently untied.

The first knot called us to unlearn and relearn—to challenge the quiet beliefs that shape how we see the world. The second turned us inward, urging us to rediscover our true essence, beyond roles, identities, and conditioned beliefs. The third revealed that life is neither a circle nor a straight line, but an upward spiral—ever-evolving, ever-inviting us to rise.

Now we enter the realm of human connection—the place where love, vulnerability, conflict, and companionship converge. Here, our relationships do more than shape our outer lives; they reflect and transform the deepest layers of our inner being.

Every bond we form is a mirror. In the embrace of love, in the tension of conflict, in the quiet of companionship—we are confronted with both our brightest light and our hidden wounds. These encounters are not merely about understanding others, but about awakening to ourselves through others.

To heal human suffering, isolated insights are never enough. Fragmented healing cannot sustain transformation. Just as the five knots represent our most profound inner struggles, they must be approached as an interconnected whole. Revisiting the past without shifting perception keeps us bound; true growth requires integration, accountability, and introspection. And within this integration, love and relationships are not secondary—they are at the core.

Our families, friendships, and romantic bonds are woven into the very fabric of our identity. They are shaped by centuries of culture, belief, and personal history. And through them all, one force remains—timeless, universal, and deeply human: love.

Love transcends time and distance, weaving invisible threads between hearts and souls. It lifts us into new heights of joy and awakens a vision of our higher selves. Yet it also unsettles us—consuming energy, clouding clarity, and drawing us into depths where our worth feels fragile and uncertain.

At its essence, love is pure and simple. But once filtered through the human psyche, it tangles with fear—fear of abandonment, echoes of unmet childhood needs, unhealed wounds, and complex attachment patterns. What was meant to connect us can just as easily divide us.

Only when we learn to love with awareness—not merely with emotion—does love transform. Then it heals instead of harms, liberates instead of confines, unites instead of fragments. The alchemy of meaningful connection lies in this transformation.

In the life lessons ahead, I will share insights drawn from experience, reflection, and observation—exploring the dance between vulnerability and resilience, joy and sorrow, unity and individuality.

For love is a paradox: it can lift us into euphoric heights, yet cast us into depths of longing and doubt. This duality does not weaken love—it reveals its depth. Joy shows love's delight, but hardship unveils its truth—for without the burn, how would the soul know it has been touched by fire? Like life itself, love asks to be understood, tended to, and honored for its beauty as well as its complexity.

And so we arrive at the threshold of love—not the fleeting feeling, but the living force that shapes destinies. To enter is to risk, to surrender, to be remade. For in every connection lies both a mirror and a fire: the mirror that shows us who we are, and the fire that forges who we may yet become. Love, in its truest form, is not just what binds us to others—it is what awakens us to ourselves.

Join me as we explore the intricate world of connection—and discover how, in loving and being loved, we come to better understand what we are, what we need, and how we grow.

51: Family Is Everything

The ideal starting point for the first life lesson in the fourth knot is family, as it serves as the foundational pillar of our existence. Whether united by blood or by choice, family forms deep emotional bonds that profoundly connect us.

From the moment we take our first breath, many of us are cradled in a two-way high love—a love that radiates from within and reaches outward. This form of love transcends all boundaries. It emanates from the baby like a silent plea—wordless yet urgent—a yearning to be held, to belong, to feel safe. In return, it surges from the caregiver like a tidal wave of devotion: fierce, instinctive, and utterly unconditional. To the newborn, it is pure trust—felt before thought, deeper than language, as natural as breath. To the mother, it is a sacred bond, so raw and consuming that she would trade her heartbeat for the child's without a moment's doubt.

This love—pure, instinctive, and expansive—soon extends to fathers, siblings, and even extended family, weaving a network of empathy, comfort, and stability that anchors us through life's storms. In a healthy family, this shared love becomes so deep that joy is multiplied and sorrow is shared. One person's triumph is everyone's celebration; one person's pain, a collective burden. A family's embrace becomes the very definition of home—and without it, even happiness can feel adrift, like a smile searching for meaning.

But this kind of love isn't automatic. It requires cultivation—attention, patience, humility, and an unwavering commitment. Investing in family may be the single most valuable decision you'll ever make.

For me, the meaning of family was etched into my soul by my Nana's gentle voice. Her words weren't mere advice—they were sacred vows wrapped in love and legacy. She taught me that to fail our family is, in many ways, to fail ourselves—to forsake the rarest gift life offers. Her wisdom still echoes through me, a quiet compass guiding my every step.

My mother, in her strength and grace, showed me that true manhood isn't measured in years but in compassion and devotion. To be a father, brother, or son isn't simply a title—it's a sacred responsibility, carried with dignity and humility. One of Nana's words still rings in my heart: *"My son, if you fail to keep the family united, you are not worthy of the milk I breastfed you with."*

It may sound harsh, but my life was never destined to be ordinary — and neither is yours. My mother raised me with the weight of purpose, preparing me for something greater. From an early age, she instilled in me a profound sense of responsibility and self-belief, calling me Baba— father—long before I could fully grasp what it meant. I could have seen this as unfair, a childhood stolen too soon — especially on that sunlit day when other children played outside, and I stood in the shadow of my father's death. But I chose not to. I chose to rise. Because I believe: it takes just as much energy to live a miserable life as it does to build an extraordinary one — so why not strive for the extraordinary?

Because I believe: It takes just as much energy to live a miserable life as it does to build an extraordinary one—so why not strive for the extraordinary?

Nana taught me how to be a man through a woman's lens, and for that, I am eternally grateful. Today, I am a family man to the core. My brother is like the soul to my body—when he is near, I am alive. My sisters are pillars of strength who lift me when I fall and soothe me when I'm broken. And my mother—she is the heartbeat of our family, her love the guiding light of my life.

But family isn't only revealed in great sacrifices and heavy responsibilities. Sometimes, its wisdom comes in the smallest gestures.

I remember a moment in Spain, on a warm summer morning. A mother and her little girl were walking down the stairs as I passed by. I greeted the mother with a smile and a simple "Good morning." She looked at me with distance in her eyes, as though quietly measuring me. But her daughter—untouched by such hesitation—looked up, smiled, and waved with such innocence that it instantly lit my day.

Children do not manufacture unity; they embody it. Where adults build walls of suspicion or judgment, they create bridges without even trying.

I've seen this again and again with my nieces and nephews. Their laughter, their play, even their clashes come from a place of untainted purity. They don't calculate whether someone deserves kindness; they simply give it. They don't ask whether someone belongs; they just include them.

That is family in its purest sense: not defined by perfection, but by belonging. Acceptance is not an achievement—it is our natural state. Children remind us of this, urging us to return to it.

Family isn't static—it evolves. Through joy and pain, triumph and trial, we forge unbreakable bonds that weather time and adversity. In our laughter and tears, we become more than relatives—we become reflections of each other. From daily calls that bridge continents to annual trips that reignite our closeness, we honor these sacred ties. And I believe this deeply: Where family exists, so does hope. If there were no hope, there would be no pain when it's missing. So, reach out. Rebuild the bridge. Forgive if needed. Apologize if you must. But don't wait. If you turn your back on the family that gave you life, how will you ever protect the family you dream to build?

Yes, some families are fractured — some demand more patience, more forgiveness, more work — but they are still worth the fight. For nothing cuts deeper than the absence of connection at home, and few wounds last longer than love left unresolved.

•••

Spiral Upward

Cherish your family as the ultimate treasure in your life, dedicating your entire being—mind, body, and soul—to them. Within the embrace of family, you uncover your truest self and discover genuine strength. Family is the cornerstone of your character, lighting your path in dark times and providing the courage to face life's challenges. United, you become a formidable force. Without them, there will always be an irreplaceable gap in your life.

52: Embracing Harmony in Gender

The sun does not compete with the moon, yet both keep the rhythm of the same light.

In a world often defined by conflict and division, these tensions can subtly infiltrate our perspectives, turning potential collaboration into rivalry and shaping fleeting emotions around gender. For the next generation, the question of gender has become a focal point, often overshadowing a deeper truth: men and women are not adversaries but complementary partners in life's intricate dance.

The discussion of gender has been a source of discord throughout human history, contributing to conflicts that have fragmented societies for centuries. But it's not history that repeats itself—it's human behavior. Until we elevate ourselves above these superficial debates, we remain trapped in cycles of misunderstanding and division. Gender, after all, is not a purely human construct; it is an intricate part of existence itself. The interplay of male and female energies is the very source of life's continuity.

Appreciating our biological and gender differences is essential. It's not just about social constructs or individual feelings—it's a profound interplay of chromosomes and energies that shapes our existence. Recognizing this complexity allows us to honor the unique strengths of each gender and fosters a harmony rooted in mutual respect and understanding.

The Dance of Energies

The interplay between masculine and feminine energy is not merely human — it is cosmic. It moves through everything that exists, shaping creation, rhythm, and change itself. From the motion of galaxies to the beating of a heart, this dual current flows in divine correspondence, each completing what the other begins.

To confine this sacred balance to the difference between man and woman is to misunderstand its vast design. These energies live within every soul — strength and stillness, will and wisdom, action and intuition — forever seeking harmony. A woman may carry the fire of masculine drive; a man may embody the calm of feminine grace. Together, they mirror the divine polarity through which all of life unfolds.

The problem has never been gender, but interpretation — how we label, limit, and divide what was meant to be whole. When we learn to see these forces as partners rather than opposites, we transcend the illusion of separation. In that awareness, we begin to see that love, creation, and balance are born of the same eternal dance — the meeting point where heaven and earth, mind and heart, finally move as one.

The masculine and feminine are not in competition — they are in conversation. One leads, the other listens; one gives, the other receives; both are essential for the harmony of existence. To suppress either is to silence half of creation's symphony.

A Complex Reality

Gender is not a social construct nor a personal choice — it is a universal principle, woven into the fabric of creation. From the balance of night and day to the dance of sun and moon, masculine and feminine energies sustain every rhythm of existence. Humanity is one of many expressions of this greater design.

Science continues to explore how the human brain and body may reflect this complexity. Some findings suggest variations that influence how individuals experience identity, reminding us that biology itself holds many layers. Yet such discoveries do not change the truth that gender belongs to a universal order — one that operates beyond human preference or perception.

Though feelings can shift and identity can evolve, the underlying design remains constant — written into the very architecture of existence. What we feel may fluctuate, but truth endures.

Our feelings, though powerful, are transient. They rise and fall like tides; they reflect, but do not define, reality. Therefore, emotion can never be the compass of truth. When we elevate feelings above divine order, confusion follows — for emotion is meant to be *felt*, not *followed*. A feeling may visit like the wind, but truth is the mountain that remains unmoved.

The gender we are born into is not an error but part of divine intention — a thread in the tapestry of the soul's journey. Just as we do not choose the time or place of our birth, we do not choose the vessel that carries us. Every challenge holds the opportunity to rise — to cultivate patience, strengthen faith, and elevate the mind above confusion.

We must approach every individual's experience with empathy and respect, but compassion does not require the abandonment of truth. The highest form of love is clarity — to help others see that beyond our forms and feelings, there exists a harmony crafted by the One who makes no mistakes. The Qur'an reminds us that "We created you in pairs" — a reflection not only of physical form but of balance itself. To deny that design is to deny the wisdom of the One who made it.

The Heart and the Brain

To debate the worth of men and women is as futile as arguing whether the heart or the brain holds greater value. Each serves its divine purpose; each sustains life in its own way. The heart gives rhythm, the brain gives reason — one feels, the other perceives — and together they create harmony.

In the same way, the masculine and feminine were never meant to compete, but to complete. They are not opposites but counterparts within creation — distinct in function, equal in importance, and interdependent by design. When we resist or distort this truth, we create conflict where there should be balance, and division where there should be unity.

To rise above such discord, we must shift our focus from competition to collaboration, from comparison to complementarity. True strength lies not in sameness, but in synergy. When we embrace our differences as gifts rather than threats, we open the path to genuine unity — a love rooted not in ego, but in the purity of the heart.

When masculine and feminine energies work in harmony, society flourishes. When one seeks to dominate, imbalance follows. Balance, then, is not weakness — it is wisdom. To align with nature is to accept our essence as it was intended — not as a flaw to be corrected, but as a note in the greater symphony of life.

A Bridge, Not a Barrier

When we honor the distinct yet complementary strengths of man and woman, we return to the harmony that nature itself designed. This union is not man's invention — it is life's intention. From our very beginnings, survival depended on this sacred partnership: two becoming one, each fulfilling what the other could not.

To recognize this truth is to see beyond hierarchy and toward harmony. It invites empathy, deepens connection, and restores balance to the way we live and love. Gender, in its truest form, was never meant to divide — it was meant to unite. It is not a wall to keep us apart, but a bridge through which understanding flows. And across that bridge moves the promise of a higher humanity — one shaped by collaboration, strengthened by purpose, and sustained by love that honors both difference and design. Where gender becomes a bridge, love becomes a language — one that transcends identity and speaks directly to the soul.

...

Spiral Upward

Recognize that gender transcends both social construct and biological form. It is the meeting of two divine currents — masculine and feminine — flowing through every note of creation. Together, they compose the eternal symphony of existence, where harmony is born not from sameness, but from balance. To embrace this truth is to awaken to the rhythm that connects all things — to free yourself from the illusion of separation, from the need to define identity through fleeting emotion or passing thought.

Rise above these limitations and return to the essence of who you are: a soul in which both energies already reside in perfect correspondence. See gender not as conflict but as communion — a sacred bridge uniting the heart and the mind, the giver and the receiver, the seen and the unseen. To live in balance with your nature is to live in obedience to divine wisdom. To rebel against that nature is to create a war within yourself that no ideology can heal.

Answer the quiet call to unity. Let difference refine, not divide. When we live in alignment with divine design, the noise of separation fades, and we begin to hear life for what it truly is — a masterpiece of perfect correspondence, conducted by the One who composed it all.

53: The Beauty of the Brain

Before we venture into the depths of love and relationships, we must first understand the very blueprint of man and woman. For just as a master painter studies each color before touching the canvas, or a composer knows every note before writing a symphony, we too must know the way we are wired. Only then can we create bonds that are not just strong, but harmonious, lasting, and alive with meaning.

Love and relationships are where biology and emotion intertwine, shaping our most profound bonds. Yet, we often navigate these intricate dynamics without fully appreciating the biological influences at play. This lack of understanding can lead to confusion, miscommunication, and missed opportunities for deeper connection.

Have you ever asked yourself: *Why does love sometimes feel like it's not enough? Why do we grow distant even when our hearts are still connected?* These questions cut to the heart of relationship challenges. Unpacking them is essential for understanding recurring struggles and nurturing a bond that can withstand the tests of time.

Understanding the Biological Dance

Growth in relationships stems from understanding not just the emotions expressed but also the silence shared. To truly appreciate love, we must explore both our emotional experiences and the biological instincts that subtly guide them.

One of the first things that draws people together when they fall in love is the diminishing of distance—physical, emotional, and psychological. Love thrives on closeness, the magnetic pull that brings two hearts into alignment. Yet, ironically, distance is also the first thing that erodes love when we begin to drift apart. As we create space between ourselves—whether through physical separation, emotional disconnection, or lack of understanding—the bond weakens, and the connection that once felt unbreakable begins to fray.

Recognizing this duality—the power of closeness to ignite love and the danger of distance to extinguish it—offers profound insight into nurturing relationships. It reminds us that maintaining intimacy is not just about staying physically near but also about remaining emotionally engaged and mentally attuned to one another. Without this effort, even the strongest love can falter.

The human brain provides further insights into these dynamics. It functions through two distinct hemispheres: the logical, rational left side and the emotive, intuitive right side. Each influences how we think, feel, and interact. Appreciating how these cerebral domains impact relationships can help couples navigate differences, fostering stronger, more empathetic connections.

What Science Reveals

Recent research from the University of Pennsylvania used MRI scans to uncover striking differences in brain connectivity between men and women. Men's brains tend to show stronger connections within each hemisphere, supporting logical and practical thinking. In contrast, women's brains exhibit more cross-hemisphere connections, enabling seamless integration of emotional and cognitive information.

These neurological distinctions help explain why men and women, though often seeking similar outcomes, approach challenges and communication in fundamentally different ways.

For instance:

- Women often emphasize emotional expression and open dialogue when resolving conflicts, seeking to connect feelings with solutions.

- Men, on the other hand, may focus on quick analysis and

practical fixes, sometimes appearing emotionally detached—not out of disinterest, but due to their innate problem-solving approach.

These differences aren't flaws; they're features of our design. Embracing them instead of trying to erase them fosters harmony and understanding.

The Power of Perspective

Recognizing these differences allows us to move beyond surface-level frustrations and into genuine understanding. When a man finds it difficult to express his emotions, it's not a sign of disinterest but a reflection of his natural wiring. Likewise, a woman's silence is not always peace; often, it conceals a quiet storm of feeling beneath the surface. Learning to read this subtle language of emotion prevents small misunderstandings from growing into discontent.

Instead of waiting for her silence to fade, lean into it with presence. Listen not only to her words but to what remains unspoken. See her stillness not as absence, but as a form of presence — a complex convergence of thought and emotion waiting to be seen. This is not about blame; it is about honoring the depth of another's experience. When we neglect these emotional nuances, distance begins to grow, eroding even the strongest connections. But when we meet them with empathy and openness, conflict transforms into understanding, and relationships evolve into something deeper, truer, and enduring.

Turning Differences into Strengths

Effective communication is the bridge between two emotional worlds — the space where understanding begins and unity takes root. When both partners recognize and value their distinct strengths, conflict loses its sharpness and becomes an invitation to grow. The masculine and feminine are not opposing forces, but complementary notes within the same melody, each enriching the other and bringing balance to love's design.

Communication does not always require words. Sometimes, it is found in silence — in holding hands when no words are enough, in meeting each other's eyes and letting presence speak, or in an embrace that quiets the noise of misunderstanding. These moments remind us that love often communicates most powerfully through stillness.

By honoring our differences rather than resisting them, we transform misunderstanding into connection and distance into closeness. When logic and emotion, strength and tenderness, will and intuition learn to move together, harmony emerges — a relationship built not on control or sameness, but on mutual respect, compassion, and the quiet grace of true partnership.

...

Spiral Upward

Life is a beautiful dance of masculine and feminine energies, each playing a vital role in shaping your relationships. Before love can flourish, take the time to understand the biological and emotional tools at your disposal. By fostering empathy, embracing open communication, and appreciating the unique ways men and women are wired, you can unlock deeper connections and lasting love.

Open your heart to the full spectrum of human emotions and bridge the divides that may separate you from your loved ones. This thoughtful approach not only strengthens your relationships but also enriches your shared experiences, creating a foundation for a more harmonious, compassionate, and enduring bond.

54: Love Is Simple

Have you ever wondered how two souls, adrift among millions, can find one another, weave their stories together, love deeply, lose their way, and in the end, return to silence — strangers once more?

I find this transformation strange and enlightening in its own peculiar manner. It evokes sadness because you lose people you once gave your heart to and is elevating because within the pain lies a lesson: We enter this world as strangers, and we depart it as strangers. No one knew us upon arrival, and with time, no one will recall us upon departure. I apologize for the sad beginning to this life lesson, but I promise it will end well. Allow me to share a perspective that resonated deeply, shedding light on the essence of love.

Love is simple; it is we who complicate it with the restless stories of our minds. You may ask, how can something that so many fail to understand be simple? Then ask yourself: Do you make your heart beat, or does it beat by itself? These are simple questions but with deep insight. If I asked you to explain the process of how the heart beats, it would be a highly complex task, if not merely impossible. But it's easy to understand that our heart beating is something that happens for us, not something of our own doing. Just like that, if we try to explain the process of love, it would be highly complicated, but it's easy to understand that love just happens, and isn't something of our own doing.

To feel love is simple—just as simple as the sound of a heartbeat. It needs no effort, no script, no control. The complications begin the moment we try to force love into being. Most people are not in love, but in love with the idea of love itself. And that is no surprise, for the spark of love in human eyes is like dawn breaking within the soul — a light that needs no sun to shine.

In our longing, we rush to name every tender feeling as love, mistaking warmth for fire and attention for affection. Yet to have never been touched by love is to have never truly been touched by life—for love colors the ordinary with wonder and makes existence shimmer with meaning. Over the years, I have witnessed countless hearts break, not because love failed them, but because they mistook desire, comfort, or attachment for what love truly is.

Perhaps this explains why people break their vows so easily even though they once sincerely told each other; "I promise to be true to you. I will always love and honor you through good and bad times." Regrettably, these promises have become beautiful words that decorated a moment in the past for most relationships.

Love isn't a fleeting emotion or a passing scene in life's film. It rises without warning, beyond permission or control. When it's real, even resistance cannot undo it. You may curse it, fight it, deny it, yet it remains. You can spend a lifetime arguing with your heart, but it always knows the truth. For just as we never decide when to give our heart, we never truly decide when to reclaim it.

Now, falling in love is not the same as being in love. Not that it's wrong — in fact, it's necessary. The heart must first fall before it can truly rise. The heart can fall for many reasons. It usually happens in the beginning, which is fascinating, because we hardly know the person. What we often fall for is not them, but the *idea* of them — the image painted by our imagination, a best-case version born of longing and hope.

We catch a glimpse of something that stirs us, and our imagination does the rest. That is why the heart falls first, and the mind follows — to assess, to interpret, to ask whether what we feel is real. Often, what we call love in those early moments is simply a reflection of what's missing in our own lives.

Imagine feeling unseen, as if no one truly cares for you — and then, suddenly, someone does. Your heart falls, not because of who they are, but because of how they made you *feel*. What you are truly touched by is not them, but the reawakening of your own self-love. That is why we need the mind — to discern whether what moves us is healing or harming.

When we confuse *falling in love* with *being in love,* we deceive ourselves. Falling in love often springs from fleeting emotion — beautiful, yet transient. That is why lasting connection remains elusive; feelings, by nature, surge and shift like tides. So never make life-altering choices in moments of anger or in bursts of joy. Perhaps that is why falling in love fades with time — and if we are fortunate, it matures into *being in love*. True love does not fade; it deepens. Falling in love needs constant tending, but being in love needs nothing, for it is unconditional — sustained not by emotion, but by truth.

...

Spiral Upward

Love is pure and unconditional — a quiet current that flows from the depths of the soul and blooms in the presence of the right person. It transcends material desire, financial comfort, and emotional dependency, embodying a steadfast devotion to walk beside one another through every season of life. Falling in love, however, often rests on perception rather than truth. In the beginning, it is easy to be swept away by the euphoria of discovery, when the mind drifts into sweet illusions. That is why love must be met with patience — allowed to unfold in its own time. Wait for the resonance that feels true in your heart. Do not rush to name it or force it to grow. For only love that blossoms freely can endure, and only what is real can remain.

55: Forged by Faith

Deep within, we all long for a love that lasts — and so we weave our hope around the notion of a soulmate. To some, a soulmate is a harmony of two souls vibrating on a higher frequency; to others, it is destiny itself — a soul fashioned to mirror our own.

I believe each of us has a soulmate — a soul whose path intertwines with ours as part of a greater design. This belief is not born of longing, but of faith in life's sacred order, where certain encounters are written long before we take our first breath. Just as Eve was created for Adam so that humanity might begin, there is someone destined for you — not to complete you, for only God can do that, but to walk beside you as you fulfill what was written for both your lives.

Let me tell you the first love story in the history of mankind — a story that endured every trial, yet they kept searching for one another, not by force, but by choice. A timeless love story.

When Adam opened his eyes for the first time, he was not alone. Before him stood Eve — not a stranger, but a soul he somehow already knew. She was not made from the dust beneath his feet, but from the rib that protected his heart. Two beings formed from one essence, destined to walk side by side beneath heaven's light.

But when they descended to Earth, their bond was tested. Adam landed upon the mountains of Serendib — what we now know as Sri Lanka — while Eve descended upon the shores of Jeddah. Between them stretched oceans, deserts, and the long silence of time.

For years they walked the earth, their hearts guided by remembrance, their prayers carried by the wind — each step a testament to faith that love, when written by God, will always find its way home. Guided by divine mercy, they wandered until their paths finally converged upon the plain of Arafat — the place of recognition. Their reunion was not merely a meeting of two lovers, but a living proof of what love can endure when anchored in faith.

"It is He who created you from one soul and created from it its mate that he might dwell in comfort with her."— Qur'an, 7:189

Their story reminds us that no distance can divide what God has destined to unite. What is meant for you will never pass you by — it will find you in its own time, and when it does, your heart will understand why the wait was necessary. And yet, even if destiny brings two souls together, love's endurance is never effortless. Fate may spark the connection, but its flame must be sustained through intention, patience, and daily acts of care. Meeting your soulmate may be written in the stars — but staying united is written by your choices.

The True Role of a Soulmate

It's a misconception that meeting your soulmate means everything will be effortless. On the contrary, a true soulmate relationship can be one of life's greatest challenges. Your soulmate is not here to simply validate your way of being but to help you grow.

They are often shaped in a way that disrupts your comfort zones, challenging habits, beliefs, and behaviors that no longer serve you. This process of mutual growth can feel uncomfortable — even painful — at times. But this friction is precisely what refines and strengthens you.

A soulmate is not merely a perfect fit; they are a mirror, reflecting both your strengths and the parts of you still in need of healing. By pushing you to evolve, they help you become the best version of yourself. True soulmates don't just walk alongside you — they challenge you, uplift you, and refuse to accept a version of you that falls short of your highest potential.

The Interplay of Fate and Will

Our life journey is shaped by two forces: fate and will. Fate governs what we cannot control — the circumstances of our birth, the people we meet, the twists of destiny. Will, on the other hand, is the domain of choice and action, determining how we respond to fate. Together, these forces weave the tapestry of our lives.

Even when we choose a path, what lies ahead remains uncertain. Here, intuition becomes our compass, guiding us through the unknown. Embracing life's unpredictability means focusing on what we can control — our actions and attitudes — while surrendering to what we cannot. This balance between effort and acceptance is the cornerstone of growth, both individually and in relationships.

Love Beyond the Fairy Tale

Imagine a vast hall filled with every person you've ever crossed paths with — friends, strangers, old loves, forgotten faces. The room hums with voices, laughter, and fragments of memory. You're told you can choose only one person to find. Your eyes scan the crowd. Chances are, they don't linger on the most beautiful or the most admired.

They settle, almost instinctively, on the one presence your soul cannot bear to lose — the one whose absence would leave you hollow, whose nearness feels like home. Who did you think of? That is the person who is truly irreplaceable.

If that person still walks beside you, treat their presence as one of life's greatest blessings. Moments are fragile, and people are not promised. To cherish them is to honor the gift of time itself. This reflection is not merely sentimental; it reminds us to discern who truly matters. Everyone we encounter is part of fate's design, but it is our will that decides whom we hold close and whom we release. Sometimes, what we once believed to be a blessing reveals itself as a lesson. Love can be powerful, yet not always enough to sustain a bond. To recognize this is not failure but wisdom — the first step toward building a connection that lasts, shaped not only by feeling, but by choice, effort, and truth.

Relationships as Partnerships

Think of a relationship as a partnership, much like building a meaningful enterprise. Partnerships thrive on trust, clear communication, and a shared vision for the future. Yet too often, we reduce love to a transactional "give-and-take," as if keeping score could measure its worth. True love transcends that mindset — it is not about balancing the ledger, but about contributing to each other's growth, joy, and well-being.

Approach your relationship with the same dedication, creativity, and passion you would give to a purposeful project. Ask yourself: *Am I putting as much effort into my relationship as I do into achieving professional success?* If not, it's time to realign your priorities.

Many relationships falter because the energy we devote to our careers far outweighs what we invest in our personal lives. Imagine if we brought the same consistency, problem-solving, and innovation to our relationships as we do to our work. How many families might still be whole? How many marriages might still thrive?

Relationships require equal — if not greater — care and attention than any other pursuit. When neglected, the cost is often far greater than we realize. It's time to invest deeply in the love that sustains us. After all, what is the value of success if it comes at the expense of the connection that gives life its meaning?

...

Spiral Upward

When fate leads you to your soulmate, recognize that this connection is a gift, not a guarantee. Lasting love is not about avoiding challenges but embracing them as opportunities to grow together. Your soulmate isn't here to make your journey easy — they're here to make it meaningful.

Celebrate your differences and let them strengthen your bond. Build your relationship on a foundation of open communication, honesty, and forgiveness. Nurture the connection with intention, and approach your partnership with the same determination you'd bring to something sacred. Be the architects of your own joy — building a life shaped by understanding, mutual respect, and enduring love.. Be the architects of your own joy — building a life shaped by understanding, mutual respect, and enduring love. True love isn't found; it's built — piece by piece, day by day — with unwavering commitment and shared purpose. Rise to the challenge and embrace the beauty of a soulmate connection that transforms and elevates you both.

56: The Paradox of Love

Love is like water—pure, essential, and life-giving. But the vessel it's poured into—our hearts, minds, and past experiences—shapes how it flows. While love itself is simple, understanding the emotions that surround it is a far more complex endeavor.

Forging lasting love requires embracing its paradoxes—the contradictions that make it both tender and intense. To love well, we must navigate not just affection, but also fears, expectations, and past wounds. It's a delicate dance between instinct and intention, simplicity and complexity.

Love thrives when we balance its purity with the emotional truths that define our humanity. It is not about perfection, but about growth—choosing to understand ourselves and one another more deeply, again and again.

Yet, understanding love requires us to explore its profound paradoxes. This life lesson ventures through the intricate landscape of love, uncovering its many forms and contradictions.

For many, love drifts through life like a wandering star—appearing in a sudden blaze, only to vanish into the dark. We chase it endlessly, yet the pursuit often leaves us hollow, and at times, we wear its mask to hide the emptiness inside. But love is a wild thing; it comes not to the hunter, but to the still and open heart. It arrives unannounced, cloaked in mystery, and in its quiet embrace, it leads us toward the purpose we did not know we were seeking.

Love's Beginnings and Its First Paradox

From the very start of life, love is intricately woven into our existence. In the womb, it reaches us through the rhythmic beat of our mother's heart—a steady, soothing sound that offers companionship and comfort. This heartbeat becomes our first encounter with love: a primal, unconditional connection that wraps us in security and peace.

But as we enter the world, that constant rhythm fades away. The steady reassurance of the heartbeat is replaced by the unfamiliar sounds of the outside world. Perhaps that's why we cry upon our arrival—we are abruptly separated from the safety and connection we once knew.

This marks our first encounter with love's paradox: while love brings profound joy and connection, it also carries the pain of separation and loss.

This early bond lays the foundation for what can be called "high love"—a love that transcends words and is felt deep within. As we grow older, we continuously seek to recreate that sense of unconditional love and euphoria we first experienced. Yet, learning to love is far more complex than simply being in love. One is conditioned by life's experiences, while the other feels predestined.

This doesn't mean we stop seeking love. On the contrary, we continue to aim for high love—a love that elevates and fulfills. However, love in its purest form is not a steady or predictable force. It takes us on an emotional roller coaster, lifting us to incredible heights of joy and plunging us into the depths of vulnerability and uncertainty.

The journey of love is as challenging as it is beautiful, demanding courage, patience, and an open heart to embrace its contradictions and rewards.

The Leap of Faith

When love enters our lives, it feels as though our feet no longer touch the ground. Yet to truly *rise* in love, we must first *fall*. Falling in love requires surrender—a leap of faith into the unknown, trusting that we'll land safely. It demands vulnerability and courage, embracing fragility as a source of strength.

This leap is inherently risky. Trusting someone, even ourselves, can be daunting. When we say, "I trust you," it often carries an unspoken plea: *Please don't break my heart*. But the truth is, heartbreak is an inherent risk of love. To love deeply is to accept that we may cause or endure pain, whether intentionally or not.

Heartbreak leaves cracks that allow emotions to surface. These cracks, though painful, create openings for growth and self-discovery. Love, then, is a paradox: it empowers while leaving us vulnerable; it builds us while exposing us to destruction.

Love Is for the Courageous

True love isn't for the faint of heart—it's reserved for the brave. It requires exposing yourself fully, without hesitation, because half-measures can never lead to the fullness of love. To give 99 percent in love is to fall short; love demands everything.

Navigating the labyrinth of love means loving unconditionally—wholeheartedly and without expecting anything in return. This is the essence of love's paradox: its purest form is selfless, seeking no validation or reward. By letting go of expectations, we open ourselves to love's transformative power, allowing it to shape and elevate us.

The Puzzle of Love

Love defies logic and resists rationality. It is a puzzle that empowers yet leaves us powerless; it builds us up even as it makes us vulnerable to being torn down. Love compels us to confront our deepest fears and insecurities, urging us to step into the unknown and embrace the uncertainty it brings.

To try to understand love only through intellect is to bring the wrong tools to the task. Love cannot be dissected like an equation; it must be lived, experienced, felt. We know when it is present, but we can never fully explain how it arrived or why it chose us. It is mystery as much as it is truth, wonder as much as it is reality.

This journey demands courage, resilience, and a willingness to walk beyond comfort. By accepting love's paradox — its power to lift and to wound, to give and to take — we uncover truths not only about love, but about ourselves. Love is a teacher that cannot be confined to reason; it shapes us in ways we could never imagine, calling us to rise, to surrender, and to grow.

...

Spiral Upward

To truly rise in love, you must first fall deeply—surrendering to its mysteries with unwavering trust. Love may leave you feeling fragile and exposed, but it is through this vulnerability that you will uncover your greatest strength.

Embrace love unconditionally, free from expectations, and allow yourself to welcome the intricate puzzle it presents. Love, in its paradoxical nature, acts as a mirror—revealing both your deepest flaws and your greatest potential. These moments of reflection will guide you to immense strength, profound beauty, and transformative growth within yourself.

Let love lead you, not as a fixed destination to reach, but as an ever-evolving journey—one that brings you closer to becoming your most authentic self.

57: The Art of Choosing the Right Partner

Love is a powerful force—almost like being possessed. It makes us feel emotions we've never known, notice things we've never seen, and do things that, outside the euphoria of love, might seem foolish—but in love, make perfect sense. Love can overtake our mood and influence our decisions, which makes it essential to engage the mind. Otherwise, we drown in the realm of feeling—submerged in a deep blue sea where solutions feel as elusive as land. When it comes to emotions, the key lies in the mind—not in more emotion. With this understanding, I'm excited to share a fascinating perspective about love and how it intertwines with the process of choosing a life partner. Each morning, after completing my routine, I prepare my morning coffee, settle into the sofa, and gaze out the window. No matter the pains or struggles of yesterday, today arrives as a fresh beginning.

In that quiet ritual, I take the time to focus on all that I am blessed with, and I feel gratitude, peace, and a deep sense of belonging—knowing I am exactly where I am meant to be. This grounding moment allows me to focus on my breathing, give thanks, and surrender to a higher plane, letting my thoughts wander and return with fresh perspectives.

On one such morning, my thoughts settled on the patterns in my choice of potential life partners. I saw that these patterns revealed far more about the way I view myself than about the women in question. It was as if each relationship had been a mirror—not reflecting them, but quietly showing me the unspoken truths I carried within.

Throughout my life, I believed we chose partners based primarily on their qualities. Yet, I've come to understand that our choices aren't just about their attributes but also deeply tied to how we see ourselves at the moment of our life. Our current circumstances, levels of confidence, and self-esteem profoundly influence what we believe we deserve in a partner.

When we step into relationships, we often bring with us unspoken expectations—hopes that someone will fill the empty spaces within us, complement our flaws, and complete the puzzle of our lives. It's why we so often find ourselves beginning with, The person I'm looking for should be...—as if the right soul could step in and complete the unfinished lines of our story, soothing our insecurities and making us whole.

However, our perception of potential partners often mirrors our own needs. If we are overly focused on our flaws or what is missing, we may project these onto our partner, creating a relationship built on expectations and a perpetual cycle of give-and-take. This insight encourages a deeper examination of not only who we choose, but why we choose them, highlighting the significance of self-awareness as the first step. Initially, the relationship might seem balanced. But we never grow at the same speed, which means that if your circumstances, confidence level, or self-esteem change over time, you might feel like you are now giving more than receiving, and the balance shifts. Our partner's personality might gradually appear different from our initial perception. Not because they have necessarily changed but because we no longer feel the void. Doubts about compatibility emerge, and we begin to question our choices. The truth is, it was not our energies that connected but our needs.

Our egos often blur our perspective, so we don't see the person in front of us; we see a potential solution to our voids. We become so fixated on what the other person can provide that we lose sight of their true essence. To cultivate fulfilling and rewarding relationships, it is crucial to consider more than just our personal needs. We must select partners who resonate with us through their individuality, values, and character, ensuring genuine compatibility. The goal is to forge connections with those who share our fundamental values and actively enrich our lives, creating a robust foundation for mutual respect and growth.

By choosing partners for their inherent qualities rather than what they might offer, we establish a foundation for authentic and enriching relationships. This approach enables us to value each other's true selves, rather than seeing one another merely as means to fulfill our own needs.

As explained in the previous life lesson, developing a sense of self-worth and self-love based on acceptance is crucial before entering a relationship. Nurturing a healthy relationship with ourselves diminishes the likelihood of seeking validation or completion from others. Instead, we enter a relationship not in a searching mode but in a giving mode. Searching implies void, while giving means contentment.

In doing so, we transform into individuals who enhance the lives of others rather than simply filling gaps in our own. This notion of wholeness does not mean achieving perfect emotional or physical fulfillment, but rather developing an awareness that allows us to foster meaningful relationships.

...

Spiral Upward

Your choice of life partner often reflects your self-image. By acknowledging your intrinsic worth and prioritizing the cultivation of genuine self-acceptance, you're better equipped to choose a partner based on their innate qualities rather than solely fulfilling your needs. Authentic satisfaction and joy in relationships blossom when both partners cherish and embrace each other for their true selves, nurturing a connection rooted in mutual respect, love, and personal development.

58: Love Is Not Enough

Understanding the internal dynamics that influence how we choose a partner was essential to unraveling the deeper layers of this life lesson. Many relationship challenges stem from the subjective nature of our minds—where the ego leads, the focus shifts to *I*, and emotions take center stage.

As noted in a previous discussion, many of us first encounter love through the intense, unconditional "high love" from our mothers. This form of love is an internal experience that, while foundational, is different from the love encountered in romantic relationships. Romantic love—unlike the idealized version often portrayed in fairytales that mimic high love well—requires development and learning; it is an external love that evolves over time.

While love is inherently beautiful and magical, the complexities of human nature can sometimes unintentionally compromise healthy relationships.

Someone once asked me if I believed love alone was enough to sustain a relationship. In its essence, love is rooted in emotions, and solely relying on these feelings is insufficient for long-term sustainability because emotions are inherently unstable. For love to thrive, it must be nurtured by both emotional depth and intellectual commitment.

Love, though essential, is not enough. A relationship may begin with love, but it cannot grow on love alone. To truly flourish, it must be rooted in trust, upheld by respect, and nurtured through consistent, mutual effort.

My experiences with the joys and pains of love have taught me a critical truth. When trust is shattered into a million pieces, and you resonate deeply with that pain, it feels as though you too are broken into a million pieces. You could spend a lifetime trying to piece it all back together in the dark, or you could choose to let the pain pass through and beyond you. Holding onto the pain turns your fears into a constant input, which, over time, can morph into a self-fulfilling prophecy. Therefore, it's essential to be mindful of what you internalize, because it directly influences your output.

While some may argue that true love can overcome all obstacles, the reality is more complex. Deep wounds like breaches of trust can fundamentally alter the foundation of a relationship. Forgiveness is vital, but it doesn't always mean that someone who has hurt you should continue to have a place in your life. The ability to discern this difference is crucial for emotional well-being and the health of any ongoing or future relationships.

The three most significant reasons for divorce often stem from a lack of communication, infidelity, and financial challenges. These problems arise when our ego overshadows our capacity for love, hindering healthy connections with others. In other words, most of us are enslaved by our own ego without even being aware of it, simply because of the intangible nature of the ego.

Although the ego appears very clearly, it's still impossible to catch, as if it's always one step ahead of us. That may be why most people spend a lifetime pleasing and feeding it, yet it's never enough.

The only way to grasp our ego begins with awareness, recognizing its influence, and relinquishing control over our actions. Ask yourself, what is the purpose of being in a relationship if the main objective is self-love? By self-love, I mean a subjective notion based on what makes you happy. And that sentence so often begins with, *I love the way you make me feel*. But when you rise into an objective state of mind, the "I" begins to dissolve into "us," and love shifts from being about how someone makes you feel to cherishing them for who they truly are.

Which leads to the question: what are the essential ingredients for a thriving relationship beyond love?

First and foremost, respect is crucial. It stands as one of the greatest expressions of love. However, the measure of respect we extend to others is rooted in our character, which blossoms from self-respect. Respect acknowledges our partner's inherent worth and value, nurturing a more fulfilling connection.

Loyalty is the quiet vow to stand where love has planted you. It is the choice to stop searching for perfection in anyone else and instead remain steadfast in your devotion to your partner. From loyalty springs trust, the safety to grow side by side, and the courage to face life's seasons together. It is the deep listening to each other's thoughts, the honoring of each other's feelings, and the weaving of perspectives into a shared tapestry of understanding.

Communication goes beyond mere knowledge exchange; it fosters understanding that allows us to be deeply known by a few, rather than just recognized by many. Investing in mutual growth and understanding significantly enriches a relationship.

Financial success is not the cornerstone of a successful relationship—gratitude is. Unlike business transactions, relationships thrive on mutual appreciation and emotional connection. By prioritizing the non-monetary aspects of our relationship, we foster a deeper sense of fulfillment and companionship.

As long as we give our best effort and work persistently toward shared goals, financial worries should not overshadow the bond we share. In fact, ungratefulness, rather than financial strain, poses a greater threat to the harmony of a relationship. By valuing and acknowledging the richness of our partnership beyond material wealth, we reinforce the bond between us.

...

Spiral Upward

Love is undoubtedly a powerful force, but its strength peaks when combined with other essential ingredients. To truly thrive in your relationships, you need more than just love; you need respect, loyalty, understanding, and gratitude. These elements form the building blocks of enduring and fulfilling connections, creating a solid foundation upon which love can blossom into something truly remarkable.

59: The Illusion of Compromise

Is compromise essential in a relationship? This question introduces an intriguing life lesson, as many people automatically assume it is. However, I'd like to offer a different perspective. After delving deeply into the concept of compromise, I've come to realize that a significant misconception about compromise has adversely impacted many lives. Typically, compromise is seen as crucial for fostering harmony and mutual understanding in relationships. In this life lesson, we will distinguish between compromising based on needs and compromising core values, questioning the prevailing belief that compromise is always beneficial in relationships.

Understanding Compromise: Needs vs. Core Values

Compromise in relationships can be divided into two distinct types: compromising based on needs and compromising on core values. Compromising on needs involves adapting to daily routines and responsibilities that are essential for the practical operation of a relationship, such as sharing household chores or managing schedules. This type of compromise is crucial for maintaining balance and harmony, fostering a sense of shared responsibility and teamwork.

Conversely, compromising on core values means sacrificing fundamental principles or beliefs to preserve peace within the relationship. This kind of compromise can be harmful, as it often requires us to suppress our true selves to fit in, potentially leading to emotional distress and undermining the relationship's foundation. It's important to recognize when compromise threatens to violate personal integrity, as this can jeopardize both individual well-being and the mutual trust upon which healthy relationships are built.

The Illusion of Compromise

Compromising on core values contributes to what I call the illusion of compromise. In essence, this type of compromise is a form of self-negation, where we sacrifice our authenticity to maintain external harmony. By suppressing our true feelings and beliefs, we compromise with our own joy and fulfillment, which can lead to a gradual erosion of self-awareness and originality.

When compromise equates to suppression, it undermines the essence of a healthy relationship. Authentic connections thrive on mutual respect and the acceptance of each other's individuality. By honoring our unique identities and values, we enhance the growth and vitality of the relationship, fostering a deep sense of connection and understanding.

Embracing Authenticity and Individuality

Rather than compromising core values, we should prioritize finding partners who share our fundamental beliefs and aspirations. Relationships built on a shared understanding and appreciation of each other's core values are more likely to withstand challenges and nurture a lasting emotional bond.

While the search for a compatible partner may seem daunting, it is a journey worth embarking on. Instead of settling for compromise, we should remain steadfast in our commitment to authenticity and self-discovery. By manifesting and visualizing our ideal partnership, we can align ourselves with like-minded individuals who appreciate and celebrate their true selves.

In a world that often emphasizes compromise as the cornerstone of relationships, it is vital to question conventional thinking. Suppression of authenticity and self-negation should not be the price we pay for love. By prioritizing authenticity and embracing individuality, we can cultivate relationships that are built on trust, respect, and mutual admiration.

Therefore, always remember that while compromise is indeed essential in relationships, it is imperative to distinguish between compromising based on needs and compromising core values. While compromising needs fosters cooperation and balance, compromising core values undermines authenticity and erodes the foundation of the relationship. By embracing authenticity and seeking partners who share our core values, we can cultivate genuine, nurturing, and enduring relationships.

...

Spiral Upward

Embrace the truth that it's all right not to fit the mold of a million eyes because finding that one soul who sees your essence is where true connection lies. Cherish the path of seeking someone who celebrates your genuine self, for authenticity is the foundation of a deep and lasting bond. Don't rush to settle for the sake of it; let your heart resolve all doubts, aligning with the answers your mind seeks.

60: The Blurred Line

A man's elegance begins with lowering his gaze,
And a woman's elegance begins with not desiring his gaze.
It's difficult not to be tempted, but we must master it,
Otherwise, we drown in lust and lose the power to commit.

The gaze is the first step toward temptation,
The second brings a quiet sense of longing.
A spark of desire makes us curious,
Pulling us gently toward what's mysterious.

Ignited by desires we claim are wired,
Neglecting the mind that once aspired.
Reflection fades, and we forget fairness,
As lust consumes with blind awareness.

Lust is often mistaken for something better,
A promise of love that vanishes like weather.
We chase fulfillment, calling it pleasure,
Replacing joy with fleeting measure.

But lust is tricky — it changes form,
When fed, it breeds greed; when denied, it breeds storm.
No wise heart seeks to conquer or to fight,
It finds its power in surrender, purity and inner light.

So lower the gaze — in body and mind,
Transform desire to love divine.

Turn passion to devotion, longing to grace,
And you'll find peace in your partner's embrace.

Temptation and Loyalty

Relationships are built upon pillars of trust, communication, and mutual understanding — yet among all the forces that test them, temptation remains one of the most formidable. In a world where desire is woven into human nature, how we navigate it determines not only the fate of our relationships but also the integrity of our souls. This lesson invites you to master self-control — to ensure that what is momentary never destroys what was meant to endure.

I, too, have been caught in the quiet grip of temptation. Though I despised disloyalty, I found myself entangled in its web, discovering that infidelity is not always physical — it begins in thought, in curiosity, in a moment left unchecked. At first, the lines between innocence and desire appear blurred — disguised as harmless words, subtle smiles, or fleeting curiosity. Every temptation is, in truth, a mirror — revealing what part of us still seeks what only God can fulfill. It is not the world that tempts us, but the emptiness within that longs to be filled.

But soon, the heart begins to justify what it already knows is wrong — dressing desire in the disguise of connection or friendship. When you strip away the excuses, the truth stands bare: you are responsible.

As I peeled away its layers one by one, I came face to face with my reflection — and it was not who I believed myself to be. That moment broke the illusion of who I thought I was and revealed the man I had become. I could not accept being governed by impulse, for that would betray the essence of self-respect.

Society romanticizes harmless admiration and playful flirtation, yet none of us would welcome the same behavior from our partner. This contradiction is revealing — we justify what benefits us and condemn what exposes us. In solitude, I wrestled with this paradox until a realization emerged: the test is not in avoiding temptation's presence, but in mastering our response to it.

Temptation is not proof of weakness; it is proof of life itself — a reminder that the lower self still whispers. The test is not to silence those whispers, but to rise above them — to let the mind lead where desire once ruled. Every temptation carries a mirror, asking one simple question: what governs you — impulse or intention?

Navigating the Path to Genuine Connections

At the heart of every lasting bond lies a truth: in a world overflowing with temptation, self-control is not repression — it is protection. To surrender to lust's illusion is to trade something sacred for something fleeting, leaving behind fractured trust and an emptiness that no pleasure can fill.

The gaze — our first bridge between thought and desire — often becomes the spark that ignites temptation. When we look outward for fulfillment, we begin to drift inwardly, away from peace. No one can complete what remains incomplete within. The same fire that fuels attraction can cloud our perception, leading us away from genuine love and clarity.

Too often we reduce our impulses to biology, forgetting that what separates us from instinct is reflection. When lust overtakes reason, choice dissolves into reaction, and the soul loses its freedom. In those moments, we become servants of desire rather than stewards of discipline.

Modern culture glorifies instant gratification — mistaking pleasure for happiness, attraction for love, and thrill for connection. Yet the pursuit of what feels good often robs us of what is good. The more we chase stimulation, the less we understand intimacy.

Lust, ever-changing in form, seduces us into a cycle that always ends in emptiness. Fed, it breeds greed; denied, it becomes anger. It disguises itself as need, as love, as destiny — but beneath every mask lies the same void. The answer is not endless resistance, but transformation — to redirect that energy toward love, respect, and reverence.

A lowered gaze is not denial; it is elevation. It is the discipline to honor what has value, to choose clarity over chaos, and devotion over desire. In choosing restraint, we do not lose passion — we refine it. From that refinement, trust blooms, and from trust, love matures into something unshakable.

...

Spiral Upward

Temptation begins with a gaze — a spark of curiosity that, if left untamed, can consume integrity itself. To confront it is not to shame desire, but to understand it. Mastery of the self is not found in avoidance, but in awareness. Recognize that temptation is born from the fleeting nature of lust, while loyalty is born from the timeless nature of love. Choose to rise — to redirect your longing toward what uplifts the soul. True elegance is not in perfection, but in discipline — in the quiet strength to remain faithful, even when no one is watching. In a world that glorifies indulgence, restraint becomes a rebellion — and loyalty, the highest expression of love.

61: The Right Person, Wrong Time

Sometimes love is not denied — it is delayed for divine alignment.

One of the most common misconceptions that keep us tied to the past is the belief that we met the right person at the wrong time. This idea may sound poetic, but it quietly imprisons the heart in regret. Words carry power—they can heal or harm, free or confine—and of all the conversations we will ever have, the most transformative one is the one we hold with ourselves.

After my divorce, it took me nearly six years to truly move on. The conviction that my ex-wife was the right person kept me trapped in reflection: *What if I had been more present, more mature, more patient?* But the truth remained—I wasn't. Her presence was a blessing; her absence became a lesson. That was our story. And in time, I came to understand that it unfolded exactly as it was meant to.

The phrase *"right person, wrong time"* often enters our lives disguised as comfort. Yet beneath its softness lies quiet destruction. It suggests that love was right but life was wrong, that destiny itself miscalculated. But what is timing, truly? Did we have any control over when we met, or was it orchestrated by a force far greater than our own?

If every encounter carries meaning, then perhaps it is not the timing that is wrong, but our readiness to meet it. The number of causes and effects required for two strangers to meet is beyond comprehension. Some call it coincidence—perhaps because that word is easier to accept—but in truth, nothing in this world is random. Everything operates within divine law, interconnected from the smallest particle to the widest cosmos.

We do not control who we meet, nor the moment we meet them.

There are countless reasons why people part, but none that can defy divine order. There is no such thing as wrong timing—only the timing meant for our growth.

If I can offer you one piece of advice, it's this: never try to stop someone from leaving—and I mean truly leaving. Let them go. Do not stand in the doorway of someone who has already chosen to walk away. I am not telling you not to fight for your relationship; I am telling you not to stand on the battlefield alone.

If their departure becomes the force that awakens your growth, then the open door is not punishment but passage—a reminder that you could have changed without being pushed, yet waited until life insisted. And if they leave because love has shifted, that too is mercy. It frees you both to live in truth rather than illusion—to love again, not from fear of loss, but from the wisdom of letting go.

Of course, the right partner will not stay in the face of betrayal, dishonor, or harm—nor should they. But when love is sincere, the right person will not walk away without cause. Love cannot be held by grip or guilt; it remains only where it is freely chosen. Never force anyone to stay. And while circumstances may compel you to move on, do not force them out of your heart. Let time take what time needs.

If we do not control who we meet, then who does? We will explore this further in the fifth knot of this book, but for now, consider this: call it fate, destiny, or divine design—it is all the same. The will of a higher power ensures that your meeting was never a coincidence.

Finding comfort in this truth comes naturally when we remember that nature makes no mistakes. It moves in perfect harmony, guided by laws that keep every part in balance. Nothing drifts without purpose. Even a leaf does not fall except by His command:

"And there is no leaf that falls but He knows it." — *Qur'an, 6:59*

This remembrance brings peace to the heart, for the Divine does not err. In truth, we cannot say, *"Destiny brought us together, but the timing was wrong,"* for such a statement contradicts the perfection of divine order. The timing of every encounter is never accidental—it is always precise. Even the briefest meeting of souls carries meaning, a purpose that must unfold before the journey continues.

We do not call the boundary between seawater and freshwater a mistake simply because they meet but do not mix. Instead, we marvel at it as a wonder of creation—a reminder of divine wisdom. In the same way, when it comes to human relationships, we must not reduce them to *"the right person at the wrong time."* What feels like misalignment is, in truth, divine design—each meeting serving a purpose in the unfolding of who we are becoming.

People enter our lives for two reasons: as blessings or as lessons. If someone brings joy and growth, be grateful, even when their chapter ends. If they bring challenge and pain, embrace the wisdom they leave behind. Both serve the same purpose—to refine you into someone wiser, stronger, and more compassionate.

Instead of mourning missed opportunities or dwelling on *what ifs*, focus on what was gained. Every encounter, whether fleeting or lasting, is part of your evolution. There is no such thing as wrong timing—only divine timing. Both joy and pain arrive for you, not against you. Each encounter—whether it lifts you or breaks you—draws you closer to the one person you must understand most deeply: yourself.

To see life this way is to rise beyond regret. For in the tapestry of existence, even heartbreak has its thread. And when you finally look back from a higher place, you'll see that every ending was not a loss—but a redirection toward where you were always meant to be.

...

Spiral Upward

A deep truth lies beyond the illusion of "right person, wrong time." Every person you meet arrives exactly when they are meant to. Each serves a purpose in your growth, whether through love or loss. When you shift your perspective from *regret* to *revelation*, you begin to see that timing has never been your enemy—it has always been your teacher.

Instead of yearning for what could have been, embrace what was. Let gratitude replace longing, and wisdom replace sorrow. For every meeting, no matter how brief, leaves an imprint that shapes who you are becoming. The impact of those who cross your path is never wasted—it echoes through your becoming, guiding you toward the person you are destined to be..

62: A Woman's Intuition

Her intuition was never wrong — only her patience to trust it.

A woman's intuition has long been described as mysterious, but mystery does not make it unreal. It is one of life's most profound forces—quiet, instinctive, and divinely placed within her nature. Science may describe it as heightened interconnectivity between the hemispheres of the brain; spirituality calls it insight from the soul. Either way, it is both biological and sacred—her built-in compass for truth.

This extraordinary inner sensitivity allows women to perceive what words conceal—to feel what has not yet been said. In relationships, this gift becomes her greatest strength. It is not suspicion; it is perception. A woman often senses the truth long before it surfaces. Deep down, she knows when something is wrong—but too often, she silences that knowing to protect a hope she's afraid to lose.

I remember my Nana, once saying: *"The foundation of a relationship rests in the hands of a strong woman."*

For a long time, I pondered what she meant. Only when I began to study human nature more deeply did I understand the wisdom behind her words. A woman's strength is not in domination but discernment. She sees beyond what is shown and feels beyond what is spoken.

In relationships, women merge instinct with awareness—blending feeling and foresight in ways men rarely can. Where a man may rely on logic, a woman perceives tone, pauses, and energy. She senses when affection shifts or when honesty fades, often before a word is spoken. Her intuition does not accuse—it observes.

Yet this advantage fades when she ignores it. An innocent hope can turn a few weeks of dating into years of unhappiness, because women often project potential into the future, convincing themselves of what could be instead of accepting what is. Men, on the other hand, understand the persuasive power of words and may say whatever is necessary in the moment—but their actions always reveal the truth.

A woman's first intuition is rarely wrong; it's her patience to trust it that falters. Her mind seeks logic, while her heart already knows. To honor that knowing is to honor the wisdom God placed within her—a compass that points her toward peace and away from pain.

Still, it's essential to distinguish between intuition and judgment. Judgment speaks from fear; intuition speaks from peace. Judgment rushes to conclusions; intuition waits, listens, and understands. Judgment divides; intuition guides.

Her intuition is the whisper of protection, not the voice of control. It warns her of danger, but never from ego—from care. It is what tells her *"this doesn't feel right"* before reason can explain why. The danger lies not in feeling too much, but in doubting what she feels.

Women hold a unique strength—the power to say *no* when something feels wrong. If it doesn't feel right, it usually isn't. By staying grounded in the present and discerning between reality and imagination, a woman protects not only her heart but her peace. To honor her intuition is to honor her soul's wisdom, to align with the truth rather than escape it.

For men, the lesson is equally vital. When a woman grows quiet, do not mistake her silence for serenity. Her stillness is not peace—it is realization. And never take her tears lightly. When a woman weeps over the same wound again and again, she is not merely grieving a moment; she is emptying her heart of what it once held. That is why many men cannot afford her tears—because with each one shed, she releases a little more of her love, until nothing remains.

From women, I have learned wisdom that words could never teach— the lessons carried in their silence, their tears, and their final decision to walk away. When my ex-wife left, I understood it in my bones: sometimes love demands distance, and true strength lies not only in holding on but in having the courage to let go.

...

Spiral Upward

A woman's intuition is not a mystery to be solved but a wisdom to be honored. When she learns to trust it fully, she aligns herself with the divine guidance placed within her. It becomes her protection from deceit, her clarity through confusion, and her quiet reminder that peace is the measure of truth.

But this gift also carries responsibility. To feel deeply is not to act impulsively; it is to discern with grace. She must stand firm in her convictions, especially when faced with men of dishonorable intent—most of all, those already bound in marriage. To silence her intuition in such moments is to risk not only harming another's life, but unraveling her own.

Your heart already knows the truth. Do not betray it. Intuition is not a whisper to be ignored, but a shield meant to protect you. Trust it without hesitation, and you will walk into a future of genuine, life-giving love—relationships that uplift, endure, and bless everyone they touch.

The voice you silence today becomes the storm that teaches tomorrow.

63: Advice for Men

A man's greatness is not in what he conquers, but in what he protects.

The most beautiful view in life appears when you rise high enough to see your own mistakes. My body bears scars, and my heart has carried its share of pain. If you look closely, you'll see stories etched in each one—lessons carved from mistakes I can never erase. We all falter, but that does not mean we must repeat what once broke us. So consider this my gift to you: be wiser than I was. Everything life has to offer already lies within you. Be grateful for what you have, not resentful for what you lack.

Becoming a Man

Manhood is not measured in years but in character. True men refuse to hide behind excuses like *"boys will be boys."* Maturity is not proven by age, but by accountability—by standing firm when it would be easier to run.

If you are blessed with a family, remember that your role is sacred: to protect, to provide, and to love with unwavering devotion. And if you are fortunate enough to love a woman deeply—to hold her in your heart as your most cherished treasure—then consider yourself wealthier than kings. Do not seek to change her. A woman's heart does not need control; it needs inspiration. When you rise, she rises beside you — not because you demand it, but because love naturally mirrors growth. Be the kind of man whose presence commands respect, not by authority, but by integrity.

A woman is like a rib—bend her too harshly, and she will break. So give her room to breathe and space to grow. Lead not through control, but through example. Become the reflection of the values you wish her to embody. Be the calm that steadies her storms, and the strength that never needs to shout.

To understand the woman you love is to understand the human heart itself. Fail to do so, and you will move through life surrounded by people yet never truly connected to anyone. True love, when found, is a rare gift; to find it twice is a miracle. And I don't mean the fleeting kind of attraction that comes and goes with circumstance—but the enduring love that survives storms and seasons, that refines rather than fades.

Stand Strong by Her Side

In a world full of noise and distraction, your steady presence becomes her peace. When life unravels, be the stillness she can lean on. A woman's strength is extraordinary—she does not need you to survive, she chooses you to belong. That choice is her deepest form of love and trust.

If you shy away from responsibility, she will carry the weight alone. And if she must lead for too long, her respect for you will quietly fade. Remember: leadership is not dominance—it is responsibility. Sometimes, she doesn't need you to fix her problems; she just needs to feel that you truly care. Presence can speak louder than words, and a sincere embrace can heal more than a thousand explanations. When she grows quiet, listen with your soul. When she feels unseen, remind her she is your world. Engage not just with her words, but with her silence. Let her know she is not only loved—but safe.

Faithfulness and Trust

It is almost comical how we fear pain yet so easily cause it. We seek mercy, yet deny it. How can we shield ourselves from heartbreak, yet justify inflicting the same wound upon the one we claim to love? Is her worth any less than ours?

Faithfulness is not a restriction; it is a reflection of your highest self. Trust, once broken, never returns unscarred. That is why fidelity is sacred—it protects not only her heart but your honor. To betray trust is to shatter your own reflection. No man can claim strength while living in deceit.

To profess love while betraying it is not love at all—it is cowardice disguised as charm. Integrity begins when desire bows to discipline.

Loyalty is not about perfection; it's about principle. The man who keeps his promises, even when no one is watching, stands taller than those who chase every passing pleasure.

Love Beyond Possession

A relationship built on materialism is not a union—it is a transaction. Gifts may sparkle, but they cannot replace presence, loyalty, or truth. To confuse compensation with affection is to mistake ownership for love. Although providing is your responsibility, your presence is your true offering. For a woman who truly loves you, your presence will always matter more than your provision. She does not crave your wealth—she craves your warmth. The moments you give her are the currency that never loses value. True love cannot be bought or bargained; it must be built. It is made of trust, empathy, laughter, and silence understood. When love is sincere, even simplicity feels abundant — because what is real between hearts can never be measured in things, only in presence. Love is not about showing up with gifts—it is about showing up with yourself. Provide not only with your hands, but with your heart. Presence is the one gift that never fades.

Attention to Detail

The secret to keeping love alive lies in never letting it grow predictable. A relationship thrives when you keep creating new *firsts*. We cherish the first call, the first embrace, *the first I love you*—because they carried the thrill of discovery. But time dulls what intention no longer sharpens. Never stop pursuing her. A handwritten note, a gentle compliment, a glance that says *you still move me*—these are not small gestures. They are reminders that love is still alive. Learn her rhythms: how she laughs, how she prays, how she drinks her coffee. The more you notice, the more she blooms.

Love doesn't die of time—it dies of neglect. Attention is the antidote.

Becoming Her Best Friend

Strive to make your partner not just your lover, but your truest friend— the one who holds your secrets, shares your laughter, and steadies you when life feels unsteady. Friendship in love is not merely comfort — it is divine alignment. Two souls learning the rhythm of life together, as one melody played on different instruments. Let your love sparkle with playfulness but root it in friendship. She should be the person whose presence makes even silence feel full. Friendship is the spine of lasting love. It's what steadies you when storms come and what turns ordinary moments into sacred ones. When your partner feels like both your home and your adventure, you've built something eternal. Be intentional about this bond. A man often sets the tone of the relationship—so let it be one of safety and warmth. When you give her freedom to be fully herself, she will give you loyalty that no force can break.

...

Spiral Upward

To be a man is not to conquer, but to cultivate. To lead is not to command, but to serve. Strength without tenderness is tyranny, and love without loyalty is illusion. Rise above the need to prove yourself through pride. True greatness is quiet—it moves through patience, consistency, and respect. Stand beside the woman you love through both silence and song. Be her protector, not her prison. Be her safe place, not her test. Keep the fire of pursuit alive long after the chase is done. Because in the end, love is not sustained by grand gestures, but by daily reverence.

Be a man who honors what is sacred. One whose strength brings peace, not fear. One whose love is proof of his faith. And when you live like that—you won't have to demand respect. You will become it.

64: Advice for Women

The beauty of a woman is not in her face or form, but in the light she carries within.

Your true power lies not only in your outward beauty, but in the essence you embody—the grace, wisdom, and strength you bring into the world. When you understand this, you protect yourself from becoming what many desire, instead of what few truly value. The line between the two is razor-thin, and many women stumble here.

What catches a man's attention is not always what keeps his respect. Desire may open the door, but it is rarely what builds a home. Perhaps that is why so much pressure has been placed on women's appearance—because desire is loud and fleeting, while true value is quiet and eternal.

The Trap of Seeking Attention

It is human to crave attention, but how you seek it defines your spirit. Too many women fall into the illusion that they must mold themselves into what others want, chasing admiration at the cost of authenticity. Attention may feel like validation, but it is temporary—it vanishes when the eyes turn away. Instead of becoming what others expect, become the woman you yourself admire. Look into the mirror and be proud of what looks back. Your worth is not found in the eyes that watch you, but in the soul that guides you. When you live aligned with your truth, you attract not attention, but respect—and the right kind of man will always recognize that light.

Trusting Your Intuition

Your intuition is not a weakness; it is divine wisdom speaking softly through you. It is the quiet knowing that whispers before reason catches up. Too often, women silence that voice—offering chances to men their spirit already warned them about. Intuition may not explain itself, but it rarely lies. Trust it. It is the compass of your soul, designed to protect your heart in a world that often seeks to distract it. Judgment speaks from fear; intuition speaks from peace. The more you honor that difference, the fewer regrets you'll carry. A woman's greatest protection has never been walls—it has always been awareness.

Love and Commitment

When you meet a good man—one whose heart is pure—do not hold back. Nurture that bond with depth, respect, and grace. Men often decide the future based on how they feel in the present; women often decide based on what they hope the future will become. Both perspectives are powerful—but balance them with wisdom.

Do not build your life on potential alone. Love what *is*, not only what *could be*. For a man, respect is love. Fear is not. The man worth your heart will never need to be feared; he will inspire reverence through his steadiness. He will be gentle in peace and unshakable in storms—tender enough to hold you, strong enough to defend you. That is balance: the lion and the light. Support his growth when he is with you, and protect his name when he is not. Speak of him with honor, even when it's difficult. A man grows when he sees pride reflected in your eyes. Nothing empowers a man more than to be seen with faith by the woman he loves.

Carrying Yourself with Dignity

When you walk into a room, let your presence speak of quiet dignity — the kind that honors both your heart and your values. Boundaries are not chains—they are the language of self-respect. Do not act available when you are committed. Loyalty is not just about what you do; it is about how you carry yourself when no one is watching. Comparison, too, is a silent thief. It steals joy and turns admiration into insecurity. True beauty radiates from within: confidence, kindness, and dignity are the traits that leave lasting impressions. Remember, elegance is not about perfection—it is about peace.

Guarding Your Self-Worth

Guard your self-worth tenderly. It was never meant to be handed over, for it was placed within you long before anyone else arrived. The moment you allow someone else to define your value, you forfeit it. Your worth is not measured by how loudly someone praises you or how closely they hold you. It is measured by how deeply you know who you are. Address conflict when it arises, but choose your battles with wisdom. Every wound does not require a war. Seek counsel if needed, but guard your relationship from outside noise—bad advice can destroy what patience could have healed. Know when to speak, when to stay silent, and when to walk away. That balance is strength.

Staying True to Yourself

Demand respect—but do not lose yourself demanding it.

Do not let disappointment turn your heart bitter. Stay gentle, but grounded. Softness is not weakness; it is divine resilience. Remain loving, even when misunderstood. Like a flower that releases its fragrance even when crushed, let your essence remain pure. And remember—you do not do this only for him. You do this because it is who you are. A woman who knows her worth, walks with dignity, and refuses to bend her truth becomes magnetic—not just to men, but to everything aligned with her light.

Choosing Love Wisely

Commit only to love that brings peace to your soul. Do not mistake intensity for intimacy or drama for depth. The allure of chaos fades; calm endures. Choose the one who steadies your mind, not the one who excites your fears. The right love may challenge you—but it will never consume you. It will call you both to growth, not destruction. The beginning of true love may not always be easy, for it asks both hearts to evolve. But if the foundation is sincere, every trial will purify rather than break it. Choose simplicity over spectacle, sincerity over charm. Real love is not loud—it is loyal. It is not perfect—it is patient.

...

Spiral Upward

Trust your intuition. Honor your boundaries. Commit to love that strengthens your peace, not your anxiety. Carry yourself with dignity, speak truth with grace, and protect your light from those who dim it. When you live from this place, you do not just love a man—you elevate love itself. You transform it into something sacred, something that reflects the very balance of the universe: strength and softness, wisdom and warmth.

That is your true power—not to compete, but to complete.

Not to chase, but to choose.

Not to please, but to *be*.

When you live this truth, love does not define you—you define love.

65: Unveiling Jealousy

Jealousy is love's shadow—it appears when the light of trust begins to fade.

Jealousy is a universal emotion—one that visits every heart at some point in life—yet its roots are rarely simple to untangle. Left unaddressed, it can evolve from a fleeting feeling into a quiet poison that corrodes love, clouds trust, and drains peace from the soul.

At its core, jealousy arises from fear: the fear of loss, inadequacy, and not being enough. It is born when we sense a threat to something or someone we deeply value. And though it often wears the mask of love, jealousy is not love's proof—it is love's distortion.

It is also important to distinguish jealousy from envy. Envy desires what another possesses; jealousy fears losing what you already have. One looks outward, the other inward. Yet both are born from comparison—a habit that blinds us to our own worth.

When understood, jealousy can remind us how deeply we care. When ignored, it becomes a storm that destroys what it once sought to protect. I have seen it break even the strongest of bonds—not because love was absent, but because fear was never faced.

The Trap of Assumptions

Jealousy thrives in the shadows of assumption. It whispers stories of betrayal that may not exist, painting entire worlds from fragments of fear. The mind, when ruled by insecurity, becomes a storyteller of suffering—turning silence into secrets and coincidence into conspiracy.

To disarm jealousy, we must cultivate self-awareness and discipline. Understand its origin. Communicate openly. Build trust—first within yourself, then with the one you love.

Jealousy wears many faces—romantic, emotional, even professional—but in every form, it reflects a lack of inner contentment. And contentment is not a destination; it is a spiritual practice. It begins by acknowledging your emotions, tracing them to their roots, and choosing reflection over reaction. When you look deeply enough, you'll see that jealousy doesn't ask you to control another person—it asks you to reclaim yourself.

Mastering the Pause

Jealousy urges us to act—to accuse, to defend, to demand before reason can breathe. Yet the most powerful response is not action, but stillness. Pause. Breathe. Let the wave rise and fall without letting it carry you away. One moment of patience can save you from a thousand moments of regret.

When you finally speak, replace accusation with honesty. Instead of saying, "Why did you look at her?" say, "When that happened, I felt insecure. Can you reassure me?"

This simple shift transforms confrontation into connection. What could have been a wall becomes a bridge. Honesty builds intimacy; blame destroys it. The difference between the two is often just one breath, one pause, one act of awareness.

Facing the Root

At the heart of jealousy lies insecurity. Remind yourself: *There will never be another me.*

Comparison steals peace because it forgets individuality. Confidence is not arrogance—it is gratitude for your own design. When fear arises, test it with truth. Ask yourself: *If my worst fear came true, could I still survive?* The answer is always yes. Fear loses its power the moment you stop running from it.

If jealousy grows because your partner's actions feed your doubt—through neglect, inconsistency, or lack of reassurance—then it may not be insecurity, but intuition. Do not silence your own truth to keep the peace. Sometimes the wound is not within you, but between you. Reflection is not self-blame; it is self-respect. The goal is not to suppress jealousy, but to understand whether your fear is real or imagined—and to act not with impulse, but with integrity.

Love Without Chains

Love cannot breathe where fear rules. You cannot protect love by imprisoning it.

Love that must be watched is not love—it is control disguised as care. If someone is meant to stay, no fear is needed. If they are meant to leave, holding tighter will not stop them. Let them go, and if they return, it will be out of choice, not control. Be protective, but not possessive. Trust is the oxygen of love; without it, affection suffocates into anxiety.

Do not let a fleeting emotion write the story of your forever. Time reveals what suspicion cannot. And if jealousy becomes a recurring storm, step back and heal. Carrying old wounds into new love only ensures you will reopen them. Sometimes the lesson is not about trusting others—it's about trusting God's plan for what's yours. What is written for you cannot be taken. What leaves you was never meant to stay.

The Gift Hidden in Jealousy

Every emotion carries a message, and jealousy is no exception. Beneath its sting lies a call to awaken—to see where your insecurities live, where trust must be rebuilt, and where love requires more care. When met with humility and courage, jealousy becomes a teacher. It reveals where fear still resides and where love has grown impatient. Managed wisely, it transforms from a destroyer into a guide—leading you toward a deeper kind of love, one rooted in understanding rather than ownership. When fear is replaced by awareness, jealousy reveals its hidden gift: a mirror reflecting not what you lack, but what you are called to grow into.

...

Spiral Upward

To rise above jealousy is to master the art of reflection. It begins not with accusation, but with awareness. Look inward. Speak with transparency. Meet your flaws with compassion instead of shame. Disarm jealousy by naming it, tracing its roots, and understanding its message. Only then can you replace fear with faith, and control with connection. Know your worth so deeply that you refuse to remain in places that diminish it. If a relationship corrodes your peace, do not confuse leaving with failure—it is preservation. Walking away from what poisons your spirit is not weakness; it is wisdom.

Remember this truth: love is not meant to cage you—it is meant to free you. And when you finally learn to trust not only your partner, but yourself, jealousy fades—not because you stopped caring, but because you started believing.

66: Listen to the Silence

Amid the highs and lows of life's journey, some lessons etch themselves so deeply into our hearts that they become part of who we are. These lessons arrive in many forms—sometimes clothed in joy and laughter, other times in pain and grief. Yet, no matter how they come, each carries wisdom.

Reflecting on my own path, I cannot ignore the profound influence women have had in shaping me. By "women," I don't just mean past relationships, but also my mother, my sisters, and the women within my closest circle. Each of them—carrying unique identities, stories, and scars—has left an indelible imprint on my understanding of the world.

From them, I have learned not only through their words but also through the language that requires no speech—the wisdom carried in their tears, their silences, and, in rare moments, their decision to walk away. In my own life, I felt this most deeply when my ex-wife chose to leave. That departure, though painful, carved its own lesson: that sometimes love demands distance, and that true strength lies not only in holding on but also in the courage to let go.

The Weight of Her Tears

When a woman cries, she doesn't shed just water from her eyes—she pours out pieces of her soul. Her tears carry the weight of love, disappointment, sacrifice, and silent hope. Each one tells a story too heavy for words, yet too sacred to keep buried.

Every tear is a story. It carries with it the memory of love, the ache of loss, the joy of belonging, or the sting of betrayal. Her tears are not weakness—they are courage. For it takes strength to stop pretending, to let the façade fall, and to confront pain head-on.

In crying, she cleanses her soul. She lets go of what corrodes her spirit and makes room for healing. And when she rises from her tears, she rises renewed—like soil after rainfall, softer, richer, and more fertile for new growth. But remember: her tears come at a cost. They demand presence, empathy, and the courage to stand beside her. To "afford" her tears means to honor her vulnerability, to truly listen, and to carry the weight of her emotions without dismissing them.

The Depth of Her Silence

Silence is often mistaken for emptiness, but for a woman, silence is rarely empty. It is full—overflowing with thought, reflection, and transformation. When she goes quiet, it is not always about withholding words from you—it is often about listening more closely to herself.

Her silence is sacred ground. Within it, she wrestles with emotions, redefines her boundaries, and sometimes reimagines her life. It is here that she grows in ways no one else can see, breaking away from the woman she once was.

Too often, silence is misunderstood as weakness or indifference. But her silence is not passive—it is active. It is her rebuilding, her protecting herself, her stepping into clarity. And by the time she emerges from this silence, she is no longer the same. Her boundaries have shifted, her perspective has widened, and her decisions—once uncertain—become final.

The Final Goodbye

When a woman decides to leave, it is never sudden. Her heart leaves long before her body follows. She detaches piece by piece, first in thought, then in emotion, until finally she has little left to give. By the time she physically walks away, she has already survived the heartbreak of letting go.

This is why convincing her to stay once she has truly left is almost impossible. Winning her back requires more than apologies; it requires transformation. It requires recognition of her pain, respect for her journey, and the humility to grow into someone new.

For her, leaving is not escape—it is survival. It is an act of self-preservation, a reclaiming of her dignity. And though it may look like loss from the outside, within it lies courage: the courage to say, "I deserve better than this."

Listening Beyond Words

A woman's tears, her silence, and her departure—each is a form of communication, each a chapter of her unspoken truth. They demand more than surface-level understanding; they demand presence, empathy, and courage. When she cries, hold her—not to fix her, but to remind her she is not alone. When she falls silent, respect it—give her the space to return whole. And if she leaves, let her go with dignity—do not beg for her return if you are unwilling to become the person worthy of it. For the wisdom of a woman does not always arrive through her words. Sometimes it comes through the very things she does not say.

The Invitation

The lesson, then, is not simply to hear her but to listen—to the silence, to the pauses, to the spaces between words. For in those spaces lie the truths she cannot always speak aloud. And if you are wise enough to listen, you will find in her not only the power to transform herself, but the power to transform you as well.

...

Spiral Upward

The unspoken language of a woman carries profound wisdom. When she falls silent, do not mistake it for peace—it is not serenity, but realization. Her silence is not a sign that she understands you; it is the quiet acknowledgment that she no longer sees you as the answer. And never take her tears lightly. When a woman weeps over the same wounds again and again, she is not only grieving the moment—she is emptying her heart of everything it once held for you. That is why many men cannot afford her tears: because with each one shed, she releases a little more of her love, until nothing remains.

67: I Deserve Better

The moment you remember your worth, everything that isn't meant for you begins to fall away.

Through my experiences counseling individuals on matters of the heart, I've witnessed the raw complexity of human emotion—the longing for love, the sting of betrayal, the silent erosion caused by neglect, and the quiet strength required to rebuild.

In these moments, I've come to see that the most powerful turning point in any relationship—romantic or otherwise—begins with three simple words—small in sound, yet immense in power: *I deserve better.*

These words are not merely a declaration; they are a revolution of the soul. Life's journey is filled with love and heartbreak, laughter and sorrow. Along the way, too many of us accept less than we deserve—mistreatment, disrespect, or being taken for granted. But the instant we affirm our worth, everything changes. *I deserve better* is not a complaint; it is a boundary, a torch that lights the path from suffering toward dignity, peace, and renewal.

The Courage to Claim Your Worth

To say *I deserve better* requires courage. At first, doubt whispers: *What if I'm asking for too much? What if this is all I'm worth?* But vulnerability is not weakness; it is the birthplace of strength. It is in daring to demand respect that we begin to reclaim our power.

Self-respect cannot survive in environments where disrespect is normalized. Every time we accept less, we chip away at our dignity. But every time we affirm, *I deserve better*, we rebuild that dignity brick by brick. We remind ourselves—and the world—that love without respect is not love at all, and kindness without consistency is nothing but a façade.

And here lies a truth many avoid: the moment you accept less than you deserve, you teach others how to treat you. The first betrayal is never from them—it is from yourself, when you silence your worth for the sake of being loved.

Setting the Standard

When you declare *I deserve better*, you don't just change your own life—you change the atmosphere around you. Boundaries are not walls; they are standards. By setting them, you teach others how to treat you. When you value yourself, people either rise to meet that standard or fall away. Either way, you win. And make no mistake—people notice. Your quiet insistence on respect, your refusal to tolerate cruelty, your choice to walk away from toxic patterns—these ripple outward. They inspire others who are watching silently, perhaps doubting their own worth, to also rise.

From Pain to Joy

Accepting mistreatment leads only to bitterness. Choosing better leads to joy. The phrase *I deserve better* is not about arrogance or entitlement—it's about liberation. It frees you from cycles of negativity and guides you toward a life where peace, love, and fulfillment are not exceptions but the rule. Even moments of self-doubt have their place; they are proof that your soul already knows when something is wrong. That restlessness, that unease, is not weakness—it is your inner compass reminding you: *this is not what I was made for.*

Recognizing your worth is the first step to breaking free, and breaking free is the first step toward healing.

Becoming What You Seek

To *deserve* better is also to *become* better. The love, respect, and peace you long for are not random gifts—they are reflections of who you are becoming. We attract not what we want, but what we are. If you seek honesty, be truthful. If you seek loyalty, be steadfast. If you seek love that endures, let that love begin within you.

Growth calls to growth. As you elevate yourself, you naturally draw people who live at that same frequency—souls who mirror the values you embody. The Qur'an reminds us of this divine symmetry:

"The good men are for the good women, and the good women for the good men." (24:26)

This truth transcends gender or circumstance—it speaks to resonance. You cannot meet what you have not yet become. The better you seek is also seeking you, and the bridge between the two is your own evolution. So when you say *I deserve better*, let it not only be a demand from the world but a promise to yourself—to rise, to grow, to reflect the very goodness you wish to receive.

A Call to Transformation

Saying *I deserve better* is not just about personal boundaries—it is about shaping a culture of respect and compassion. When we honor ourselves, we set an example. We remind others that dignity is not negotiable. And as more people embrace this truth, a shift happens. We begin to build communities where kindness is the standard, not the exception.

This affirmation becomes both personal and universal. It is not only your shield against mistreatment—it is your sword against despair. It empowers you to heal, to grow, and to demand not perfection, but what is real: respect, love, trust, and peace. So let these words take root in your heart. Speak them when you are mistreated. Whisper them when you doubt yourself. Shout them when you are ready to rise.

Because you do deserve better. Always.

•••

Spiral Upward

The mantra *I deserve better* carries the power to redirect the course of your life. It is more than words—it is a vow to yourself, a declaration that you will no longer settle for what diminishes your spirit. It reminds you that joy, love, and respect are not luxuries but birthrights.

Embracing this truth requires both courage and vulnerability—the courage to walk away from what wounds you, and the vulnerability to believe you are worthy of something greater. In that act, you reclaim what is yours: your dignity, your honor, your self-worth.

But *I deserve better* is not only about what you demand from others—it is also a mirror held up to yourself. The energy you attract is often the energy you give out. If you continue making the same choices, you will meet the same outcomes. Declaring you deserve better must therefore be followed by living better—by choosing differently, giving differently, and aligning your actions with the life you claim to seek.

Each time you affirm this truth, you raise the standard of your own life. You ignite change within yourself, and in doing so, you invite others to rise with you. This is how transformation begins—not in grand revolutions, but in the quiet strength of someone who refuses to settle.

Remember this: *you deserve better*. And when you truly live by that truth, doors open—doors to peace, fulfillment, and joy beyond anything you once thought possible.

The Great Orchestra

Does God Exist?

The God-Centric Path

From Connection to Harmony

Having learned to love others, the soul now longs for something greater — to understand the unseen design that binds everything together. Every joy, every loss, every connection has been guiding you toward this realization: that nothing stands alone. The same intelligence that moves the stars moves within your breath, your choices, your heartbeats.

Knot Five is where the individual merges with the infinite. It is not about learning something new, but remembering what has always been true — that every encounter, every challenge, every prayer was part of a larger harmony, conducted by a wisdom beyond our own.

Here, we no longer ask *why* things happen. We begin to see *how* they belong. This is the Great Orchestra — where every sound, silence, and soul finds its place in the divine symphony of existence.

As we near the end of this book, we embark on a pivotal exploration—the fifth knot. Without it, the other four knots would leave a critical piece of the puzzle of human suffering unanswered: *Does God exist, and what is the purpose of life?* These questions arise from our innate curiosity to understand our existence, yet many of us avoid confronting them.

Consider this analogy: imagine returning home to find clear signs of a burglary. Would you ignore it and continue your day as if nothing had happened? Of course not. You would investigate, call the authorities, seek answers. Now imagine the authorities dismissing the evidence and insisting, *"Nothing happened here."* Would you simply accept that? Unlikely.

In the same way, when we look at the universe—the galaxies, the laws of physics, the precision of nature—can we truly believe that all of this appeared from nothing? From nothing, nothing can appear. The very presence of *something* demands an origin; every effect requires a cause. The existence of creation, therefore, implies a Creator. To deny this is to accept an impossibility—that order, beauty, and life itself arose without source or intention.

As human beings, we are naturally inclined to seek connections between the what, the why, and the how of everything around us. Consider this book as an example: you engage with it, seeking answers to fundamental questions. What is its purpose? Why was it written? What value does it offer, and how might it enrich your life? These inquiries are foundational to every action we take. Similarly, we contemplate the purpose of various aspects of existence, from the sky above us to the function of our nails—we question everything, driven by an innate curiosity about our world and our place within it.

The creation can never be equal to the Creator, but rather, the creation longs to be reunited with the Creator.

Much like the drop of water that falls from the sky—unsure of its purpose, drifting between faith and uncertainty—so do we. As the drop falls, it wonders: *Does this fall mark the end, or am I becoming something greater?* It mirrors the way we question our purpose, balancing between doubt and faith. Yet, each drop ultimately finds its place—some nourishing the earth, some melting into mountain streams, and others merging into vast oceans.

This is where the true beauty lies: the drop, though small and fleeting, is part of something infinitely greater. A single drop becomes the ocean, just as we, in our journey, merge with something far beyond our individuality. In this, the creation mirrors the Creator's divine plan.

As human beings, we long for love and connection, failing to realize that we are not separate from love—we are love, just as the drop of water is not apart from the ocean but is the ocean. Perhaps that is why God says: *From water, We made every living thing.* Longing for love implies separation, but being love itself is to embody the divine every day.

In the same way, our quest to understand God is not merely about intellectual curiosity; it's about merging into something greater, recognizing that the very essence of life is the Creator's reflection. The miracle of water is not in the ocean but in the essence of each drop. Similarly, the miracle of life is not in the complexity of the universe alone but in the soul of each person, each moment of existence.

As we explore the purpose of life, we are reminded of the connection between the creation and the Creator. Our purpose is to seek that reunion, to understand that we are not accidental beings in an accidental world. Much like the drop of water, we are on a journey of faith and purpose, merging into something far more significant than ourselves—where individuality fades, and unity with the divine emerges.

A true love story, yet untold.

68: The Beginning of the Universe

How did the universe begin? This question of how the universe began leaves us grappling for a starting point, its enormity often rendering us speechless.

I recall a particular night at the age of 14, lying in bed and thinking, *If there is a God, then who created Him? And where exactly is He?*

I often saw my mother raise her hands in prayer, looking upward as she spoke to God, so I assumed he was up there somewhere—but how do we know what up is?

Given the Earth's gravitational pull, everything remains grounded, and considering the planet's orbit and yet not knowing the position of the Earth in the universe, our concepts of up and down are fundamentally challenged.

In space, what we perceive as up could just as well be down. In this context, both directions are equally plausible and equally ambiguous, which shows how little we know. I wasn't sure where all these thoughts originated, but they constantly surfaced, leading me quickly to the conclusion that everything that exists must have a beginning.

I began to explore a variety of viewpoints from different religions, tribes, scientists, philosophers, and gurus, each offering their unique perspective. My goal is not to disprove any particular view but to reassess conventional teachings and encourage an open-minded approach. Let's embark on an intellectual and rational exploration, setting aside emotions and spiritualism. This is crucial because when emotions are involved, we can be biased. Let's strive for clarity and understanding through a more detached, analytical lens.

The universe is in a state of constant expansion, a phenomenon first scientifically validated in 1929 by Edwin Hubble. Using the most powerful telescopes of his time, Hubble observed that galaxies are receding from us at speeds proportional to their distances—a discovery that implies the farther away a galaxy is, the faster it appears to be moving away from us. This discovery suggests that the universe is expanding uniformly in all directions. When we consider this expansion, it implies that if we were to reverse the process, eventually everything would converge into a tiny, dense point.

Let's consider that tiny dense point as our starting point. Before anything can exist, three fundamental components are necessary: time, space, and matter. Time marks the beginning, matter consists of particles, and space provides the environment where these particles can exist.

The interdependence of time, space, and matter suggests that they must have arisen simultaneously—each necessitating the others for their existence. To illustrate, consider the analogy of painting: you need time to plan, space as your canvas, and tools (matter) to paint. The absence of any one of these elements makes painting impossible.

Let's now consider time in a practical sense; time is a tool we use to measure existence. This doesn't imply that time didn't exist before humans; rather, it suggests that an intellectual mind is required to comprehend time. In other words, the universe does not perceive time; it simply exists.

Space is often overlooked because we tend to focus more on the bright, luminous points we see as stars. However, it's essential to recognize that the existence of stars depends on the vast expanses of space around them.

Matter comprises everything that exists, with all matter made up of atoms. Intriguingly, atoms themselves are lifeless. Since everything in existence is composed of atoms, including us, a fundamental question arises: What is the source of life, often referred to as the soul, within the physical form?

It also implies that the human body gradually evolved into an embryo, yet initially showed no signs of life. According to the National Institutes of Health (NIH), the first heartbeat of an embryo begins after the fourth week of gestation. This scientifically confirms that life in the embryo has a beginning. So, what ignited the heart to beat? What energy sparked life into the embryo? Could it be a soul that is injected into the human body and then departs upon death, and if so, by whom?

Turning our attention to the dense point before the universe expanded, a concept widely accepted by scientists as the Big Bang, we acknowledge that everything within time, space, and matter has a beginning and, therefore, likely an end. The Big Bang marked the start of the universe about 13.7 billion years ago, heralding the inception of time. The ongoing expansion of the universe signifies that space also had a beginning. Therefore, matter, composed of lifeless atoms, likewise had a beginning.

Let's revisit the painting analogy. Suppose you have the time to paint, a canvas, and the tools needed. Would the painting create itself? Clearly not—your will is essential. In the realm of painting, it's understood that without your intention, no painting would materialize; if it did, we'd call it magic.

Yet, when considering the creation of the entire universe, with its intricate systems and laws, which itself seems magical, many are inclined to believe it emerged without an Orchestra, that no will was behind it; it simply came into existence. The right question then is: if time, space, and matter are the evidence we see today, who "painted" the universe?

Imagine displaying your painting to people who have never met you. You observe them as they try to interpret it, speculating about its message, your reasons for painting it, and its purpose. As you watch, one person asserts the painting is purposeless; in fact, they claim, no one painted it. Another counters, arguing that the painting itself is proof of the painter's existence. As the discussion unfolds, the majority begin to disregard your existence, despite the evidence right before them. They deny your existence simply because they haven't seen you. How would that make you feel?

Imagine entering a room and noticing nine stones meticulously arranged to mirror our solar system. You might recognize the pattern and think, *This represents our solar system; if this stone is the sun, then these must be the eight planets.* Now, consider this scenario: what if I told you that these stones had flown in through a small gap in an open window and landed in this precise arrangement? You would find it implausible. You'd question how none of the stones scratched the window or how they aligned so accurately without any guidance. Your skepticism would be well-founded; such a scenario is indeed beyond belief, even with simple stones. If we cannot accept that a simple model of our solar system could form by chance, how can we believe that the entire universe, with all its complexity, is merely a product of coincidence?

Now, let's return to the concept of the universe; everything within it serves as evidence of a creator. For the purposes of this discussion, we'll refer to this creator as "X- factor." Let's avoid using the term *God* for now, as it may preempt certain assumptions. Who created the "X"? Is it possible there is more than one creator? These are intriguing questions worth exploring.

For time, space, and matter to exist, it implies that the "X-factor" exists outside these realms, much like you, the painter, exists outside your painting. Consider this fascinating perspective: whatever you paint is fundamentally different from you—you are alive, the painting is lifeless; you possess will and desires, while your painting does not; you think, your painting cannot. Everything we create is essentially the opposite of ourselves.

Just as you are the opposite of your painting, the X-factor is the opposite of everything it has created.

This means that X- factor has no beginning or end, is boundless, has always existed, and is beyond our comprehension. Now, addressing the question: What if there is more than one creator?

If we entertain the notion of multiple creators, we must consider the principle of duality that pervades existence. Everything within time, space, and matter typically exhibits dualistic properties, such as positively charged protons and negatively charged electrons, or the complementarity of masculine and feminine elements. Since the creator exists beyond these dimensions and contrasts sharply with his creation, the oneness of the X- factor becomes a logical necessity. Proposing multiple creators introduces limitations, which contradicts the very essence of the "X-factor" as the ultimate creator. Therefore, the creator must inherently transcend the dualities and limitations of creation.

Reflecting on the universe's origins leads us to consider the complex interactions of time, space, and matter. Scientific evidence suggests that the universe is expanding, indicating that it is not infinite and must have had a beginning. According to the principle that anything which begins to exist has a cause, we must then ask: What kind of cause could bring the universe into existence?

This cause must be transcendent, existing independently from the creation it brought into being. It must be timeless and eternal, having existed before physical time was established. Additionally, it must be immaterial, predating the physical universe. Given the vastness and precision of the universe, this cause must also possess immense power and intelligence. Furthermore, the cause must be caring, having meticulously designed such a hospitable environment for life. Lastly, it must be personal, as the act of creation implies a deliberate choice, not an accidental event.

...

Spiral Upward

I invite you to reflect on your beliefs in light of this discussion. By applying Occam's Razor—a scientific principle favoring simpler explanations over more complex ones—we find that the hypothesis of a singular creator provides a plausible explanation for the universe's origin. This suggests that God, or whatever name we give to this creator, is fundamentally distinct from His creation. This insight emerges not just from faith or spiritual belief, but from a rational and intellectual exploration. I encourage you to contemplate deeply on this reasoning, as it may guide you to similar conclusions.

69: Decode the Messages

If you now consider that the universe must have a creator who shaped everything from nothingness, it's natural to feel overwhelmed. Such a realization can fundamentally shift your perspective on life, propelling you into a deeper quest to understand the intentions behind creation. This journey of discovery can reshape how you view your place in the cosmos and the purpose of existence itself.

Let's revisit the painting analogy once more. Just as you, the artist, are the sole interpreter of its true purpose, so too the infinite artist behind all creation is the only entity capable of fully articulating life's deeper meanings.

Like recognizing a painting as the work of an artist, we can acknowledge the presence of a designer behind the canvas of life. Yet, grasping the full significance of this design demands direct communication from the artist; without this, we risk drowning in assumptions.

The infinite artist might choose to reveal the message in mysterious ways that might not make sense to us at first, but that doesn't change the existence of the creator. Just because the people you were observing gave up trying to analyze the purpose of your painting doesn't mean your painting lacked purpose, right? This teaches us that the presence of a creator's intent doesn't always align with our immediate understanding, yet it exists, influencing and defining the essence of creation.

Imagine discovering an anonymous note left at your door. You can decipher the message based on the language and handwriting used, even if you don't know the author. Suppose the note is written in a foreign language; the message remains, but you would need help translating in order to understand its relevance to you. However, it would be illogical to assume the note was intended for the pets in the building, as they lack the capability to read or write. Similarly, you wouldn't entertain the notion that it was written by someone devoid of intellectual capacity. At first glance, the very existence of the note implies that both the sender and the intended receiver possess intellectual minds.

In a similar way, everything in life can be viewed as a coded message within a formula. Each piece of this cosmic formula is akin to a note, and it is our responsibility to decode it. The message is always there; understanding it is our task. Let's explore how this applies.

Decoding the Formula of Life

Just as a note can be decoded, so too can many aspects of life be understood through careful analysis. Consider water, for instance, which can be broken down into its molecular formula, H_2O. This formula reveals that water is composed of one oxygen and two hydrogen atoms, linked by covalent bonds. The existence of such a precise formula suggests that an intelligent mind established what we now recognize as the laws of physics. Yet, it requires another intelligent mind to comprehend and interpret this arrangement. In other words, water itself cannot understand its own composition because it lacks the cognitive capabilities. Therefore, the molecular structure of water isn't a message for the water itself, but a message for humans to decipher and understand.

The Human Struggle

The creator not only embedded messages in every aspect of creation but also endowed humans with an intrinsic curiosity to seek understanding. Unlike inanimate elements like water and the sun, humans possess the unique ability to question and search for purpose. We continuously ponder the meaning behind our existence and strive to decipher the world around us, propelling us upward in our life's spiral. This innate curiosity stems from an understanding that the messages woven into the fabric of life are meant for us to interpret. We alone are equipped to unravel the purposes behind the intricate behaviors of bees, the growth patterns of trees, and the broader phenomena of life. This realization underscores our exceptional role in the grand design of the universe.

The Existence of an Intelligent Mind

While we may not fully comprehend or articulate the intelligence orchestrating everything, we cannot ignore its presence or the messages it imparts. The note serves as a reminder of a greater power guiding and shaping the intricate dance of the universe. Just as the note is crafted with a specific intent, every aspect of life—from the smallest organisms to the expansive cosmos—bears a message. It is our responsibility to decode and interpret these messages, enabling us to appreciate the beauty and complexity of creation.

Reflecting on the Divine Favors

As we decode the messages embedded in life, it's important to pause and reflect on the blessings bestowed upon us by a higher power. Each day, we are graced with countless gifts, both visible and hidden. Every detail, from the air we breathe to the relationships we treasure, has been meticulously crafted. Through this process of interpretation, we develop a deeper appreciation for the wonders of existence and the divine intelligence that orchestrates it all.

...

Spiral Upward

Life is akin to a symphony; each note is a message awaiting your keen interpretation. Just as an anonymous note piques curiosity and stimulates the intellect, so too does the world around you invite you to unravel its mysteries. By recognizing that every facet of existence carries a message hinting at a higher purpose, you embark on a journey of discovery and enlightenment. While the intelligence behind it all may be elusive, take comfort in knowing that these messages are intended specifically for you. As you delve into the purposes behind the existence of bees, trees, and life itself, you forge a deep connection with the divine. Remember, you are not alone in deciphering the symphony of life.

70: Thinking Has Different Planes

To observe reality is to see its surface, but to understand it is to touch its soul. Sight reveals form, yet thinking unveils meaning—and thinking itself unfolds upon three planes: **basic, deep**, and **transcendent**. These are not merely levels of intellect but gateways of consciousness, each shaping how we perceive the world and who we are becoming within it.

Wisdom mirrors the ocean. Its surface welcomes all, glimmering with the comfort of the known. But as one dares to descend, the water thickens, the currents strengthen, and silence begins to speak. In those depths, light bends differently. Here, truth is not read—*it is felt*.

To think deeply is to dive beyond the surface of existence, and to think transcendentally is to touch the very rhythm of the Great Orchestra—the divine intelligence that moves through all creation. Such thought demands discipline, openness, and courage, for the deeper we go, the more the illusions dissolve, and the clearer the melody of truth becomes.

The ocean does not change as you dive deeper; **you** do. And in that transformation lies the beginning of wisdom.

The Three Planes of Thinking

Basic thinking is perception. It is the first opening of the window to the world, where we encounter reality in its simplest form. At this level, the mind observes without questioning; it accepts what the senses reveal and processes information directly. Here, understanding is rooted in the tangible—the fire burns, the water quenches thirst, and life appears as it is seen. It is the realm of the immediate and the evident, where truth is measured by sight and experience. Yet even this simplicity is sacred, for it forms the foundation upon which all deeper and higher thinking begins.

Deep thinking is illumination in motion. It is the act of stepping through the window of perception to separate truth from illusion, cause from effect. At this level, the mind no longer drifts upon appearances—it begins to dive beneath them, tracing the invisible threads that bind all things together. Here, we analyze not merely to conclude, but to *understand*. We seek the patterns, meanings, and purposes hidden beneath the surface of events. Such thinking demands stillness of mind, openness of heart, and the humility to see beyond the narrow horizon of our own perspective.

Transcendent thinking is surrender. It is the quiet dissolving of the self into the vastness beyond the window—where separation fades and all of existence reveals itself as one. In this realm, the mind no longer seeks to control or define; it simply *beholds*. Here, the boundaries that once shaped your identity—how you were raised, what you believe, how you feel—lose their grip. Emotion, memory, and perception no longer dictate truth; they simply fall silent before it. You do not interpret reality—you *merge* with it. At this depth, thinking rises beyond intellect and becomes wisdom. It touches the eternal questions that echo through every soul: *Who are we? Why do we exist? How are we woven into the fabric of creation?* This is the plane of awakening, where the seeker and the truth are no longer two. To think transcendentally is not to reach outward, but to return inward—to the divine intelligence that breathes through all things, the Great Orchestra itself.

Making It Practical

- At the **basic level**, the ocean is simply a place to swim— salty, restless water where one learns only to float or sink. It is experienced, but not yet understood.

- At the **deep level**, the ocean becomes a field of inquiry. We begin to study its patterns, its chemistry, its living ecosystems, and the hidden currents that move beneath the surface. Knowledge grows, but it still observes from a distance.

- At the **transcendent level,** the question itself transforms. We no longer ask *what* the ocean is, but *why* it is. Why water—of all elements—as the vessel of life? What truth does its endless depth whisper about existence itself?

- Each level of thinking expands not only our understanding, but our very way of being. As we descend from surface awareness to transcendent insight, we don't just learn about life—we begin to *participate* in its mystery.

The Particles of Reality

At the surface, reality feels fixed and obvious. With deeper thought, we learn it can be influenced, shaped, even directed by choice and intention. But at the transcendent level, reality itself begins to dissolve into mystery.

Modern physics offers startling proof of this. Consider the observer effect: when electrons are observed, they move predictably; when unobserved, they scatter unpredictably. Observation changes behavior. Consciousness does not merely witness reality — it interacts with it.

This truth echoes what spiritual traditions have taught for centuries. Islam describes existence as vibration: every thought, intention, and remembrance sends ripples into the unseen. The Qur'an reminds us: "Indeed, in the remembrance of God do hearts find rest." That remembrance is not passive — it reshapes our inner rhythm and perhaps even the very particles that compose reality.

If fear vibrates louder than trust, fear manifests as reality. If intention vibrates stronger than doubt, life bends toward that intention. The resonance we emit is the life we attract. Both science and mysticism converge here: the world outside is never separate from the world within.

Attempts to force joy rarely succeed, for effort born of tension carries the vibration of struggle—and struggle only multiplies itself. True joy cannot be manufactured; it must be *aligned.*

The key lies in choosing gratitude, hope, and surrender. These are not acts of weakness but of harmony, tuning the soul to the rhythm of divine order. Just as prayer does not command the Divine but opens the heart to His will, so too does alignment invite joy to flow naturally, without resistance. Transcendent thinking reminds the mind of its sacred dependence on a higher order—an order sustained by Him alone. In surrender, struggle dissolves, and what remains is peace: the quiet recognition that all things unfold as they are meant to.

Even quantum entanglement reflects this unity: two particles, separated by great distances, still move in harmony, as though connected by an invisible thread. The mystics would say: so it is with souls, bound within one divine tapestry of creation. What touches one, in some way, touches all — by the wisdom of the One who sustains them. Therefore, transcendent thinking is not simply higher reasoning — it is higher living. Reality is participatory. It bends not only to what we do, but to the energy of who we are.

The Great Orchestra

Think of existence as a vast orchestra. Basic thinking hears only noise—many instruments playing at once without order or meaning. Deep thinking begins to notice patterns: moments of harmony and dissonance, melody and rhythm, cause and effect. But transcendent thinking hears the full symphony—the rise and fall of every note, the purpose behind every silence, and the invisible connection that unites them all. Every sound, every pause, every instrument has a place in this grand composition. Nothing plays alone; everything contributes to a masterpiece far greater than itself. At this level, life no longer appears random. Design reveals itself in the smallest details, meaning shines through the quietest moments, and unity is found even within contrast. You realize you were never merely an audience member; you were created to *respond* to the music. Your life reflects the divine rhythm, your choices echo within the vast harmony conducted by the Great Orchestra.

...

Spiral Upward

Your perception of the world is inseparable from the level of thought you cultivate. Without elevating your consciousness, transcendent thinking—the pinnacle of awareness—remains beyond reach. But as you rise through these planes, you begin to see existence not in fragments but in wholeness: creation united in its dependence on the Creator, each part fulfilling its role within His design. Therefore, we must strive to rise beyond the basic and deep planes of thought, and ascend into transcendent thinking. For it is there that we encounter God—not as an abstract idea, but as the living truth that illuminates every atom of existence.

At this level, faith and intellect no longer stand apart but converge, harmonizing reason with revelation, logic with love, and knowledge with worship. Every question points back to its Source. Every mystery reflects its Maker. Every longing is answered in the Divine.

Every time you choose to think deeper, you spiral upward. Every time you align your vibration with truth, gratitude, and love, you spiral upward. And in transcendent thinking, you discover what was missing all along—that the final key to understanding existence is not out there, but within your own mind.

It is here, at the highest plane of thought, that the restless mind finds stillness, the doubting heart finds clarity, and the weary soul finds home. For in transcendent thinking, we do not merely think about God—we find Him, intellectually, spiritually, and existentially. And in finding Him, we finally find ourselves.

71: The Source of Wisdom

As we explore the layers of thinking, we find that even at a transcendent level, we discover the limits of our understanding. This journey into wisdom is humbling; it quiets us, making us speak less, even as our knowledge expands. Wisdom carries a significant weight—it is both vast and infinite. This might explain why one of God's names is the All-Knower, symbolizing that He is the ultimate source of wisdom. Wisdom, then, did not originate from us; it existed before us. We do not invent wisdom; we discover it. And perhaps, this is why the pursuit of wisdom so often leads us toward a divine connection with God.

Understanding is the foundation of love. Whatever we do not fully understand, we cannot deeply love. Hence, God is wisdom itself, then the only way to draw closer to Him is by elevating ourselves in wisdom. The higher we ascend in wisdom, the better we understand God; the better we understand God, the more deeply we can love Him. Therefore, we must question everything, because within the answers lie glimpses of God's wisdom and signs.

Human existence is a complex puzzle, with experiences, emotions, and reflections shaping us into unique beings as distinct as our fingerprints. We stand apart based on what we know, for knowledge shapes our actions and ultimately our lives—a truly fascinating concept. As we gradually unfold the layers of understanding in life, the truth, like a gift, awaits our discovery.

The beautiful part is that lives unfold within two distinct spheres: control and surrender, or will and faith. A significant portion of our existence is shaped by faith, which signifies the will of God. This suggests that we are all being guided toward wisdom in one way or another, affirming that we are never truly alone.

This might explain why wisdom is held in high esteem as a noble virtue across cultures and philosophies. It transcends knowledge and intelligence; wisdom necessitates a deep exploration of life's intricacies and a deep understanding of human nature. Those endowed with wisdom bear the responsibility to offer guidance and insights, profoundly impacting the lives of others.

But how do we gain wisdom?

To answer this question, we must first examine the process of thinking and judging reality. Effective judgment of any reality requires several key elements:

- **A tangible reality** — something that exists independently and can be observed or measured.

- **Our senses** — the instruments through which we perceive and gather information about that reality.

- **A sound and healthy mind** — capable of processing, reasoning, and interpreting the sensory information.

- **Prior knowledge and experience** — the framework that shapes how we understand, connect, and give meaning to what we perceive.

Consider a practical scenario: imagine I'm holding something behind my back and ask you to guess what it is. Without seeing it, your guess would be based purely on speculation. Now, suppose I reveal that it's a Chinese dictionary. If your vision is impaired, you might still struggle to perceive it accurately, affecting your ability to judge what it is. Even if you can see clearly, if your brain isn't processing information correctly, you may look at the dictionary but not be able to understand or process that it is indeed a dictionary.

Let's say your senses and brain are functioning adequately, and you recognize from the cover that it's a Chinese dictionary. However, without prior knowledge of the Chinese language, you'd be unable to understand a single word inside it. Imagine I allow anyone to help you, as long as they don't speak Chinese. Could you translate a word without guessing? Likely not, even given a lifetime.

This scenario reveals that true wisdom transcends sensory perception and ordinary knowledge—it depends on prior information, on something that precedes human experience itself. If the first human had emerged from a womb, then whose womb was it? Who named the stars, the rivers, and the creatures before him? Who taught him the meaning of language, of self, of existence?

Such understanding could not have arisen from nothingness. It points to an origin where the first human was not born but *brought forth*—complete in form, mind, and purpose. His wisdom was not learned but bestowed. For wisdom does not originate from within humanity; it flows from a higher source. It is the signature of a transcendent intelligence—the Great Orchestra himself—who composed the harmony of creation and whispered knowledge into the human soul.

...

Spiral Upward

Always pursue wisdom, for it is a journey that stretches beyond the limits of human capacity. True wisdom is not merely gathered through experience; it is drawn from the Great Orchestra of existence, the eternal source from which all understanding flows.

Reflect on the vastness of time. The Earth has turned for nearly 4.5 billion years, while humanity has walked upon it for only a fleeting moment, barely 200,000 years. Whenever you feel enlightened or believe you have grasped the essence of truth, imagine dipping your finger into the ocean and pulling it out. The droplets that cling to your skin represent the sum of human wisdom; the ocean that remains is the infinite intelligence of creation itself.

Let this awareness humble you, yet also ignite your thirst to seek not just knowledge but the wisdom that echoes from eternity. In that pursuit, you align yourself with the harmony of the Great Orchestra, and your understanding becomes part of its divine symphony.

72: Divine Guidance

One morning during my fifteenth year, I awoke from a dream so vivid and powerful that it haunted me for days. Eventually, I decided to discuss it with my mother. "Nana," I began cautiously, "I had a dream that I think was a calling to Christianity." Bear in mind, I was raised as a Muslim. My words hung in the air, leaving her momentarily speechless. When she regained her composure, her curiosity was piqued. "What happened in your dream?" she asked gently.

I described the setting to her: It was a serene Friday afternoon, and our entire family was gathered in a park, basking in peace. Suddenly, a sound like a deafening horn echoed—a sound humanity recognized instantly as the trumpet of Judgment Day. Panic and chaos erupted rapidly, with people running in all directions, though escape seemed hopeless. My surroundings devolved into a scene of indescribable horror. I, too, found myself running until the ground beneath me crumbled into dust. Collapsing onto the ground, I resorted to crawling on my elbows. To my astonishment, I encountered bare feet just before me. As I raised my gaze, I realized it was Jesus. Instinctively, I pressed my lips to his feet. He reached for the soil beside me, gently stroked it through my hair, and then I awoke.

This dream marked the beginning of my profound journey into exploring various religions and life philosophies. Later, as I delved deeper into the Quran and Islamic narrations, I encountered verses describing the events of Judgment Day. To my astonishment, I found striking parallels between my dream and these descriptions—the appointed day, the trumpet-blowing angel, the onset of chaos, and even the return of Jesus. These discoveries left me in awe and deepened my reflection on life's ultimate truths.

The Quran vividly describes the cataclysmic moment when the Trumpet is blown, initiating the Day of Judgment:

- **Surah Az-Zumar (39:68):**
  "And the Trumpet will be blown, and all who are in the heavens and all who are on the earth will fall dead, except whom Allah wills. Then it will be blown again, and behold, they will be standing, looking on."

- **Surah Al-Haqqah (69:13-15):**
  "Then when the Trumpet is blown with a single blast, and the earth and the mountains are lifted and leveled with one blow—then on that Day, the Event will occur."

These verses vividly align with the imagery of a deafening sound, the ensuing chaos, and the inevitable collapse described in my dream.

The Quran also captures the overwhelming panic and terror that will seize humanity on that fateful day:

- **Surah Al-Hajj (22:1-2):**
  "O mankind, fear your Lord. Indeed, the convulsion of the [final] Hour is a terrible thing. On the Day you see it, every nursing mother will be distracted from that [child] she was nursing, and every pregnant woman will abort her pregnancy, and you will see the people [appearing] intoxicated while they are not intoxicated; but the punishment of Allah is severe."

These verses mirror the fear and chaos I witnessed in my dream, where humanity's sense of control shattered in the face of an overwhelming divine reality.

The return of Jesus is a significant event mentioned in the Quran, resonating deeply with the encounter in my dream:

- **Surah Az-Zukhruf (43:61):**

  "And indeed, he [Jesus] will be a sign for [the coming of] the Hour, so be not in doubt about it, and follow Me. This is a straight path."

- **Surah Aal-e-Imran (3:55):**

  "When Allah said, 'O Jesus, indeed I will take you and raise you to Myself and purify you from those who disbelieve and make those who follow you [in submission to Allah] superior to those who disbelieve until the Day of Resurrection. Then to Me is your return, and I will judge between you concerning that in which you used to differ.'"

- **Surah An-Nisa (4:157-159):**

  "And [for] their saying, 'Indeed, we have killed the Messiah, Jesus, the son of Mary, the messenger of Allah.' And they did not kill him, nor did they crucify him; but [another] was made to resemble him to them. And indeed, those who differ over it are in doubt about it. They have no knowledge of it except the following of assumption. And they did not kill him, for certain. Rather, Allah raised him to Himself. And ever is Allah Exalted in Might and Wise. And there is none from the People of the Scripture but that he will surely believe in him before his death. And on the Day of Resurrection, he will be against them a witness."

In my dream, the appearance of Jesus brought both awe and reverence, reflecting the Quranic emphasis on his role on the Day of Resurrection. The vividness of these descriptions left me astounded; how could I dream so vividly about something I had never even thought of?

This dream ignited a journey to intellectually and rationally connect with God. It was a search for evidence of His existence—a quest that has spanned over two decades of dedicated study. For me, this dream represents divine guidance.

Just as the eyes are made to see, ears are made to hear, and the brain is made to think, everything in existence serves a purpose. I equally believe that humanity's biggest questions are there for a reason. Perhaps this is why humanity is driven to seek meaning in life—to make sense of it all. Not being able to answer these questions or suppressing them leads to one of the greatest sources of human suffering. We try to fill the void within ourselves with pursuits that do not resonate with both the mind and the heart.

By alignment with the mind and the heart, I mean a rational pursuit supported by evidence that also brings inner peace. Consider the analogy of a magnificent statue being presented as God for worship but made with human hands. Rationally, it defies logic to worship a creation as the Creator. Seeking protection from an object that cannot even protect itself doesn't bring peace to the heart. Therefore, both the mind and heart must be in harmony, guiding our understanding and actions.

Another example is Darwin's theory of evolution attempts to describe how life diversified, yet even this process remains incomplete and unproven. The so-called "missing link" between species continues to elude discovery, leaving vast gaps in our understanding of how one form of life transitions into another. More profoundly, the theory offers no explanation for how the very first spark of life emerged from non-living matter—a question that stands at the heart of existence itself. To this day, there is no universally accepted scientific theory that explains how consciousness and life arose from chemistry alone. Therefore, evolution may outline fragments of life's story, but it fails to address its origin or essence—offering neither rational completion to the mind nor lasting peace to the heart.

The existence of an intelligent force is woven through the very fabric of reality. Even if our minds cannot fully grasp its magnitude, its traces are undeniable. Just as footprints in fresh snow reveal the passage of someone unseen, the patterns, precision, and harmony of our world reveal a mind behind the movement. Every law of physics, every rhythm of nature, every breath of life whispers of design, not accident. This silent intelligence orchestrates existence—from the pulse of an atom to the dance of galaxies—inviting us to listen, to observe, and to interpret the language through which creation speaks.

I perceive this message as a love letter imbued with guidance—We all receive guidance in various ways, tailored to our unique circumstances and journeys. In my understanding, the way we are guided does not make us special; rather, it is how this guidance shapes our actions and transforms our character that defines our uniqueness. True significance lies in how we respond to this divine nudge—whether we choose to grow, reflect, and act in alignment with our higher purpose.

...

Spiral Upward

Life is filled with divine guidance; you simply need to observe it. This guidance is hidden in how the skies pour drinking water, the mountains are firmly rooted beneath the earth, and in the remarkable creation of the camel. Recognizing that every aspect of existence carries a message from the divine is essential. The origin of the first life from non-living chemicals doesn't make sense and therefore doesn't align with the mind or the heart. The origin of first life can only blossom from the source of life—the one true Creator who exists beyond time, space, and matter.

73: Explore the Depths of Explanation

Allow me to ask a question that appears simple yet hides profound depth: What is the difference between describing and explaining?

To describe is to tell what something looks like, to outline its features so others may picture it in their minds. To explain, however, is to pierce deeper—it is to reveal the hidden "why" and "how," the forces and purposes that lie beneath appearances.

Take the camel. We can describe its broad, padded feet that keep it from sinking in sand, its long lashes shielding its eyes from storms, or its hump rising like a monument on its back. These details are useful, even fascinating. But description only scratches the surface. True wonder awakens when we explain: how its body can drink forty gallons of water at once and endure days without another drop; how its kidneys conserve every ounce of moisture, producing dry waste so nothing is lost; how its hump stores fat that can be transformed into water and energy; how its body tolerates desert extremes—from freezing nights to burning days—without breaking. Even its milk, rich in vitamin C and minerals, sustains life where little else survives.

Through description the camel may seem odd, but through explanation it becomes sublime—a creature whose every detail speaks of intentional design.

Now consider the fly. At first, nothing seems more ordinary—perhaps even bothersome. Yet move from description to explanation, and the ordinary becomes astonishing. Its wings beat faster than the blink of an eye, carrying it in dizzying patterns no human eye can fully trace. Its compound eyes perceive hundreds of angles at once, granting it a vision far beyond our own. Within its tiny frame exist systems of flight, digestion, and reproduction—each more intricate than the most advanced machines we have ever built.

Think about this: one of humanity's greatest accomplishments is the invention of the airplane. We marvel at its engineering, its weight defying gravity, its ability to carry hundreds across continents. Yet imagine if we could build an airplane the size of a fly, with wings that move faster than thought, with sensors that perceive the world in hundreds of directions at once, with self-repairing systems and perfect energy efficiency. We cannot.

So I challenge you: go deeper. First describe the fly, then explain it—and I promise, you will never see a fly the same way again.

And what about us? Most of humanity suffers from a mere description of existence: we are born, we grow, we work, we die. This shallow view blinds us from the true beauty of existence. But where is the explanation? Science tells us nothing can arise from nothing, yet here we are—the pinnacle of complexity and consciousness. Such a paradox cannot be ignored; it demands an answer. Perhaps it points to a divine Creator, and if so, then our lives carry a weight far beyond our ambitions and dreams. That possibility is unsettling—for it forces us to ask not only what we are, but why we are.

Yet overwhelming as it may be, we cannot turn away. There is a truth waiting to be unveiled. A life lived only in description is flat and soulless. A sunset described is merely the sun descending; a sunset experienced is a symphony of light and time unfolding before our eyes. In the end, all true explanations lead us upward, toward the Great Orchestra—the grand harmony in which every note of existence finds its place.

...

Spiral Upward

Do not settle for mere descriptions of existence—there is no beauty in that. The magic lies in the explanation. To accept that intelligent life arose from an unintelligent origin is like claiming that water came from sand. Such a paradox demands more than passive acceptance; it calls for fearless inquiry.

This pursuit is the key to unlocking reality's hidden depths. It will compel you to confront your deepest fears, dismantle your oldest assumptions, and strip away the veil of the ordinary to reveal the truths beneath. Commit to this path, and your life will rise to a higher vibration.

And as you ascend the spiral of existence, you will begin to see the intricate interconnectedness of all things—the breathtaking beauty of a world that was always before you, but never truly seen.

74: Seeking Purpose

Sometimes, to transcend upward, we must look inward. What if the answer to why we seek purpose in life is embedded within our biological essence? We did not create ourselves; rather, we were crafted by a higher power, perfect in our imperfection, and destined for a purpose. Could it be that our imperfections are designed to bridge the gap between ourselves and God?

To understand human behavior more deeply, let's explore the instinctive needs that drive our actions toward purpose. The first is the survival instinct, which motivates us to overcome life's challenges, especially when we face any type of danger. Every cell in our body is a marvel, perfectly engineered with complex defense mechanisms to protect, repair, and rejuvenate itself.

The second is the social instinct, compelling us to forge relationships and build communities. This instinct arises from both a need for companionship and the survival of our species.

The third is the worship instinct. Humans have an inherent pull toward worshiping transcendent entities, often manifesting in religious or spiritual practices. This reflects a surrender to a higher power, indicating an inherent aspect of our nature.

These instincts are universal to all humans; however, their fulfillment varies widely. Some people suppress or substitute these needs with other things, but because they are inherently part of our nature, they will always resurface. Perhaps our purpose lies in understanding why God created us with these instincts to begin with. Interestingly, engaging with these instincts often leads us toward a divine path, suggesting that they are not just aspects of human nature but also bridges to higher understanding.

Therefore, everything we engage with in life must have a purpose; without it, we tend to disengage. This may explain why a lack of purpose often leaves us feeling insignificant and contributes to human misery. After all, can bees, with their single-minded dedication to their roles, truly be more purposeful than humans?

The key distinction lies in our capacity for reflection. Unlike bees, who are bound to their roles by instinct, humans can ponder their purpose. Armed with free will, we hold the power to either save or destroy our planet, depending on how we choose to fulfill—or neglect—our roles.

So how do we correctly understand our purpose? Just like a single bee fulfills its daily purpose, collectively, it significantly impacts the entire ecosystem. Similarly, we need to comprehend not only our purpose but also the broader purpose of our existence within the totality of life.

To illustrate this concept, consider a competitive team game: the ultimate goal is victory, and each player's unique role is pivotal to achieving this overarching aim. However, victory becomes elusive if players do not fully grasp their roles and the game's purpose. It is therefore crucial that the game's creator, who established the rules and objectives, imparts this knowledge. Seeking guidance from any source other than the creator risks misunderstanding the game's true intent, potentially leading us astray.

Similarly, understanding the broader purpose of life is essential before we can fully realize our individual roles within it. This understanding leads us to a crucial question: from where and whom should we seek guidance in this challenging pursuit?

It's no secret that many of us have taken it upon ourselves to search for our purpose within the confines of time, space, and matter, yet we often find ourselves feeling insignificant and without purpose. For years, I grappled with this persistent void, striving to understand it. It wasn't until I approached the question with transcendent thinking that a new perspective began to emerge, offering a glimpse into a broader, more meaningful existence.

As we've learned from previous life lessons, it is a fundamental truth that everything within time, space, and matter is composed of atoms. These minuscule building blocks form the foundation of our physical reality, shaping everything from the air we breathe to the majestic mountains we admire. Science teaches us that 99.99 percent of an atom is space, with the remainder consisting of protons, electrons, and neutrons. The illusion of solidity that atoms present is simply due to the rapid vibration of these particles.

In light of this, when we seek purpose within the confines of time, space, and matter, we are, in essence, grasping at emptiness. Perhaps this is why nothing in this world completely satisfies us. True fulfillment, therefore, must lie beyond these limits.

Now, to address the question: From whom should we seek guidance? The creator of life, responsible for defining the purpose of life and its rules, is the ultimate source of this wisdom. Attempting to define our purpose on our own could lead to chaos, as each person has different ideas and perspectives on how life should be lived.

The wisdom behind our purpose lies in the realm of the infinite, with the creator who is whole and encompasses all, unlike creation, which is inherently marked by emptiness.

Acknowledging that the fulfillment we yearn for surpasses the emptiness of mere creation opens us to embark on a profound spiritual journey. This acceptance confirms the presence of a higher power. God can reveal the purpose of our existence either directly or through chosen individuals. Since there has been no direct revelation to all of humankind at once, it logically follows that we must rely on the second option. We seek understanding through those chosen to convey His intentions, with direct proof that they are indeed the messengers of God. Ultimately, however, it remains our responsibility to actively seek out this purpose.

...

Spiral Upward

The purpose of life can't be grasped from within time, space, and matter. Realizing that atoms, the building blocks of our universe, are predominantly empty space provides a powerful metaphor for the emptiness often felt in life. Rather than letting this emptiness lead to dissatisfaction, shift your focus toward the divine creator—the source of completeness and genuine fulfillment. By acknowledging your inherent connection to God and nurturing your spiritual growth, you empower yourself to rise above the material realm. This transcendence allows you to discover enduring joy, purpose, and peace that far outweigh any temporary challenges.

75: Find Your Purpose

We have arrived at the final life lesson, and I am profoundly grateful for your unwavering companionship. By now, you know me deeply—perhaps even more intimately than those dearest to me. Much of what I have endured has remained unspoken, hidden even from those who love me most, for fear my pain might weigh too heavily upon their hearts. But I see now that keeping it to myself was a mistake.

Pain is not merely ours to endure; it is the soil where wisdom takes root. And when pain is understood, it is transformed into wisdom—and wisdom is the greatest charity. For what greater gift can one human being offer another than to help them rise, not by carrying them, but by teaching them to carry themselves? To heal someone's wound is mercy; to help them discover their own strength to heal is virtue of the highest kind.

And so these pains are not mine alone. They belong to you as well. You have the right to witness them, to learn from them, to rise beyond them—and to carve your own path toward understanding and peace. If my pain becomes your wisdom, then it has served its purpose. If my scars become your light, then they were never in vain.

This is the moment to unlock your full potential and embrace the calling that is yours alone. Just as the work of a single bee may seem small, yet sustains the balance of life, so too does your presence—though it may at times feel insignificant—remain an irreplaceable thread in the grand design of existence.

Everything in creation is born with a gift perfectly aligned to its purpose—a purpose meant to serve something greater, like a vast symphony in which every note, every instrument, plays in harmony with the whole. In the same way, our body, heart, mind, and eyes are gifts with meaning, given not merely for themselves, but to serve the highest truth of who we are.

Lessons from Nature

Consider the sun, the moon, and the trees. Their existence and contributions are not self-serving; their gifts enrich and sustain life around them. Take water, for example, one of the essential sources of life. It doesn't cling to where it has been, nor does it hesitate to go where it's needed. It moves not for its own gain, but so that others may thrive. Water teaches us that our purpose often lies in movement—in our willingness to adapt, connect, and sustain others through our journey.

Consider the flower, delicate yet resilient. Its nectar and pollen are offered freely to pollinators, enabling the cycle of life to continue. The flower may never witness the fruits of its gift, yet its existence sustains the entire ecosystem. It reminds us that sometimes, our greatest purpose is to give without expectation and to sow seeds of impact we may never see. And then there is the river, which never stops flowing. It delivers fresh water to distant lands, bringing life to fields, forests, and every living thing it touches along its journey.

Even when faced with obstacles—rocks, hills, or dams—the river finds a way. It teaches us that our purpose doesn't fade in the face of challenges; instead, it grows stronger as we discover new paths to serve others. So, what is our gift, and who is it for? It can't be for Mother Nature, as it has survived eons without us. On the contrary, humanity depends entirely on nature for its survival.

Your Gift and Purpose

Just as water flows, flowers bloom, and rivers run, we too have a gift—a purpose. But here's the truth: our gifts, your gifts, are not here to serve your ego. Even in death, whales provide for over 12,000 organisms through their "whale fall," embodying nature's ultimate act of giving. Your words, talents, and love—these are the waters that sustain those around you. Your ideas, creativity, and kindness—these are the nectar that nurtures dreams and futures. And your resilience, determination, and ability to rise—these are the rivers that guide others when they feel lost. These are your gifts, and your purpose is to reflect the divine: to give without condition, love without expectation, and be a light in the world.

Our purpose is intrinsically tied to the unique gifts we possess, and our gifts are never truly for ourselves—they exist to serve others. Our intelligence, our ability to think, and our free will set us apart from everything else in existence, but their true value lies in how we use them. Are we using our intelligence to unlock the secrets of existence and understand our purpose, or are we driven by greed, focused solely on improving our own lives?

Are we exercising our free will to enhance life as a whole—from how we treat the vulnerable among us to how we preserve the ecosystems that sustain us—or are we neglecting the interconnectedness of all things? The truth is, humanity is suffering, hearts are whispering, and tears are flooding. The world is heading in the wrong direction, and your gift is needed.

So, how will you flow?
How will you bloom?
How will you persist?

Trusting the Infinite Artist

Watching an artist at work reveals a quiet magic. In the beginning, as the first strokes touch the canvas, there seems to be no clear purpose— only scattered colors, shapes without meaning. The early stages may feel chaotic, even trivial.

But with time, the artist's hand moves with intention, weaving brushstrokes into patterns. What once appeared aimless begins to form a composition that captivates the eye and stirs the soul.

Our lives unfold in much the same way. Like a painting, reality holds intricate designs that often escape our notice at first. We move through our days—meeting challenges, navigating uncertainty, gathering moments—rarely aware of the larger tapestry being woven.

Yet, just as an artist's vision emerges with each deliberate stroke, so too is our purpose interlaced into the fabric of our lives by the Infinite Artist—the One who crafted all things into being. With perfect precision, the Infinite Artist blends color with shadow, joy with sorrow, and triumph with trial, shaping a unique expression of existence within each of us.

To glimpse the fullness of our purpose, we must learn to see in two ways: close enough to notice the fine details, yet far enough to behold the entire canvas.

Your gift, like every gift in nature, was never meant for you alone. A river does not drink its own water; a tree does not eat its own fruit. Your purpose is to discover your gift and channel it toward the service of others. In doing so, you align with the natural harmony of existence.

By stepping back from life's immediacy, we begin to discern the hidden patterns—moments of reflection that reveal how even chaos holds its place in the design. Fragments that once seemed unrelated merge into a whole.

Life unfolds one moment at a time, often without clarity on how the pieces fit together. Only when we look back do we begin to see the threads of meaning—how every joy, loss, delay, and breakthrough was woven into a larger plan.

To live well is to trust this process. Through both high and low tides, through gains and losses, we hold faith that there is intention behind it all. What feels meaningless today may tomorrow prove essential to the beauty of the whole.

For just as an artist pours vision and soul into every creation, so too does the Infinite Artist shape our days with purpose. Though we may not always understand the meaning in the moment, time will unveil the truth. And when the patterns finally emerge, we will see not randomness, but art—intricate, intentional, and alive with the richness of the journey.

...

Spiral Upward

Live as both the artist and the observer. Treasure the delicate brush-strokes that compose your life, and trust that from chaos, clarity will one day emerge. By holding two perspectives—seeing each detail and beholding the whole—you begin to uncover hidden meanings and glimpse the shape of your purpose.

Know that your gift is not merely yours to keep; it is your offering to the world. In giving it, your purpose will reveal itself. Let this truth steady you in both storms and still waters. And when the night feels deepest, remember: you are the spark. Light the path before you. Take the first step. Watch as the way rises to meet your feet, and feel yourself spiraling upward into the life you were always meant to live.

Exercise: Write a letter to your future self, summarizing the key lessons you've taken from the book and your intentions for living a more harmonious and purposeful life. Seal the letter and set a reminder to open it in six months.

The Return to Stillness

And so, the spiral continues. Every truth you have met along the way — every moment of doubt, courage, and surrender — was never random. Each played its note in the great symphony that is your becoming. You have learned that growth is not a race upward, but a rhythm — expansion and return, ascent and rest. Even as you rise, life invites you to pause, to breathe, to be.

Even as you rise, life invites you to pause, to breathe, to be. You were never moving away from yourself, only closer. Every lesson, every love, every loss was guiding you home — to the still point within, where the soul meets its Source. There, in that peace, the journey begins again. For life is not a single climb but an eternal unfolding — a spiral upward, forever reaching, forever returning, forever becoming. Because God's wisdom is infinite, and we can never grasp what has no end. We rise to understand, only to find there is more to know, more to love, more to become. And so the spiral continues — each turn drawing us closer to the One who is whole.

Life Is a Game

Imagine being handed a chessboard without instructions. You're intrigued, curious even—but quickly overwhelmed. No rules, no strategy—just pieces on a board and the pressure to play.

Now imagine you do know how to play. You understand the rules, the goals, the strategies. The game isn't suddenly easy—it becomes meaningful. The challenges remain. The complexity remains. But now, you're not lost. You're engaged. You're growing. This is life.

And here is the paradox: life is not a game, yet it must be played like one. It is not meaningless, but it must be carried with a spirit of play. Without joy, struggle hardens into bitterness. Without purpose, play collapses into distraction. To live fully, we must hold both—the seriousness of purpose and the lightness of play.

Without an understanding of life's principles, we stumble through our days disoriented and defeated. With clarity, life does not become effortless—it becomes purposeful. Knowing the "rules" doesn't remove the obstacles; it redefines their value.

If chess had no challenges, it wouldn't be worth playing. Its brilliance lies in the struggle. Every obstacle is what gives each move weight. And the same is true in life. Without trials, there is no triumph. Without sorrow, no depth to joy. Yet we are taught to treat opposites as enemies: ease is good, struggle is bad; smiles are welcome, tears must be hidden. As if one could exist without the other. But this is the illusion.

There is no joy without sorrow. No light without darkness. No peace without pain. What appears to be separation is, in fact, unity—each side completing the other. Together, they form the full spectrum of what it means to be alive. We chase comfort while fleeing discomfort, not realizing both are teachers. Contrast is what reveals meaning. Just as chess needs both offense and defense, life needs both challenge and clarity.

Often, our suffering doesn't come from pain itself, but from not understanding its place in the game—from resisting the very process designed to shape us. Life is not here to punish you. It is here to polish you. The path isn't meant to be smooth; it's meant to be real. And it is in navigating that reality—with wisdom, intention, and heart—that you rise.

This book cannot decode every intricacy of existence, just as no player can master every possible move. But it can offer a foundation—a way to begin. A lens to see more clearly. A compass for your upward spiral. And yes, it ends with God—not because He is last, but because to understand Him, you must first come to understand yourself. Self-discovery is not separate from the divine. It is the doorway to it.

You are here for something real—
Not to impress, not to be liked, but to become.
To set fire to the illusion,
And rise from the ashes of every falsehood.
For when you are reunited with God,
Only your truest self will be called forward.

Your journey doesn't end here. Like a chess master reviewing old games, revisit the exercises, the reflections, the moments that moved you. See how far you've come. Look again. Think again. Feel again.

Ask yourself:

- What new patterns have you uncovered?

- How has your understanding evolved?

- What are your next moves?

With each return, each reflection, you rise. The spiral continues—not in circles, but in ascent.

And as you rise, may your life become a light—radiant with purpose, grounded in truth, and vibrant with spirit.

The board is yours. The game is life.
Spiral upward—always.

The Riddle

When we began this journey, I posed a riddle. At first, it may have seemed like a playful introduction, a moment of curiosity to set the stage. Yet, as we navigated the lessons, untangled the knots, and ascended through the challenges of existence, the answer has quietly revealed itself.

The path with twists and turns, the steps that climb higher with every challenge, the lessons learned at every stage—that path is life itself. And life, as we have discovered together, is an upward spiral.

This spiral is not about perfection but about progress. It reminds us that life does not move in straight lines. It loops and circles, returning us to familiar emotions and challenges, but always from a higher vantage point. Even when it feels as though we are stuck or regressing, the spiral carries us upward, teaching us to grow, adapt, and rise.

As you reflect on the journey we've shared, think of the spiral in all its forms: the golden spirals of nature, the swirling galaxies, the intricate patterns of DNA. These are reflections of the same upward movement that shapes our lives. We are part of this infinite design, continually rising through our experiences, our struggles, and our triumphs.

The upward spiral also calls us to action. It invites us to embrace life's twists and turns with courage and grace, to view setbacks as stepping stones, and to find meaning in both joy and pain. The spiral teaches us that every challenge is an opportunity to ascend and that progress is the true measure of a life well-lived.

So, as this book comes to an end, the journey continues. Take with you the lessons, the wisdom, and the inspiration to face each day with renewed purpose. Remember that life will always challenge you, but it will also lift you higher. Trust the process, embrace the spiral, and know that even the smallest steps take you closer to the extraordinary.

Life is not about arriving—it is about ascending. The answer to the riddle lies in the title of this book: Life Is an Upward Spiral.

Acknowledgments

To my beloved mother,

Words can never fully capture the depth of my gratitude, but I hope this book stands as a humble testament to your unwavering love and sacrifices.

You once asked me to let you know if I ever uncovered the reasons behind human misery. Nana, I didn't just seek answers—God blessed me with the experience of living through them. Those who guide others through darkness are not the same as those who become light within it. My body bears scars I have kept hidden from you, some of which are revealed in these pages—woven into the lines and the spaces between them.

The irony is that you will never read this book because even the ability to read and write was a sacrifice you made for us. Yet, something tells me you always knew the answers. You embodied contentment even as you endured the greatest suffering. The truth is, even my proudest achievement feels incomplete without your and Baba's validation.

But that is the lesson you've always imparted to me—that life's value is not found in external validation but in the strength to rise above challenges. As you always taught me, it doesn't matter how many times you fall; what matters is how many times you rise again. Nana, I promise to always stand up for what is right until my last breath.

You have been both mother and father to me, filling my life with warmth, guidance, and strength. Your resilience, compassion, and unwavering perseverance have shaped not only this book but every step of my journey. I've seen you endure sleepless nights, empty stomachs, and the uncertainties of a new land—all to provide us with safety and a brighter future. You taught me that any roof, whether clay or brick, becomes a home when it is filled with love.

Your prayers, whispered into the night, always seem to reach the divine. Perhaps it is because your love reflects God's essence—a pure, selfless devotion. You have carried the weight of your own burdens and ours, often at great personal cost. Through it all, you have shown me that love is the greatest force in the universe, capable of transforming even the harshest realities.

When life threatened to break me, it was your wisdom, your prayers, and your love that sustained me. Though circumstances kept us apart at times, your presence has always been my guiding light.

This book is a tribute to you and the extraordinary person you are. From my earliest memories, I've watched you face life's trials with unparalleled grace and courage. You are my first teacher, my eternal inspiration, and my greatest source of strength.

Indeed, a mother's love is a son's first and purest bond, and a son's love becomes her enduring legacy. This bond—profound, unbreakable, and eternal—is the truest testament to love.

With endless love, your son, Ansar

*

The Wind Beneath My Wings

There are moments when gratitude swells so deeply within us that words feel too fragile to hold it. Yet still, I try — because to leave it unspoken would be to leave it unseen. With humility and boundless love, I write these acknowledgments to honor the guiding lights who have carried me, lifted me, and shaped the creation of this book.

First and foremost, my gratitude belongs to God, the divine orchestrator of all existence. By Your constant presence and quiet guidance, I have been led into this journey of reflection and discovery. Your wisdom has steadied me, Your mercy has renewed me, and Your love has given me the courage to share these lessons with the world.

To my beloved family, my pillars of strength — thank you for being the wind beneath my wings. Your faith in me has carried me through storms, your love has been my refuge, and your sacrifices have been my foundation. To my nephews and nieces, who have carved out a sacred space in my heart, you are among my greatest blessings. Though I may not yet have children of my own, you have shown me the pure joy, responsibility, and tenderness of parenthood. In your laughter, I see my hope. In your eyes, I see the future.

This book is my gift to you — and to all future generations. May these pages guide you when life feels heavy, inspire you when the path feels dark, and encourage you to rise higher than I ever have.

To the countless souls who have touched my journey — some knowingly, others without realizing — thank you. Every word of encouragement, every spark of inspiration, has been a reminder that our stories are not just ours. They ripple outward, shaping lives in ways we may never see.

To my cherished friends, Anders Eriksen and Jens Eriksen — thank you for filling my life with laughter, loyalty, and memories I treasure. You are the family I chose, and your friendship is one of my life's greatest gifts. To my collaborators: Crystal Nero, whose guidance was a compass; Vanessa Ta, whose precision gave these words their clarity; and Christian Tupac, whose artistry breathed life into this vision — my gratitude is immeasurable.

And finally, to you, the reader — thank you for meeting me here. You now hold not just a book, but pieces of my heart, written with the hope that they resonate with your spirit, comfort your wounds, and strengthen your will to rise. May these words remind you that you are never alone, and that every struggle can be alchemized into light.

References

Hubblesite. *One of Hubble's Key Projects Nails Down Nearly a Century of Uncertainty*. Accessed 7 July 2024. https://hubblesite.org/mission-and-telescope/hubble-30th-anniversary/hubbles-exciting-universe/measuring-the-universes-expansion-rate.

Kybalion, The. *The Seven Hermetic Principles*. Accessed 7 July 2024. http://www.kybalion.org/kybalion.php?chapter=II.

Lewis, Natalie, and LiveScience. *How Men's Brains Are Wired Differently Than Women's*. Accessed 7 July 2024. Scientific American. https://www.scientificamerican.com/article/how-mens-brains-are-wired-differently-than-women/.

Medical College of Georgia at Augusta University. "Gene variants provide insight into brain, body incongruence in transgender." ScienceDaily. 5 February 2020. <www.sciencedaily.com/releases/2020/02/200205084203.htm>.

Meyer, Stephen C. *Return of the God Hypothesis*. New York, NY: HarperOne, 2021.

Operation Echo. *Unlocking Creative Genius: Impact of Education 98% to 2% Change*. Accessed 7 July 2024. https://medium.com/@operationecho/from-98-to-2-how-schooling-affects-creative-potential-080a5fb72bbe.

Singer, Michael A. *The Untethered Soul*. Oakland, CA: New Harbinger Publications, 2007.

The Holy Quran. Accessed 7 July 2024. https://quran.com/en.

Tolle, Eckhart. *The Power of Now*. Novato, CA: New World Library, 1999.

Valenti, Oriana et al. *Fetal cardiac function during the first trimester of pregnancy*. NIH. Accessed July 7, 2024. https://www.ncbi.nlm.nih.gov/pmc/articles/PMC3279166/.

Watts, Alan. *Be Here Now Podcast*. https://www.youtube.com/@BeHere-NowNetwork.

Ansar Yawar

Ansar Yawar is a multifaceted serial entrepreneur, motivational speaker, business and life coach, and author of the groundbreaking book "Life Is an Upward Spiral." His journey as a writer began in 2021, fulfilling a promise to his mother to unravel the causes of human misery. Ansar's impact as a motivational speaker is profound, with his videos amassing over 30 million views.

He has successfully launched and developed businesses across diverse sectors, including manufacturing, fashion, marketing, and IT. One of his latest ventures, EduSpace, is anticipated to be the first global educational platform that enhances communication and collaboration among students and educators, effectively breaking traditional barriers in education by connecting the global learning community.

Deeply passionate about philosophy and human behavior, Ansar specializes in its analysis, dedicating his career to elevating individuals and businesses. With a focus on personal growth and innovative strategies, he expertly utilizes technology and sales to catalyze rapid business growth and success. Originating from the diverse backgrounds of Afghanistan and Mongolia, Ansar was born in the small city of Quetta, raised in Denmark, and currently resides in the United Arab Emirates.

THE END OF MY BOOK IS

The Beginning of Your Next chapter